SOCIOLOGY OF PERSONAL LIFE

Sociology of Personal Life

Edited by

Vanessa May

with contributions by

Wendy Bottero, Katherine Davies, Gemma Edwards,
Anna Einarsdottir, Jennifer Mason, David Morgan,
Carol Smart, Dale Southerton and Becky Tipper

*Morgan Centre for the Study of Relationships and
Personal Life, University of Manchester, UK*

First published 2011 by
PALGRAVE MACMILLAN

Palgrave Macmillan in the UK is an imprint of Macmillan Publishers Limited, registered in England, company number 785998, of Houndmills, Basingstoke, Hampshire RG21 6XS.

Palgrave Macmillan in the US is a division of St Martin's Press LLC, 175 Fifth Avenue, New York, NY 10010.

Palgrave Macmillan is the global academic imprint of the above companies and has companies and representatives throughout the world.

Palgrave® and Macmillan® are registered trademarks in the United States, the United Kingdom, Europe and other countries

ISBN 978–0–230–27896–7 hardback
ISBN 978–0–230–27897–4 paperback

This book is printed on paper suitable for recycling and made from fully managed and sustained forest sources. Logging, pulping and manufacturing processes are expected to conform to the environmental regulations of the country of origin.

A catalogue record for this book is available from the British Library.

A catalog record for this book is available from the Library of Congress.

10   9   8   7   6   5   4   3   2   1
20 19 18 17 16 15 14 13 12 11

Printed and bound by CPI Group (UK) Ltd, Croydon, CR0 4YY

Contents

List of Tables, Figures and Boxes

Tables

Figures

Boxes

Notes on Contributors

Wendy Bottero is Senior Lecturer at the University of Manchester, a member of the Morgan Centre for the Study of Relationships and Personal Life, the Mitchell Centre for the Analysis of Social Networks, and is affiliated to the ESRC Research Centre for the Study of Socio-Cultural Change (CRESC). Wendy's research interests are focused on how networks of social interaction and patterns of friendship, partnership and kinship are bound up with inequality, hierarchy and class. She is currently working on the 'Who do you think they were?' research project, which looks at the different ways in which family history research is conducted, and how family historians situate themselves, and their ancestors, within narratives of social historical change and 'the past'.

Katherine Davies is Research Associate in the Realities Node of the ESRC National Centre for Research Methods based in the Morgan Centre for the Study of Relationships and Personal Life at the University of Manchester. Her research interests span the sociology of personal life, particularly kinship and friendship relationships, and qualitative methodologies. Having previously studied the social significance of family resemblances, Katherine is currently involved in research exploring the positive and negative significance of critical associations in personal lives, as well as working on a PhD investigating sibling relationships and the construction of the self in secondary education.

Gemma Edwards is Lecturer in Sociology at the University of Manchester. Her research interests include politics and personal life, social movements and social network analysis. She has written *Social Movements and Protest* (Cambridge University Press).

Anna Einarsdottir completed her doctorate study at London South Bank University in 2008 and is Research Associate at the Morgan Centre for the Study of Relationships and Personal Life at the University of Manchester. In her research Anna has specialized in same-sex relationships, focusing on formalized unions both within the UK and in Iceland. She is currently working on an ESRC-funded study 'Just like Marriage? Young Couples' Civil Partnerships' with Dr Brian Heaphy and Professor Carol Smart.

Jennifer Mason is Professor of Sociology at the University of Manchester, and Co-Director of the Morgan Centre for the Study of Relationships and Personal

Life. She also directs the Realities Centre, which is part of the ESRC National Centre for Research Methods. She has written several books and many articles and chapters on family, kinship, relationships and qualitative methodology. Recent research projects, all conducted with colleagues and all ESRC-funded, include: critical associations; inter/generational dynamics; living resemblances; family backgrounds and everyday life; and children creating kinship.

Vanessa May is Lecturer in Sociology at the University of Manchester and a member of the Morgan Centre for the Study of Relationships and Personal Life. Her research interests include lone motherhood, post-divorce parenting, intergenerational relationships, the self, belonging, narrative analysis, biographical methods and mixed methods. She is currently writing *Connecting Self and Society: Belonging in a Changing World* (Palgrave Macmillan).

David Morgan taught Sociology at Manchester University for over 35 years and has also been Visiting Professor at the Norwegian Technological University, Trondheim, and Keele University. Publications include *Family Connections* (Polity, 1996), *Acquaintances: The Space between Intimates and Strangers* (Open University, 2009) and *Rethinking Family Practices* (Palgrave Macmillan, 2011). He is also a former President of the British Sociological Association.

Carol Smart is Professor of Sociology and Co-Director of the Morgan Centre for the Study of Relationships and Personal Life at the University of Manchester. She is author of *Personal Life: New Directions in Sociological Thinking*, published by Polity in 2007. Her research projects include studies on same-sex relationships, friendship, family secrets and donor conception.

Dale Southerton is Professor of Sociology at the University of Manchester. He has conducted several influential studies in the field of consumption and consumer culture. He has published extensively on these subjects, with particular reference to: time pressure and temporalities; sustainability; everyday life; identity and lifestyles; theories of social change; technologies, innovation and material culture. Previous publications include *Sustainable Consumption: The Implications of Changing Infrastructures of Provision* (Edward Elgar, 2004).

Becky Tipper worked as a researcher before studying for her PhD in sociology at the University of Manchester. Her research looks at relationships between humans and animals in suburban Britain. Her other research interests include qualitative research methods, children and childhood, and domestic and kin relationships.

Acknowledgements

Sociology of Personal Life is written by members of the Morgan Centre for the Study of Relationships and Personal Life at the University of Manchester. The book is very much a team effort, which we hope is reflected throughout the present volume.

The author and publishers wish to thank the following publishers, organizations and authors for granting permission to reproduce copyright material: the Australian Institute of Family Studies for Figures 4.1 and 4.3, originally from www.aifs.gov.au; the Office for National Statistics, for Table 5.1, originally from *Statistical Bulletin: Civil Partnerships in the UK 2009* (Office for National Statistics, 2010) and *Statistical Bulletin: Marriages in England and Wales 2008* (Office for National Statistics, 2010) reproduced under the Open Government Licence v.1.0; the Office for National Statistics for Figure 4.2, originally from *Social Trends* 34 (Office for National Statistics, 2004) reproduced under the Open Government Licence v.1.0; Institute for Social and Economic Research for Table 11.2, originally from *Working Papers of the Institute for Social and Economic Research*, Paper 2005–9 (Colchester: Institute for Social and Economic Research). Mass Observation material in Chapter 7 is reproduced with the kind permission of the Trustees of the Mass Observation Archive, University of Sussex.

The authors extend their warmest thanks to Hazel Burke for her excellent proof-reading and to Mark Hampson for redrawing (also excellently) some of the graphs.

Every effort has been made to contact all the copyright-holders, but if any have been inadvertently omitted the publisher will be pleased to make the necessary arrangement at the earliest opportunity.

Introducing a Sociology of Personal Life

Vanessa May

What is 'personal life'?

What comes to your mind when you hear the words 'personal' and 'personal life'? Take a moment to think about this, and perhaps to jot down what you associate with these words. Family and friends are probably on your list. But what about the laws which limit what we may or may not do, the ways in which the demands of work shape our lives, and the ways in which we participate in political life – did you consider these as part of personal life?

The aim of the little exercise above was to encourage you to think about how you would define 'personal life', but also to consider why you might define it in a particular way. In *Sociology of Personal Life* we wish to question and extend conventional, and narrow, notions of the personal as comprising only 'private' issues such as close relationships. Our aim is to highlight that personal life covers a multitude of spheres that traditionally get divided into discrete sociological sub-disciplines such as Sociology of Families, Sociology of Childhood, Sociology of Sexuality or Sociology of Consumption, to name a few. By examining seemingly separate spheres of life in one volume, and by exploring some of the links between them, we seek to blur these distinctions that sociology textbooks tend to draw. We argue that this is an important thing to do because, in day-to-day life, personal life is 'lived in many different places and spaces ... and it forms a range of connections' (Smart, *Personal Life: New Directions in Sociological Thinking*, 2007, p. 29). For example, personal life includes not only family life at home but also going to school or to work, taking part in financial transactions in shops, and engaging with public policy – for example, by filling in official forms or by voting in elections.

However, by saying that we wish to question the primacy of family relationships as *the* stuff of personal life, we are not claiming that these are not central in personal life, quite the contrary. We still view these 'traditional' topics as major components of personal life, but we would argue that these can only be fully understood if explored in relation to other spheres significant to everyday personal life.

What is sociological about personal life?

A sociology of personal life is concerned with investigating what is *sociological* about personal life, that is, what individual people's personal lives say about society more generally. The aim of such a sociology is thus not only to understand the experiences of individual persons, but also how and why these experiences may in the aggregate follow some general patterns.

For example, there are lifecourse transitions that most Westerners go through in their personal lives, such as the transition from adolescence to adulthood, that many of our readers are probably familiar with. This transitional phase often involves moving out of the parental home, continuing in further education or seeking a job, and at some point setting up a home with a partner. Although many people may feel that the events in their lives are unique to them, taking a broader view enables us to see that in fact many aspects of people's lives are socially shaped. In current Western societies, the transition to adulthood is something that most people go through at roughly the same age. Furthermore, it is shaped by the provision of education or housing, affecting whether young people have access to university education, or whether they're able to set up an independent home at an early age.

The aim of the present volume is to highlight that a variety of 'public' issues, such as politics and the economic sphere, not only influence personal life but are also *shaped by* personal life. An example of the latter is the way in which women have been able to influence legislation around marriage and women's employment, or how non-heterosexuals have succeeded in pushing for legal recognition of same-sex relationships. In other words, personal life matters not only on the level of individual persons, but also more broadly on the level of the **'public' sphere.**

Some illustrations of personal life in sociology

There is within sociology a long history of different approaches that have focused on various aspects of personal life, though not necessarily by that name. Because it would take up too much space to go through all of them here, I offer instead a few illustrations taken from sociological writings over a century or more. A good place to begin with is Emile Durkheim, often referred to as one of the founders of sociology. His classic book *Suicide* (1970 [first published 1897]) is a sociological study of how a highly personal and private act (suicide) can be interpreted as a response to particular social conditions as well as seen to be socially patterned (for example, men are more likely to commit suicide than women are).

Between 1918 and 1920, William I. Thomas and Florian Znaniecki published five volumes of their work called *The Polish Peasant in Europe and America*, which has since become a classic within sociology (the first two volumes were published in a new edition in 1958). This work dealt with a major social question that has resonance even today, namely immigration. The authors sought to show that the problems of the immigrant community were due to the transition from one society to another very different one, which requires a series of adaptations. Thomas and Znaniecki used a wide range of materials, including individual life histories and letters, accounts from Polish newspapers, as well as social work and court records.

Thomas and Znaniecki were part of a sociological tradition called the Chicago School (so named because its members were based at the University of Chicago), which had its heyday in the 1920s and 1930s. Studies within the Chicago School explored everyday life, and many of them used the life histories of individual people as a way of studying the social world. An example is Clifford Shaw's (1966[1930]) study of Stanley, a Chicago delinquent. Stanley was part of a larger study of delinquents, but Shaw aimed to show how his life story could be used not only to understand how Stanley viewed his own life, but also to gain a picture of his social world – for example, how his background, his family and the gangs he belonged to helped shape his life.

An important milestone in the study of personal life comes in the form of C. Wright Mills's book *The Sociological Imagination* (1959). Mills defined the task of sociology as the investigation of both individual biography and history, and of how these intersect within a society. He argued that sociologists should question the distinction that is generally drawn between 'private' and 'public' issues for two reasons. First, because 'many personal troubles cannot be solved merely as troubles, but must be understood in terms of public issues', and, second, because 'the human meaning of public issues must be revealed by relating them to personal troubles – and to the problems of the individual life' (Mills, 1959, p. 226). In other words, public issues such as gender equality cannot be understood in the abstract, but must instead be viewed in terms of relationships between individual men and women in the home or the workplace. Therefore, sociology must include in its studies 'both troubles and issues, both biography and history, and the range of their intricate relations' (Mills, 1959, p. 226).

This call to study personal life as a public issue has perhaps most famously been taken up by feminist researchers. Since the 1950s, feminists have conducted many important pieces of research into various aspects of women's lives, with the aim of showing how 'public' definitions of what a woman should or could be (including, for example, **social norms** and legislation) have influenced the personal lives of women. Thus, women's 'personal troubles' (to use Mills's terminology), such as the gender inequality they faced within their couple relationships with men, were revealed as 'public issues' that originated from outside the individual women's lives. In other words, heterosexual couples were living their lives within societies that were structured around gender inequality. Thus, women's 'personal troubles' were revealed to be collective issues that therefore required collective action (Edwards, present volume). Important areas of research have been family life and the unequal distribution of money, power and housework between husbands and wives, but also the restrictions that have historically been placed on women's participation in 'public' life outside the home – for example, paid work and politics – and how these have affected women's lives (for example, Kanter, 1977; Delphy and Leonard, 1992).

Perhaps the most clearly delineated area of sociology that has focused on personal life is the field of 'family sociology'. Social scientists have been interested in families from the outset. For example, in 1884, Friedrich Engels wrote in *The Origin of the Family, Private Property, and the State* (1986[1884]) about the effects that capitalism had had on family life, particularly women's lives. Engels argued, for example, that by looking after children at home, women's labour is crucial for the success of capitalism – in effect, women were involved in the production and care of healthy workers. Due to limited space, I cannot offer an exhaustive history of family sociology, but instead I discuss a few turning points in terms of its development.

Family sociology, which could be defined as those theoretical approaches that attempt to link family life to wider social influences, emerged as a distinct field in the 1950s and 1960s when it was largely dominated by Talcott Parsons's functionalist theories (Parsons, 1955). The functionalist view of family was based on the idea that the modern nuclear family has a positive function in industrialized societies, and that each family member had a distinct role to play (men as breadwinners, women as caregivers). Mainstream functionalist family sociology was challenged in the 1970s, mainly by feminist and Marxist sociologists. They maintained that **functionalism** in effect held the male-breadwinner-and-female-carer nuclear family form as ideal, a family form that in fact benefited men and capitalism. Feminists and Marxists argued that the modern nuclear family was a prime example of discrimination against women (who were relegated into roles as unpaid care workers) and the working classes (who could not hope to obtain such a way of life because many could not survive on one wage only). This led to what David Cheal (1991) has called the 'big bang' in family sociology, and, since then, the field has been characterized by innovative theorizing on how family life is lived, and on the connections between families and other social institutions.

There have also been debates over how families should be conceptualized. For example, David Morgan argued influentially in *Family Connections* (1996) that family is not a single pre-given 'thing', but rather that families are something that people *do*, and therefore fluid and liable to change. He urged sociologists to focus on the family practices that helped make up families, and inspired, for example, work on how family members negotiate their obligations to one another (Finch and Mason, 1993) and how parents settle their parenting responsibilities post-divorce (Smart and Neale, 1999).

A further broadening of scope came with the studies that focused on the family lives of non-heterosexual people, conducted by Kath Weston (1991) in the USA and Jeffrey Weeks and colleagues (2001) in the UK. They argued families are not necessarily restricted to blood relations, but can be created by choice – hence the term **'families of choice'** that has since become widespread within family sociology. The research participants in Weston's and Weeks and colleagues' studies spoke of their families as having fluid boundaries, and consisting mainly of other lesbians and gay men, former lovers, partners, as well as relatives, biological or adoptive children, and people with whom they lived. A great deal of importance was placed upon *creating* networks of relationships that were conceived of as 'families', in the sense of providing support, care and commitment, but that were *chosen*.

Of late, it has become customary for sociologists to talk of 'families and intimacies' (for example, Jamieson, 1998) as a way of reflecting a move towards a broader perspective to include also non-familial relationships such as friendships. Carol Smart's book *Personal Life* (2007) is, however, the first attempt to develop a coherent conceptual framework for an even broader field of study within sociology that looks beyond close relationships. In its approach and focus, *Sociology of Personal Life* is heavily indebted to Smart's groundbreaking work. Below, I turn to discuss two further sociological traditions within which our work can be situated: a relational view of people and **social constructionism**.

The 'personal' is relational

At this point the reader may be wondering why we have decided to talk about 'personal life' rather than 'individual life'. On the face of it, you may think that there is little difference between the two terms. But within sociology, as in any other discipline, concepts come with a history of how they are used and in relation to which theories and arguments. Smart (*Personal Life: New Directions in Sociological Thinking*, 2007) argues for the use of the concept 'personal' instead of 'individual' because of the theoretical baggage that is associated with the latter due to its usage in what is called 'the **individualization thesis**', also known as the **de-traditionalization thesis**. This is a thesis that has been the focus of much debate within many areas of sociology since the 1990s, including areas that focus on family, work and consumption. The key argument of this thesis is the increase in individual choice (hence the term 'individualization').

In a nutshell, the individualization thesis proposes that Western societies have undergone a significant shift that has led to the traditional social structures of, for example, gender, class and family losing much of their influence. As a result, individuals have become 'disembedded' (Giddens, 1991) from traditional roles, leaving them with more freedom (or agency) to decide how they wish to live their lives. In the past, the lives of, for example, women and working-class people were clearly defined so that many knew from an early age what their life would be like. In contrast, people in contemporary societies have fewer such certainties or fixed roles to follow. In Beck's (1992) terms, the standard biography has been replaced by the 'do-it-yourself' biography that contemporary individuals must construct for themselves.

One of the areas that Anthony Giddens (1992) and Ulrich Beck and Elisabeth Beck-Gernsheim (1995) have focused on is family life. They argue that marriage as an institution has weakened. Fewer people, for instance, feel they *have* to marry in order to live together or have children, while divorce is now a real option for married couples. In other words, marriage is neither a must, nor is it 'til death do us part'. Giddens argues that this reflects a significant shift in how relationships are viewed by people. Traditional relationships were largely held together by external constraints such as the marriage contract and by powerful social norms against extra-marital sex and divorce. In contrast, contemporary relationships are, according to Giddens, based on romantic love, communication, openness and trust, and survive only for as long as they satisfy both partners. Relationships are, in other words, based on a 'rolling contract' that can be terminated at will. Such a relationship Giddens calls 'the **pure relationship**':

> [The pure relationship] refers to a situation where a social relation is entered into for its own sake, for what can be derived by each person from a sustained association with another; and which is continued only in so far as it is thought by both parties to deliver enough satisfactions for each individual to stay in it. (Giddens, 1992, p. 58)

The individualization thesis argues that such choice has become a prevalent element in most areas of life, including, for example, consumption. Zygmunt Bauman (1990) has proposed that people have more freedom to choose what they consume and how, and that these consumption choices are now a basis for identity. In other words, people no longer have to stick to a given identity pre-determined, for example, by their class background. Instead, they have more freedom to choose among the many 'lifestyles' on offer and to choose the one that they feel best represents who they think they are.

As you will see in the chapters that follow, this individualization thesis has been strongly criticized within sociology, among other things for its rather simplistic depiction of life in the past and for its exaggerated emphasis on individual choice. Although there is some empirical evidence that supports the individualization thesis (such as increased variability in the age at which people get married or have children, or the increases in divorce and cohabitation rates), traditional categories and norms have not weakened to the extent that the individualization thesis claims. It still matters whether one is born into a working-class family or a middle-class family in terms of one's future chances, and traditional institutions such as marriage have not lost their cultural and moral significance. Why else would we continue to have public debates about whether same-sex couples should be allowed to marry or about whether the children of divorced parents fare worse than children whose parents have stayed together?

Another reason for preferring the term 'personal' above 'individual' is that the latter depicts people as autonomous, isolated individuals. Think back to Giddens's pure relationship – what image do you have in your mind when you picture Giddens's couple who are weighing the options of either staying together or splitting up? Here we have two individuals who seem somehow free-floating, not connected to other people in any significant way. The chapters in this book are, however, based on the notion that people are fundamentally relational. This means that their sense of self is founded on and shaped by the relationships they are embedded in from birth, and that they make important life choices with significant others in mind. We are using the term 'personal' as a way of signalling that people are not isolated individuals, but rather inherently connected to others (Smart, *Personal Life: New Directions* in *Sociological Thinking*, 2007; Morgan, Chapter 2).

One of the most famous theorists to address the relational nature of people is G. H. Mead (1934), who studied how children come to develop a sense of self. According to Mead, a baby is not born with the capacity to understand herself as a person, but rather develops this in interaction with others. During these interactions, the child also learns how she 'should' behave (also called the **socialization** process). A 'real' boy does not cry (at least not as much as his sister does), and a 'moral' person does not lie or cheat. At the same time, the child comes to understand herself as more (or less) extrovert, funny, or intelligent than those around her. Our sense of self is in other words relational, because it is constructed *in relationships with* others, and *in relation to* others and to social norms. By 'others' I mean not just immediate family and friends, but also other children we interact with in the playground, our teachers and neighbours. And later in life, 'others' include also our colleagues at work.

Personal life is socially constructed

Sociology of Personal Life falls, broadly speaking, within a sociological tradition called social constructionism. 'Social constructionism' is a term that describes a particular way of looking at the nature of reality. Whereas many people might assume that social reality as they have come to understand it 'just is so', a social constructionist approach wishes to explore how a particular way of defining something came about, and why it continues to be so. A prime example of a socially constructed phenomenon is 'sexuality'. The common belief is that sexuality is a given, and that a person's sexuality defines their identity (Einarsdottir, present volume). Many people think that this 'just is so', and cannot conceive of any other way of looking at this issue. Yet the term 'sexuality' was invented in the nineteenth century by a new occupational group called 'sexologists' (Weeks, 1991). Before then, different types of sexual activity, such as heterosexual sex between people of different genders, and homosexual sex between people of the same gender, did take place, but these were not seen to define a person's *identity*. In other words, there was no conceptualization of people as either 'heterosexual' or 'homosexual' because these terms did not yet exist.

The above example illustrates that to propose that something is 'socially constructed' is not to say that it is simply a matter of 'choice' or that it can be changed at whim. A person cannot very easily decide *not* to be defined by their sexual practices if this is how people are defined in a society. In fact, not many people would even think of doing so because these socially constructed categories feel very real and inescapable to us. They inform our view of our self and of the surrounding social world at such a fundamental level that they seem unavoidable. The key to the power and longevity of established social categories lies partly in the fact that they feel 'natural', even unquestionable. Sociology could be described as the art of shifting our perspective on the world and opening up fresh ways of looking at social reality (not unlike someone using a kaleidoscope), allowing sociologists to question and be critical about such taken-for-granted assumptions.

As sociologists, we are interested in how socially constructed categories such as gender and class help pattern and structure personal life, but also in the variety that exists within these. Thus, we can see that women as a group or the working class as a group share *on average* some common characteristics. For example, women earn on average less and tend to do more housework than men do. But despite these general patterns, it is important to always keep in mind that not all women are the same. A sociology of personal life is interested in examining both the broader patterning of personal life in a society, and how individual people live their lives within these structures.

The chapters

In summary, we argue that 'personal life' encompasses a broad range of issues, the following of which are examined in this book: family formation; heterosexual and same-sex couple relationships; the significance of relatedness; the role that friendships and pets play in our personal lives; the personal lives of children; personal lives in public spaces; the ways in which changing notions of time, as well as consumer culture, have shaped our personal lives; and the interconnections between personal life and politics. The topics covered in this book are by no means intended to be exhaustive, but rather our central aim is to introduce students to a new sociology of personal life that re-draws traditional sociological boundaries.

Sociology of Personal Life consists of 15 chapters. The book proceeds with Chapter 2 by David Morgan, which acts as a conceptual basis for the chapters that follow. Morgan focuses on the meaning of the concept of 'personal'. A key question he poses is: how can a word, which seems so tied to ideas to do with possessive individualism and the private, be seen in relational terms and, therefore, as a key idea in understanding social life in modern society?

These conceptual issues raised by Morgan are, in Chapters 3 to 13, examined in relation to different areas of personal life. These chapters are organized in such a way that they move from the inside out as it were. We begin with intimate relationships, which, as Morgan explains, are most commonly associated with the concept of the personal. Step by step we move our way outwards, first to relationships with kin and friends, as well as animals, as well as considering the personhood of children, before turning our attention to topics that are perhaps not as routinely thought of as related to personal life. These are: public space, time, consumption and politics.

In the first few chapters we explore couple relationships, both past and present, and both heterosexual and non-heterosexual. In Chapter 3, Wendy Bottero examines heterosexual sexual activity in the past, and how it was regulated. She also discusses what the consequences of such practices were for how people experienced intimate personal relationships. In the process, she explodes some popular myths about sex and intimacy in the past (for example, that people in bygone times were prudes about sex).

Chapters 4 and 5 examine contemporary intimate relationships. Chapter 4, by Carol Smart, explores how heterosexual couple relationships have changed recently. The focus is on marriage and cohabitation, divorce and separation, as well as solo living and 'living apart together' – living arrangements that are currently on the rise (and receiving increasing media and academic attention). Throughout, she discusses these developments in light of sociological theorizing about personal life in contemporary societies.

While much of the preceding discussion has focused on heterosexual relationships, in Chapter 5, Anna Einarsdottir turns to focus on same-sex relationships, and more specifically on the legal recognition of these and what impact this has had on the personal lives of same-sex couples. She questions the assumption that such public recognition automatically has a positive impact. It may be the case for the community as a whole, but on a personal level the story is more complicated.

In Chapter, 6 Jennifer Mason extends our focus from intimate relationships by examining extended family or kin, and what relatedness itself means. She counters the common assumption that these matter less now than in the past; relatives and kin continue to be significant in people's personal lives.

So far the chapters in this book have focused on couple and family relationships. In Chapter 7, we move further outwards towards another form of relationship that is central in personal life, namely friendship. Katherine Davies explores the significance of friendship in personal life, looking at the meaning of friendship and the suffusions between different categories of relationship such as friend, colleague, family member and acquaintance, and questions the adage 'you can choose your friends but not your family'.

Thus far, the chapters have examined the meanings and practices attached to a variety of relationships that are generally seen as central in personal life, such as family, partners and friends. While most sociological work would stop at these human-to-human relationships, in Chapter 8, Becky Tipper argues that, for many, relationships with animals are also a significant aspect of personal life. Focusing specifically on the case of pets, Tipper examines how we can understand these relationships sociologically, and asks what such an analysis can add to our understanding of personal life.

Much of the discussion in the preceding chapters has focused on the personal lives of adults. In Chapter 9, Carol Smart turns to examine the personal lives of children. Many normative assumptions are attached to this period – for example, that childhood should be a period when a child is free from responsibility, when a dependent child will be protected and nurtured. Smart argues that, although children's lives are still closely connected to kin and family, they are increasingly assuming a greater sense of personhood.

The remaining chapters in this book extend the focus beyond topics that are customarily thought of as 'personal' into other areas that also have a central place in personal life: public space, time, consumer culture and the interlinking of the personal and the political.

'Personal life' and 'personal relationships', as discussed in previous chapters, are usually understood as taking place in the 'private sphere', that is, in the home and generally within families and networks of friends. In Chapter 10, Vanessa May argues that what goes on in public spaces, such as interactions with strangers and acquaintances, but also with intimates, is an important dimension of our personal lives. In Chapter 11, Dale Southerton turns our attention to the relationship between time and personal life. He proposes that accounting for the temporal organization of daily life is critical to any understanding of personal life. In Chapter 12, Dale Southerton goes on to examine the impact that one of the most profound social changes of the post-war period, that is, the rise of **'consumer culture'**, has had on our personal lives. He explores competing sociological accounts of the emergence of consumer culture and examines the implications of these social changes for personal life.

Chapter 13, by Gemma Edwards, extends the discussion in the previous chapters by focusing on the overlap between the 'personal' and the 'political' that are commonly seen as two distinct spheres. Edwards examines how the personal is political by exploring how social movements such as **feminism** and the LGBT movement have transformed aspects of personal life into matters of public debate and political action. The second half of this chapter examines how the political is personal – that is, the importance of personal relationships in political action.

In Chapter 14, Vanessa May explores how personal life can and has been researched by sociologists. This chapter provides a discussion of qualitative and quantitative approaches, and of the types of data that could be collected by a student interested in studying personal life. The chapter ends with examples from the work of members of the Morgan Centre for the Study of Relationships and Personal Life at the University of Manchester.

Finally, Chapter 15 by Vanessa May draws together and discusses central themes and concepts that have cut across the different chapters, focusing on the relationship between the individual and the social, and the impact that a sociology of personal life has on how we view society.

As has been outlined above, the chapters are organized following a particular logic and they contain many links between them. Thus, the chapters as a whole make up a narrative that we hope will help the reader gain a coherent picture of personal life and of a sociological approach to the study of it. However, each chapter does also constitute an independent whole, and they can be read separately from each other as well.

Conceptualizing the Personal

David Morgan

Introduction

In the course of a recent radio news programme, listeners heard of an individual politician who resigned from his office 'for personal reasons'. Later, in the same half-hour broadcast, a statement by a senior military figure was described as being his own 'personal opinion'. Readers will be familiar with these, and many similar, usages of the word 'personal'. The word is, after all, used very widely; the *Oxford English Dictionary*'s online entry for 'personal' runs to 25 pages.

What are people trying to convey when they use the word 'personal' in this or in a similar way? Taking these two broadcast statements, we can tease out the following strands of meaning:

- We are dealing with something that is attached to a particular identifiable individual – *this* politician, *this* senior Army officer – and not to anyone or anything else.
- We are dealing with some kind of distinction between the public and the private. The politician's resignation has nothing to do with his public position; the officer's statement is not a statement of public military policy.
- In the first case, there is a sense of the individual saying, 'Please keep off – no further questions!' Listeners are being requested to accept this statement at face value and not to probe further.
- In the second case, there is a suggestion that the officer's statement is of a lower value than it might have been had it been seen to represent official, public policy. It is 'just' his personal opinion.

Readers will no doubt be able to provide other strands of meaning in these or in similar statements using the word 'personal'.

While, as the *Oxford English Dictionary* (OED) entry suggests, there are numerous ways in which the word is used, two or three core ideas seem to dominate. The first is a sense of an individual 'in the round' as opposed to a role in an organization or some public position. This overlaps with another core idea, the distinction between the public and the private. There is also a third core idea which is to do with 'ownership' (as in 'personal belongings' or 'personal computer').

It might also be noted that these core ideas often have strong moral or emotional connotations. Thus, a sense of the individual and a sense of ownership combine when someone reacts against what might be taken as 'personal remarks' or is seen to be taking something 'personally'. A further moral dimension becomes apparent when 'personal' is contrasted with 'impersonal', where the latter term conveys ideas of abstract bureaucratic rules or unfeeling processes such as the operation of the market. Once we begin to explore the range of meanings around the word 'personal' we quickly enter a complex world of claims and counter-claims, yet a world that is of immediate and continuing relevance.

The question which this chapter intends to explore is this: how is it possible to provide a *sociological* account of an idea which seems to be so firmly attached to notions of the individual and individual ownership? Given that sociological enquiry seems to be centrally concerned with social processes, collectivities (communities, families, states and so on) and social structures it would appear that research into the personal is more the responsibility of psychologists. What, in short, can sociological enquiry tell us about the personal?

Is 'the personal' socially constructed?

A first answer to this question might be to argue that the very idea of 'the personal' is socially constructed. This is an approach which is familiar within sociological enquiry and one that is used in relation to a wide range of institutions and practices. The argument is one of some complexity although, in this case, what is being suggested is that 'the personal' is not something that is unchanging, arising out of human nature, biology or individual psychology but which is shaped by particular historical or cultural circumstances. This would seem to be a challenging idea. What appears to be so strongly connected to individual lives and experiences can, in fact, be seen as arising out of particular social contexts.

This chapter has shown, through exploring the many usages revealed in the *OED*, that the idea of the 'personal' is linked to a variety of other ideas, namely, the individual, the distinction between the public and the private, and with ownership. These ideas seem, naturally, to hang together. However, it can be argued that these ideas and the links between them are products of modern societies where they are frequently given a prominent place. Sometimes these ideas are challenged. Individualism may be thought to have gone 'too far' or becomes identified with a selfish 'looking after number one'. The boundaries between the public and the private are often uncertain and contested. How far, for example, are the sexual orientations or practices of politicians or sportsmen and sportswomen matters of public interest? Nevertheless, the fact that these ideas are sometimes so vigorously debated attests to their continuing importance in modern cultures.

There are two main ways in which modern society might be seen to contribute to these key aspects associated with the idea of the personal. In the first place it can be argued that capitalist economies are based upon particular understandings of 'the individual' and of individual ownership. We see these in the values and ideas associated with the individual entrepreneur, the individual consumer, the individual worker. At the same time, the operation of an abstract and remote 'market' together with the development of rational and bureaucratic means of state control create an intense longing for the comforts and support of personal life as a counterbalance to these distant and dominating impersonal forces.

Rather than continuing to discuss these ideas, and their connections, in the abstract, this chapter will focus upon one particular issue which brings them together. This is the idea and the practices associated with home ownership. In a variety of modern societies, such as Britain and Australia (Savage *et al.*, 1992; Richards, 1990), the ideal of owning one's own home is very much emphasized. This is partly because the idea of home itself is so powerful, one which is frequently identified with security, warmth and intimacy (Holdsworth and Morgan, 2005). It is also linked to ideas of family and creating a good environment in which to raise children. And it is also linked to the ideas of private property and ownership, key concepts in capitalist societies.

How this works in actual practice is beautifully demonstrated in a study of a new Australian suburb conducted in the 1980s (Richards, 1990). Nearly all the inhabitants of the suburb, named 'Green Views', had bought their own home; rental was not seen as an option by the overwhelming majority. The author writes: 'Home ownership, like motherhood, had until recently an almost unspotted record in Australia as a "good thing"' (*ibid.*, p. 94). The reference to 'motherhood' is not accidental. Home ownership, marriage and parenthood are linked in with some widely held popular understandings and this 'package' is still often seen as desirable and even natural. Home ownership is identified, like the idea of home itself, with security, which means having a measure of control over one's life and one's immediate environment. This sense of personal control contrasts with the more abstract ways in which individuals are controlled by the market and the state in modern societies. The private worlds that are created in this process provide the opportunities to be oneself and to be free from dependence on others (*ibid.*, p. 125). Although this study relates to Australia in the 1980s, some of the central ideas such as the importance of home and the linking of home and family are still valid in a range of modern societies (Holdsworth and Morgan, 2005).

The home, therefore, can in one sense be seen as an environment in which the idea of the personal can be realized and reinforced. Within the limits imposed by income and other circumstances, individuals chose the kind of property and location in which to bring up their families. The home is a personal space within which one's personal taste and preferences can be displayed. The home can be seen as not simply a physical place, a building, but a symbolic space which brings together dominant ideas of family, ownership, individuality and privacy.

It does not matter that some people, as a matter of principle, might reject the ideal. It does not matter, either, that for some people it is just an ideal and one which is far from immediate realization. In recent years, the shocks to the global economy and to the private property market have called into question the idea of 'security' linked to home ownership. Mortgages may be less easy to obtain and homes can be repossessed. But the centrality of the private property market and the consequences that this can have for the wider economy highlights the continuing importance of the idea of home ownership and of having a place of one's own.

I have chosen this idea of home ownership as an illustration of how dominant certain ideas are in modern societies and how they can be seen to influence what might seem to be individual decisions. These ideas are those of ownership and private property, privacy and individual choice. Although these ideas have their own complex and different histories in different societies they can all be seen to be linked to capitalism and to much that we regard as characteristic of modern societies. Ulrich Beck and Elisabeth Beck-Gernsheim (2002), for example, see individualization and increased individual choice as a distinguishing characteristic of modern societies (this **individualization thesis** is discussed in more detail in Chapter 1). The paradox is that individuals are *required* to choose at different stages of their life; they are not free not to choose even if the options may not always seem very attractive (to drive one's own car through busy, sometimes blocked roads or to have an uncomfortable and equally uncertain ride on a bus or a train, for example).

The argument, therefore (for which home ownership provides an important illustration), is that the idea of the 'personal' has a complex history through its connection with other ideas such as ownership, privacy and the individual. These ideas themselves have complex and interwoven histories but the main point is that the sphere of the personal does not arise out of basic individual needs or characteristics but must be understood as, in part, being shaped by wider social and cultural factors. The idea that what appears to be most individual is in fact, in some measure, a product of social circumstances is a familiar paradox within sociology. But is that all that there is to be said?

A digression: persons and selves

One response to the argument about the social construction of personal life is that it seems very over-deterministic, perhaps pessimistically so. The idea that when we think we are making individual life decisions (partnering, having children, making homes) we are in fact conforming to a complex predetermined social script is, to say the least, not a comfortable one. And in fact the balance between individual life choices and pressures arising from the ways in which societies are structured and organized are core concerns of sociological enquiry, appearing and reappearing in many different guises (Cohen, 1994; Giddens, 1984). Further, these uncertainties about social constructionism are not simply present in sociological theory but have their manifestations in everyday life.

One radio interview programme presents itself as 'showing the person behind the persona'. The idea behind this tag-line was that the skills of the interviewer aimed to go behind or beneath the public face that the interviewee (politician, artist, scholar or whatever) routinely presented – the mask – and highlight the 'real' person in so doing. A distinction was made, therefore, between the social roles or positions that an individual occupied and a more interesting and more complex person apart from these.

A very everyday experience, familiar to many readers, may illustrate this further. Consider another kind of interview, one undergone in the course of applying for a particular job or position. From time to time the individual undergoing this interview will get a sense of herself as presenting herself in a particular way to these other people in this limited circumstance. She may have decided how to adjust her physical appearance so that it is in keeping with what, she imagines, the interviewers may expect and many of her answers may have been rehearsed in advance. From time to time she may get carried away in this performance but at other times she may be aware of herself trying to make an impression and wondering if this was, really, her 'true' self.

Within the social sciences, perhaps the most influential statement of this distinction (one which readers will recognize from their everyday experiences) was G. H. Mead's discussion of the 'I' and the 'Me' (Mead, 1934; Rose, 1962). In the course of their everyday lives, individuals encounter a variety of other individuals and institutions and adjust their behaviour and orientations accordingly. These responses to 'external' expectations or 'roles' constitute what Mead calls the 'Me'. The individual's reflections on these expectations and performances (so that, for example, some expectations or roles might be thought to be more important or more enjoyable than others) constitute the 'I'. A little reflection will show that both the 'I' and the 'Me' are necessary for social and personal life and that some kind of balance needs to be attained between them. The actor, the politician or the salesman, totally absorbed in the performance at the expense of any sense of self or personal identity is seen to be a tragic or a comic figure. But similarly, the person who makes no concessions to the expectations or responses of others would be impossible to live with. We may also see that these are not two completely distinct facets of an individual person but are in constant dynamic relation with each other.

We may find echoes of Mead's theoretical distinction in several anthropological accounts from a range of different cultures. Here we shall begin by looking at what are sometimes described as 'traditional' societies, before considering the implications of Mead's distinction for modern societies. Traditional African societies are frequently portrayed as societies where ideas of the individual self are muted and subsumed by complex sets of collective and kinship rules and expectations. Yet Godfrey Lienhardt recorded encountering frequent expressions on the lines of 'one never knows what is another person's heart', phrases pointing to some idea of the self that is apart from social roles (Lienhardt, 1985). In a similar vein, J. S. La Fontaine writes: 'If the self is an individual's awareness of a unique identity, the "person" is society's confirmation of that identity as of social significance' (La Fontaine, 1985, p. 124). One consequence of this distinction is that, in some societies, some individuals (often women and children) are not 'persons' or their sense of personhood is less than others within the same society:

> The personhood of women among the Tallensi [Ghana] is of a lesser order than that of men for women lack the domestic and lineage authority of men. For the Taiti [Kenya] ... the full range of ritual powers is not open to women so that they reach the limits of their achieved personhood sooner than men. (*Ibid.*, p. 130)

Yet, it may be suggested, because an individual is not in some senses defined as a 'person' does not necessarily mean that the individual concerned lacks a sense of 'self'. In other cultures in history, for example, a slave may not be, legally speaking, a 'person' but numerous oral or written accounts attest to a sense of 'self'.

This chapter has suggested that, in different ways, in sociological theory, individual experience and anthropological fieldwork certain distinctions emerge. These distinctions revolve around the individual and the person (or the self and the person) and the 'I' and the 'Me'. At this stage in the argument it is important not to get too involved in the finer details. The core idea, this chapter suggests, is a distinction between the more social, interacting with others, aspect of an individual and the more internal, reflecting self. Let us, for the sake of simplicity, state this as a distinction between the person and the self.

With this in mind, we can return to the idea of the social construction of personal life discussed in the previous section. When we talk about the social construction of personal life we are arguing that personal life is differently organized and valued in different societies. In some cases this may entail that some individuals are not accorded the status of 'person'. This does not mean that individuals in such societies do not possess a sense of 'self'.

Looking at modern societies and restating some points made earlier, the following considerations may seem to be important:

- Ideas of the person and personhood are strongly linked to ideas of human rights and democracy. One consequence of this is that there are constant debates about whether particular categories (children, prisoners, refugees, immigrants) should be allowed the status of full personhood.
- Ideas of the personal are strongly linked to notions of ownership and choice. To say that 'this is my personal opinion', for example, is to state some degree of ownership of that opinion.

- There is a heightened awareness of the distinction between the 'person' and the 'self'. This is probably a consequence of increased rates of social and geographical mobility and more complex divisions of labour. Under these circumstances it is possible to argue that the sets of others with whom we interact are too diverse and, often, too weakly connected to each other to provide a stable sense of personal identity.

- At the same time there appears to be an increasing value placed on the 'real' and 'authentic' self and an increasing desire to discover this by whatever means are available. If we consider public figures recognized throughout the world (Queen Elizabeth II, for example) we find that the question most frequently asked of that person is 'What is (s)he really like?'

This is not a complete list but points to some of the ways in which the personal is understood in modern societies, although there may be considerable variation within these societies. To say that the personal is socially constructed, therefore, is to say that there are social, historical or cultural causes of these various ways in which the personal is understood and valued.

Personal practices

This chapter has explored some of the range of meanings associated with the word 'personal' and the links between these meanings and the way in which the idea of the person can be seen as being shaped by numerous social and cultural influences. One thing should have become clear in the analysis so far. Although we have made a distinction between the self and the person (very roughly corresponding to Mead's distinction between the 'I' and the 'Me') it would seem that, in modern times, there is some desire to explore the relationships between the two and to colour the latter with a touch of the former. In other words, modern ideas of the person seem to point to something more or other than an assemblage of roles. For this reason the account provided of the socially constructed character of the personal, while it may seem plausible in some respects, may seem in some other ways unsatisfactory.

Part of the reason for this is that much of the argument seems to be operating at a high level of abstraction. Notions such as democracy, choice, privacy, ownership and so on are big words. They are no doubt important and influential but they frequently seem removed from, say, our example of the Australian suburban house-owner seeking to construct a living family environment. What needs to be done is to move from these public or scholarly discourses about the person and personal life to explore the actual practices of the personal. In other words, we need to see people in terms of all their actual interactions, past present and anticipated future, rather than in terms of more abstract categories or processes.

In talking about 'practices' this chapter draws upon a wide and complex range of sociological thought including symbolic interactionism, **ethnomethodology**, **feminism**, post-modern thought and the writings of Pierre

Bourdieu (Morgan, *Family Connections: An Introduction to Family Studies*, 1996; Morgan, *Family Practices Revisited*, 2011). Without over-elaborating, this chapter argues that a core idea of 'practices' is an emphasis upon doing and upon the everyday. This is close to familiar distinctions between 'theory' and 'practice'.

There is, however, a further dimension involved in the understanding of practices and that is the argument that practices are carried out in relation to certain specified 'others' (family, workmates, fellow members of a sports club) and that, in carrying out these practices, these sets of others are defined and redefined. For example, I may be defined as a 'neighbour' simply through virtue of the fact that I live near or next to a particular other person. But if I engage in 'neighbouring' I engage in a whole host of everyday practices such as keeping an eye on her house or watering plants if she is away and so on. Sometimes these practices may involve not doing something, such as not peering too intently if my neighbours are having a row in their back garden. All these practices, positive and negative, are in relation to another person and, in conducting them, I am creating or recreating or redefining a neighbourly relationship. Practices, therefore, are loosely structured activities which define certain kinds of relationships such as those between neighbours, family members, friends or colleagues.

These examples of relationships point to one issue which is relevant in considering the personal, namely that this is a sphere of life which is built up over time through interaction with others who are, or who become, in some way significant. The sense of what is personal is established on a day-to-day, even moment-to-moment, basis through interaction with or through taking account of these others. Again, this chapter will try to develop this theme with one or two illustrations.

Names and naming

In English-speaking countries the naming of individuals tends to follow the pattern of family name (surname) prefaced by a more freely chosen given name or names (Finch, 2008). Indeed, these other names may sometimes be described as 'personal names'. As Janet Finch demonstrates, everyday naming practices (naming a child after a grandparent, for example) provide valuable clues to family and other personal connections and values.

But there is a difference between allocating or ascribing an individual's name and in using a name. On a day-to-day basis we are frequently engaged in making small decisions about what to call another person. Do we use some formal mode of address or do we, if we know it, go straight for the first name? Do we ask permission to use a more personal name? How do we address a person from some other culture? The process of using particular names or not using particular names or of giving permission to use a particular name is part of the process of establishing personal relationships. Thus, the novelist E. M. Forster was known as 'Morgan' within his personal circles, while the British comedian

Frankie Howerd preferred to be known as 'Frank'. The British sociologist, A. H. Halsey is widely referred to as 'Chelly' (Morgan, 'The Gentle Art of Name-dropping', 2008). In order to be able to use these names, some kind of personal knowledge and some kind of personal relationship is presumed. In my own case, I prefer not to have my name abbreviated to 'Dave' and, again, this personal knowledge is known to people within my circles.

These everyday naming practices provide links between the self and the person. Over time, names (including nicknames) become part of our personal identity. They are both part of the way in which we present ourselves to the outside world, to significant or less significant others, but also part of the way that we feel about ourselves and who we are.

Seeking and receiving informal help

Among the various troubles and problems that individuals routinely encounter are those events which have been described as 'biographical disruptions' (Ketokivi, 2008). These are problems which are so severe that they cause some kind of re-evaluation of the self and one's personal biography; Kaisa Ketokivi talks of 'the wounded self'. In her qualitative Finnish study she includes cases where family members fall seriously ill, where there is a loss of a spouse or cases of unexpected divorce. While some individuals may seek, and confine themselves to, professional help of one kind or another, in most cases approaches are made to family or friends. In this study, she deploys the idea of 'family configurations' (Widmer and Jallinoja, 2008), an idea that stresses the idea that individuals are located in networks of family and friends that extend beyond any one particular household:

> Thus, disruption puts pressure on family configurations, but only some family members get mobilized to care for the wounded. These people become significant in a pronounced way while others stay in the background. At the same time, unexpectedly, other people step in as significant due to their responsiveness to the disruptive event. (Ketokivi, 2008, p. 255)

Ketokivi gives as an illustration the story of 'Sari', a woman of 44 with two children, whose husband died after a serious heart attack. In her case she was able to mobilize two significant others, her father and a friend, whom Sari had helped just two weeks prior to her husband's death. These two significant others had different ways of helping: 'her father made sure everyday life would continue for her children, but her friend took care of her basic needs' (*ibid.*, p. 261). The kind of material that Ketokivi presents vividly illustrates the relational character of personal life. Particular relationships within a wider configuration are given significance at the time of this crisis. These relationships are personal in that they are special to the individual involved and in that they reaffirm more general ideas of family and friendship and how they impact upon the self. Ketokivi, later in the same article, notes how there may be different responses which also impact on an individual's sense of the personal. Some apparently significant others (family or friends) may impact through their avoidance of the individual and her personal disruptions. And yet others (say workmates or acquaintances), outside the everyday configurations, may offer valuable sympathetic support. Thus, in different ways, others may contribute to the structure of personal life at a time of biographical disruption.

Concluding remarks

This chapter has considered a range of meanings attached to the word 'personal' and shown that it is frequently and strongly related to other ideas such as the individual, the distinction between the public and the private and with ownership. This would seem to suggest that it is more a matter for psychological than sociological enquiry. However, this chapter suggests that, in a variety of ways, personal life is socially constructed. This is not simply in terms of major historical shifts such as the developments of global capitalism but also in terms of more immediate, day-to-day interactions. In considering these personal practices we can still retain some sense of the self.

Indeed, what this discussion of personal practices illustrates is that the distinction, explored earlier, between the self and the person, cannot be readily sustained. Carol Smart's core concepts, which she develops in the course of elaborating her discussion of personal life, demonstrate this. These are: memory, biography, embeddedness, relationality and imaginary (Smart, *Personal Life: New Directions in Sociological Thinking*, 2007). In different ways these core concepts direct us to consider both the person, in the sense of the individual in his or her ongoing sets of relationships and institutional ties, and the self, responding to, evaluating and reflecting upon these others. Thus, when people talk about what they see as personal, they are claiming ownership of these values, ideas and experiences and stating something about their lives and their personal biographies. There is a constant reflexivity in the establishment and the mobilization of personal ties. Through the practices of interacting with these others, these ties are reaffirmed and given ongoing meanings.

Let us consider one final example; the shedding of tears (Carmichael, 1991). Weeping, and the feelings that give rise to tears, might seem to be deeply personal, beyond the reaches of sociological enquiry. But how and where we cry and in whose presence may tell us a lot about our personal life and the relationships that make up this life. Tears may come easily or with difficulty. They may reflect our sense of gendered selves, our positions in organizations and those who we trust or mistrust. Almost anything that we do within our everyday lives may provide points of entry into understanding the personal.

At the end, there is perhaps something mysterious and elusive about personal life. But this should not inhibit our attempts to understand this important sphere, so long as we conduct these attempts with sensitivity and tact.

Questions for discussion

■ Take any two everyday uses or dictionary definitions of the word 'personal' and discuss what these tell us about the place of personal life in modern society.

■ In what ways is personal life 'socially constructed'?

■ How does G. H. Mead's distinction between the 'I' and the 'Me' illuminate our understanding of personal life in modern society?

■ Is it helpful to talk about personal life in terms of practices? Illustrate your argument with reference to any relevant piece of sociological research, work of fiction or autobiographical writing.

Personal Life in the Past

Wendy Bottero

Introduction: the 'facts of life' (or what the great-great-great-great-grandparents got up to)

There have been dramatic shifts in patterns of sexual activity in Western countries over the last 200 years: what have been the consequences of these changes for intimate personal relationships? To understand the impact of social change in the *present*, we must first get a sense what people did in the *past*. But our view of 'the past' is often based on misconceptions or sweeping generalizations. This chapter examines social change in personal life, and explodes some popular myths about sex and intimacy in past times.

We are all familiar with the idea that people in the past were prudes about sex, or that our ancestors had very large families, or that the decline in family size is the result of the contraceptive pill. However, prostitution was endemic in Victorian England, very large families were relatively unusual in the eighteenth century in Europe and North America, and as for 'sexual liberation' and the pill, the British decline in family size, for example, can be traced to the 1870s – long before any reliable method of contraception was widely available. So we need to be careful when we make comparisons between 'then' and 'now'. Historically, people's sexual lives *were* organized very differently, but this varied at different times and in different places.

Because we have to be quite specific about the sorts of comparisons that we make, this chapter looks at Northern European practices, from the late seventeenth century on, focusing on the particular example of Britain (though it is worth noting that similar practices were occurring in North America and Australia, colonial countries receiving large numbers of European migrants). It also focuses on reproductive *heterosexual* sex, because this is the type of sexual practice that is most apparent in the historical record (though it was certainly not the only sort of sexual activity – this issue of the 'invisibility' of nonheterosexuals will be examined more closely in Anna Einarsdottir's chapter in the present volume). As we shall see, the sexual practices of people living in the 1850s were not the same as *their* great-grandparents, and both seem pretty different to those of people today.

Beneath the sheets: documenting sexual activity

How is it that we know about people's private sexual lives in the past? Some people's letters and diaries refer to this, but such fascinating personal documents are rare, and usually only offer a glimpse of the intimate lives of a rich or well-educated minority. For the vast majority of people we have just the bare bones of their lives as they survive in the historical record – chiefly through the church or civil registration of births, marriages and deaths which become the subject matter of historical demography – telling us about the fertility, death, marriage and illegitimacy rates at different times. But what can these rather dull-sounding facts and figures reveal about how people lived their personal lives?

Actually, fertility and illegitimacy rates can tell us rather a lot about sexual activity. Because before the widespread availability of (reliable) contraception heterosexual sex always carried a strong risk of conception, the clues about reproductive sex that we get from fertility and illegitimacy rates can tell us quite a bit about people's sex lives more generally. This is not to say that people *only* had sex to have children, or that they did not engage in sex for pleasure (as we shall see) but, without reliable contraception, people's sexual practices, and their views about sex, were strongly affected by the potential impact of having a child. For *reproduction* was always linked to *production* – the need to ensure economic survival for parents and children. Amongst ordinary folk, no one minded much if marriage (official or common-law) followed shortly *after* a baby, and, indeed, the sexual activity of engaged couples frequently anticipated the marriage banns. But unwed mothers struggled to support their children, and illegitimate children were seen as both a burden upon the rate payers of the local community, and a source of shame and ruin for their parents, who could face ostracism and the loss of 'respectable' employment as a result. And just as views about sex *outside* marriage were affected by fears over who would support the children that might result, so too attitudes to sex *within* marriage were affected by the need to balance 'hands to work' and 'mouths to feed' within households, since too many children could mean economic ruin for families. Prior to the widespread use of contraception (from the 1920s in Britain) sexual activity was always framed by the risks of reproduction (Seccombe, 1993; Cook, H., 2004).

Let's think about that. The 'natural' fertility of a healthy, sexually active woman would potentially allow her to bear a child every eighteen months, from the onset of menstruation to menopause. What would that mean for a woman's life? To help think this through, Box 3.1 gives a model example of a woman – 'Eliza' – whose reproductive history is close to a 'natural' fertility career.

We might suspect that bearing 22 children made Eliza's life physically hard. Her last child was born when she was 47, so she was either pregnant, breast-feeding a baby, or had young children underfoot, for around 35 years of her adult life. And that many mouths to feed could cause economic hardship, so, however pleasurable she might find sex, she and her husband would always

Box 3.1 An example of 'natural' fertility: Eliza and her family tree

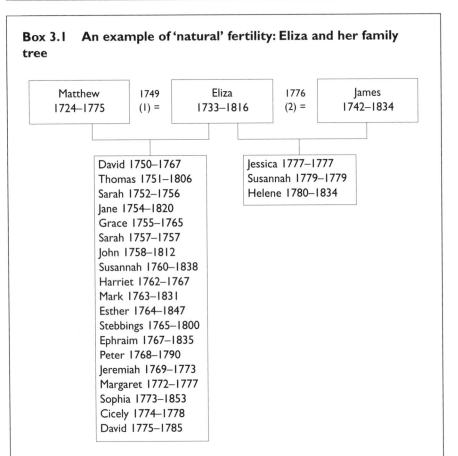

Eliza lived from 1733–1816, and had 22 children from two marriages. She married at 15, had her first child at 17, and then a child roughly every 12 to 18 months, bearing 19 children in total, until 1773 when her first husband, Matthew, died. The following year, aged 43, she married again, to James, and had another three children. She had 22 children in total, although ten died at birth or in childhood. What would be the impact of this reproductive career on her personal life: for her relationship with her children and husbands, and for her view of sex?

have to think that another child could result, and might damage Eliza's health or the household finances. So we might also suspect that her views about pregnancy, and sex, would not be wholly positive. However, if we thought this we would be wrong.

Eliza's fertility history is based on that of a real-life historical figure, Emily Lennox, who lived from 1731–1814. We still have Emily's letters and journals, which make it clear that Emily enjoyed a passionate and pleasurable sex life with her husbands, so much so that her sisters' letters teased her about her enthusiasm for the marital bed. And not just the marital one! Emily conducted an affair with her children's tutor (and nine years her junior), for several years before her first husband's death. She caused a sensation when, at 43, she later married him. Her last child from her first marriage, was probably fathered by her lover.

As you may have guessed from this, one factor in Emily's enthusiastic sex life was her social position. The impact of Emily's fertility on her life was strongly affected by the fact that Emily was a British aristocrat (daughter of the Duke of Richmond, great-grand-daughter of King Charles II of England, and wife of the Duke of Leinster) living a wealthy and privileged life, with many servants (for more information about the life of Emily, and her husbands, children, and sisters, see Tillyard, 1995). We can see the clues of this privilege in the key demographic facts of her life. Despite her many children, Emily lived to the age of 83. This was a long life at a time when complications from pregnancy were the major cause of death amongst women, and shows her affluence and good overall health. But we can also detect her privileged background in the size of her family, and her early age at marriage. It is sometimes assumed that, in the past, early marriage and very large families were the norm, but in fact, during Emily's life-time (the eighteenth century) it was only the wealthy or the aristocratic who did this, because only they could *afford* such practices. Ordinary people had fewer children, and delayed marrying until they were in their mid- to late twenties, when they could afford to start a family.

In much of North-West Europe, before and during the 1700s, the average completed family size was around five to six children (although families of ten children were not uncommon) (Anderson, 1980). Family size was a little higher than this in the United States (Klein, 2004). High infant and child mortality (which we can also see in Emily's family tree, by the way) meant many children did not survive to adulthood. However, it was not only high mortality that affected family size, since couples were able to limit their fertility by marrying later in life. For example, in the early 1700s in England, the average age at marriage was around 25–6 for women, 27–8 for men; and around 25–6 for men and 22–3 for women in parts of America (Wrigley *et al.*, 1997; Klein, 2004). Before the nineteenth century, this later age at marriage was the main way in which couples limited the number of children that they had. Compared to Emily Lennox (who married at 15 and had her first child at 17) a delay in marrying until the age of 25 could mean around four to six fewer pregnancies in an average woman's life.

The weight of numbers: the North-West European marriage pattern

In fact, historians looking at population demography have shown that delaying marriage was such a common and widespread practice that it is called the 'North-West European marriage pattern' (Hajnal, 1965). It was prevalent throughout North-West Europe (excluding Ireland) from the fourteenth century to the early 1700s, when the industrial revolution started to change things (more on that later). It was a 'low-pressure' demographic system (Wrigley and Schofield, 1989) because it was restrictions on fertility (rather than high levels of mortality) which limited the growth of the population. In the North-West European marriage pattern a set of linked practices acted to limit fertility:

- A widespread cultural expectation that couples should not marry until they could set up their own financially viable household, independent of their parents.
- A late age of marriage, which restricted fertility *within* marriage.
- Social disapproval for, and restrictions on, extra-marital sex, which limited fertility *outside* of marriage.
- High rates of 'celibacy': around 10–14 per cent of people never reproduced (usually because they could not afford to marry).

This set of practices was characterized by the heavy regulation of the sexual activity of young adults, as work and family arrangements in the pre-industrial economy combined to restrain young people from having children without the resources to support them. A new couple were expected to set up their own independent household on marriage, and not live with their parents. For this reason, and because of high mortality rates, the North-West European marriage pattern is not characterized by extended families where several generations live together – instead we see smaller 'nuclear' households.

For those families with some resources to pass on (a small plot of farmland, household goods, tools or a business) a couple could marry when they inherited at the death of their parents. The majority of folk, with no such resources, however, had to wait until they had a secure work position, or had saved enough, to allow them to marry. For most young people in Britain, for example, entering work meant entering a shop or craft apprenticeship, domestic service, or working on a farm; and all of these jobs put young people in situations which monitored their sexual activity, and heavily penalized them if they stepped out of line.

Domestic servants, farm workers and apprentices lived where they worked, under the watchful eye of their employers, and by the terms of their labour contracts were not permitted to marry. If they did, or were caught in sexual impropriety, they were dismissed without a 'character' (that is, without a reference), so they could not get another job. Since farm workers and domestic servants were typically 'tied' labourers (hired on a year's contract, receiving board and lodging, but only getting their year's pay at the very end of the contract), to be dismissed in this fashion could mean losing an entire year's wages.

If all this was not restriction enough, there was a heavy social stigma attached to illegitimacy. This was not merely symbolic, since unwed mothers (or fathers who shirked their responsibilities) would be subject to 'rough music', a social shaming in which rural villagers gathered outside the miscreant's house

---

Box 3.2   The North-West European marriage pattern in North America?

The North-West European marriage pattern was very distinctive, but what happened when people migrated? The early pattern of family practices in North America 1600–1800 was strongly influenced by successive waves of migrants who (initially at least) helped to create America and Canada as colonial 'settler' societies. Early migrants were often indentured servants from Europe (selling a contract on themselves to pay for their passage) or were slaves from Africa, and for such groups the unfree conditions of their labour restricted their family practices. More generally, migrants were young, and there were greater numbers of men than women; this sex-ratio imbalance meant that American men in the 1600s were marrying at an older age than in North Europe, while American women were marrying younger than their European counterparts (because it was harder for American men to find wives).

- In New England in the 1700s, for example, white men typically married at 25–6 years of age and white women at 22–3, around two years earlier than in England at the same period.
- This earlier age of marriage for white women in New England meant that their marital fertility was a little higher, with a completed family size of six to eight children in the 1700s, compared to an English norm of five to six children (Klein, 2004, p. 50).

However, despite these variations, and the higher overall fertility rates in the USA, we can still see many of the key elements of the North-West European marriage pattern in America during the 1600–1700s: a delayed age of marriage linked to the setting up of independent households, and tight restrictions on fertility outside of marriage, both of which combined to limit the numbers of children that were conceived (Klein, 2004).

---

to shout and sing rude songs, throw stones and sometimes to even physically harm the offender.

Around the mid-eighteenth century (during Emily Lennox's life), this set of practices began to change in Britain. A series of shifts in working and living arrangements, the beginning of the industrial revolution, started to relax some of the social restrictions on young people's sexual activities. As result, there was a move away from the 'low-pressure' demographic regime of the North-West European marriage pattern, with an increase in fertility and illegitimacy rates, and a resulting population explosion. A similar population explosion occurred in the United States, but can be dated from a little earlier (partly due to continuing and growing immigration, but also linked to the earlier age of marriage and the resulting larger family sizes among Americans) (Klein, 2004). In 1751, the population in England, Wales and Scotland was about 7.5 million: this had ballooned to nearly 21 million by 1851 and to 37 million by 1901 (Woods, 1992, p. 10). So what changed?

With the start of the industrial revolution, a period of rapid industrial change and economic growth, there was a decline in agricultural and tied labour and a move to a wage labour economy. Fewer young people had to serve out a set term of labour living in their master's household, as more impersonal and more limited contractual ties emerged between employers and workers. In factories, for example, workers were hired by the day or week, a big change from the year-long contracts of domestic or farm servants. And with rapid urbanization, young workers moved away from the watchful gaze of small rural communities to the thronging cities, which provided more impersonal, and transitory, environments. All this meant less surveillance of workers' personal lives, and fewer constraints (and penalties) on their sexual behaviour. The changes conspired to relax the limits on fertility: illegitimacy and childbirth rates went up, and the average age at marriage went down, leading to a population expansion and a shift in the age structure, with a big rise in the proportion of young people in the population.

In thinking about the implications of this for personal life, we need to be careful not to overstate the extent of the changes. Big shifts in the population can emerge from smaller changes in the personal and sexual life of individuals. Take the change in the age of marriage. By the 1800s in Britain, as elsewhere in Northern Europe, this had fallen, by about two and half years, to around 23 for women, 25 for men (Wrigley *et al.*, 1997). This would not make a huge difference in the behaviour or marital fertility of a couple: they would still wait to marry and start a family, and could expect about two more pregnancies from the earlier start to their married life (although it has been argued – by H. Cook (2004) – that these extra pregnancies would have increased the burden on mothers and adversely affected their overall health). However, a small increase in family size has a *geometric* effect on population size (that is, population size grows exponentially). Imagine if every extra surviving child born to a family had six or seven children *themselves*, and then each of *these* six or seven children had six or seven children too. In just three generations, a large number of people would be added to the population. So a shift of a few years in the marriage age can lead to a population 'explosion'.

However, it seems that in the second half of the nineteenth century a population shift occurred which *was* the result of a major change in people's personal lives. This led to a transformation in (heterosexual) sexual activity in many countries in Northern Europe and North America.

A sexual revolution: the first demographic transition

In the second half of the nineteenth century a fertility decline started across Northern Europe which has continued to the present day. We can date the change rather differently for different places (it started earlier, by the early 1800s, in France and the USA, for example), but we can see very similar patterns in many countries. Social historians often describe these changes as a 'revolution' in family and sexual practices – a 'demographic transition' to the lower fertility rates which characterize many contemporary societies. It is called the 'first demographic transition' for two reasons. First, it is argued that the changes were not just a gradual shift in demographic behaviour (as in the shift away from the 'low-pressure' North-West European marriage system), but a substantial and rapid break with what people had done before. Second, it is the *first* demographic transition because demographers believe that we are currently in the midst of another break, a '*second* demographic transition' (on which more below).

What made the first demographic transition so different? One key difference was that fertility was affected not just by variations in the age or incidence of marriage as before, but also for the first time by shifts in sexual behaviour within marriage. People moved swiftly to having fewer children, accomplished through a big shift in marital sexual relations, and without the widespread use of contraceptive methods.

The fertility decline started first among the middle classes (which is probably why people often think, wrongly, that middle-class families were *always* smaller than working-class families). But by the end of the nineteenth century, the decline was evident among all social classes. For example, in Britain between 1870 and 1920, the mean completed family size fell rapidly, from just over six children per family to around two children (Anderson, 1980; Gittins, 1982). In the United States, the total fertility rates in the 1870s were already lower, at about 4.5 children per woman, and family size dropped from then on in a manner which roughly matched the decline in Europe (Klein, 2004, p. 121). And, as Diane Gittins (1982) has pointed out, this was not just a shift in average tendencies but also in distributions (the variability in family sizes was also reduced). There was a greater homogeneity in lifecourse transitions, as smaller families became overwhelmingly the typical experience:

- of marriages taking place in 1860 in Britain, 20 per cent had two children or fewer;
- of marriages taking place in 1925, 67 per cent had two children or fewer (Gittins, 1982, p. 33).

How was this shift in marital fertility achieved? There *was* an increased use of contraceptive devices, but only after the 1920s, long after the fertility decline had taken hold. Before this period, 'mechanical' contraceptive devices (like the sheath) had a strong social stigma, because they were associated with prostitution and venereal disease, and were not readily – or cheaply – available to the working classes. From the 1920s on, contraception became more respectable, with an increased demand for 'female' devices (such as caps, diaphragms and pessaries), made available to married women through 'family planning' clinics, like those set up by the birth control activist Marie Stopes. However, in the late nineteenth century, it seems that couples limited their family size through three much more difficult methods – abortion, withdrawal and abstinence. But how do we know this?

Our knowledge comes from different sources: chiefly from a number of social surveys conducted in the early 1900s; but also from the letters written by members of the public to birth control pioneers (like Marie Stopes) asking for advice; from the records of the early birth control clinics; from the oral histories collected from those who were young women in the first quarter of the twentieth century; and also from hospital records (Fisher, 2006; Seccombe, 1993).

From hospital records we have evidence of a rise in the incidence of induced abortion in the late nineteenth century, through the use of abortifacient remedies and backstreet abortionists. Abortion was illegal, but abortion remedies ('renovating' or 'periodic' pills and potions) and services were widely advertised in the press. Many did not work, but those that did could be extremely dangerous, hence the visibility of abortion in hospital and mortality records. It is estimated that in Britain around 16–20 per cent of pregnancies were deliberately terminated, with most abortions occurring among married women in their later child-bearing years (Seccombe, 1993, p. 158).

We also know that couples increased their resort to sexual abstinence, generally by reducing coital frequency (the 'spacing' of intercourse at intervals), but also by 'stopping', the cessation of sexual activity (usually when a set family size had been reached). But abstinence was hard to maintain, and so couples also practised the withdrawal method (although the safest techniques for this were poorly understood).

All these were difficult methods of family limitation, with couples often struggling with the problems that abstinence and withdrawal created. Correspondents to Marie Stopes in the 1920s wrote eloquently of their problems with these methods, desperately asking for contraceptive advice:

- 'My husband is very good and for three years has not had a real "pleasure" in order to keep me right.'
- 'My husband had been withdrawing all that time and the only time I had any suspicion he was not so careful was on his birthday and [nine months later] my second boy was born ... I make my Husband and myself miserable by always worrying in case I have another baby. Please do help.'
- 'At certain times of the month we nearly get beyond control ... it is strange for us to go four years without proper connections.'
- 'When the last baby was born the doctor said can't you finish up but when I asked him how ... he just laughed. What's the use of saying finish up when they won't tell us poor women how to.'
- 'I was so afraid of being caught again that I stopped all intercourse, then my husband fell ill and of course I had to humour him a bit, the result was another baby.'
- 'My husband tells me to control and hold myself in check, well I can, but we do without kisses, and oh, lots of other little things that help make life pleasant.' (Correspondents to Stopes, quoted in Seccombe, 1993, pp. 170–2)

With such difficult (and, in abortion, dangerous) methods adopted, we can see that couples must have been strongly motivated to limit their families. Clearly a very significant change had occurred in people's attitudes to sex and child-bearing within marriage. But why did it happen? And why then?

How many children shall we have? Birth control and family planning

Though there are many theories, no one is entirely sure why the decline occurred. We can see a division between those emphasizing economic factors (which look at the effects of economic changes on people's motivations) and cultural factors (which look at shifts in attitudes and values in their own right). One problem in explaining why people changed their fertility behaviour is that we also have to explain the *timing* of the changes. One obvious reason to have fewer children within marriage is that a higher household standard of living is possible as a result. But why did not people realize that sooner? What was stopping people having fewer children before?

One potential explanation might be a shift in the economic 'costs' and 'returns' of having children. So, for example, Joseph Banks (1954) argues that the fertility decline can be traced to rising standards of affluence among the middle classes. During the nineteenth century, middle-class parents were increasingly obliged to devote more of their income to schooling their children (with the increasing importance of education in public life, and the rise of expensive private schooling). They were also tempted to spend more on con-sumer goods (such as a carriage, servants and a 'respectable' address), to main-tain a good appearance. The solution to this increased economic and status pressure was smaller families, with parents having fewer children but invest-ing more in each child. A similar economic explanation has been put forward for the working classes' behaviour. In the early 1800s, children were put to work at the age of five or six, and so could contribute early to the family finances. But by the late 1800s, child labour was outlawed and compulsory schooling introduced (in the 1870s in Britain). This meant children were eco-nomic costs to their parents for far longer than before. As a result, working-class families could no longer afford so many children.

However, it is not clear that this fully explains fertility behaviour. The eco-nomic value of children did fall, but children are valued in other ways, and this too is bound up with fertility behaviour. People had already begun to have dif-ferent ideas about what children's lives should be like, which was one reason why child labour was banned and compulsory schooling introduced in the first place. So, children may have become less economically valuable *as a result* of shifting cultural attitudes to child-rearing, not vice versa. John Gillis (1992) argues that the fertility decline in industrial countries resulted from a shift in how 'mothering' and 'fathering' were understood. 'Father' and 'mother' were once roles which were held by virtue of being heads of a household, and always involved 'familial' relations with non-kin (such as servants, apprentices, lodgers and so on). Death and hardship meant households often sent their children off to be cared for by others, or looked after other people's children.

However, during the course of the nineteenth century, this became increasingly impossible for 'respectable' families, as parenting roles became associated with a much more moralized view of biological parenting. Parenting became a more intense and exclusive relationship. Mothers, for example, were now expected to physically care for their own children for much of their time, and to have an intense emotional bond with them. So the burden of parenting became greater (and could no longer be shared with non-kin). According to Gillis (1992), it was the increased emotional and caring costs of looking after children, rather than the economic costs, which affected the family size of the middle classes.

So when we consider the economic motivations for fertility behaviour we also have to think about the cultural and social values that people have about children and families, and the role of sex within marriage. Before the demographic transition, there was a strong belief that sexual intercourse was intended primarily for procreation within marriage, not for pleasure. Married couples did not weigh up the 'costs' of how many children they should have, because there seems to have been little notion that they *could* control the size of their family. The timing of a marriage might limit the number of children, but once they were married couples were 'fatalistic' about the arrival of children. These ideas had changed by the end of the nineteenth century. Couples now began to see that it was possible and permissible to limit family size, and family limitation was more widely discussed (Seccombe 1993; Hawkes, 1996). Robert Woods (1992) argues that the dominant religious code (the belief that sex was intended only for procreation) began to lose its force, both because of secularization (as organized religion lost its sway on urban populations) but also because women had become more independent and assertive in their attitude to marital relations.

Wally Seccombe (1993) makes a similar argument about the fertility decisions of the working classes. He argues that the economic model of the 'costs' of child-bearing fails to see that the risks and interests in sex were not the same for women and men. Working-class women, he argues, *always* had a greater interest in controlling marital fertility. Ill-health through pregnancy, child care, the economic battle to run households, all these costs were borne more by *women* than men, which affected women's desire to have children – and sex. The 'differential distress' of repeated pregnancy (women suffered more than men) affected the 'ratio of sexual desire'. What changed at the end of the nineteenth century was that women's power within households grew (women were more literate and better educated, and there were shifts in women's role in society, with increasing numbers of women employed outside the home) so that women had a greater say in when they had sex and when they had children. The shift in gender relations led to greater discussion between men and women about family size and joint practices of limitation.

In this argument, for fertility decline to be achieved within marriage, men and women had to agree that family limitation was a good thing, and they also had to agree on how to put it into practice. Women, suggests Seccombe, had always wanted smaller families (hence the high levels of abortion among married women), but it was only in the late nineteenth century that they could do something about it in partnership with their husbands. Given the other techniques of family limitation at the time (withdrawal and abstinence) men had to cooperate with women in family limitation. Seccombe argues that it was shifts in gender relations that affected the timing of fertility decline.

Whatever the reasons for the fertility decline, the consequence was a big change in personal lives. A reduction in family size meant different relations between parents and children, and also in women's lives, with a significant reduction of the proportion of a woman's lifecourse spent child-bearing and child-rearing. And, for the first time, marital sexuality was 'decoupled' from fertility, and was instead seen primarily as part of the intimate connection between husband and wife. Marie Stopes, who pioneered family planning clinics in Britain, gives us a good example of this changing view of marital sexuality. Her book *Married Love*, published in 1918, was enormously successful, selling over 400,000 copies in under six years. In it, Stopes stressed the importance of sexual fulfilment for a successful marriage, and linked control over fertility to sexual pleasure (the last chapter is called 'The Glorious Unfolding'). This sexual pleasure was now increasingly seen as an issue of appropriate technique and sex education.

Concluding remarks

This chapter has examined social change in personal life, and has suggested that to understand the impact of social change in the present, we must first get a sense of what people did in the past. Currently, demographers believe that post-industrial societies like Britain and the United States are undergoing a 'second demographic transition' (Lesthaeghe, 1994). This is a shift in people's fertility patterns, and household and partnership arrangements, which is having significant impact on personal life.

The second demographic transition is characterized by high levels of people living alone, high levels of cohabitation and child-bearing outside of marriage, delayed fertility and high rates of union disruption. So, for example, in Britain, we see high rates of divorce and remarriage, a declining marriage rate and an increase in the proportion of people never marrying (the impact of these on personal life are further discussed in Chapter 4 by Carol Smart). At the same time, there has been an increase in the average age at which women have their first child (27.1 years in 2000), and an increase in the proportion of women remaining childless (one in ten women born in 1945, rising to one in five women born in 1961) (Office of National Statistics, 2010a, 2010b). Similar statistics could be presented for other Western countries. For example,

America shows similar long-term shifts. In the United States there has been a rise in divorces, cohabitation and in births outside of marriage, the average age at which women have their first child has risen from 21.4 years in 1970 to 25.0 years in 2006 (Matthews and Hamilton, 2009), and the increase in the proportion of women not having any children has nearly doubled, from 10 per cent in 1976 to 18 per cent in 2008 (Dye, 2008),

These developments certainly amount to a substantial change from say, the 1950s (for a discussion of how the contemporary 'demographic transition' is affecting personal relationships, see Irwin, 2005). But many of these patterns – for example, delayed child-bearing, and high proportions remaining unmarried and childless – would be very familiar to people from the 1850s or 1750s. The shifts have also meant greater *variability* in household forms and in the timing of lifecourse transitions – something which also echoes those earlier times. Of course, there are big differences too. Historically, sexuality was always con-structed within the need to control fertility, and was regulated by marriage and the birth of children, and by the organization of work and economic subsis-tence. This is not to say that people did not take pleasure in sex – as Emily Lennox's diaries and some of the Stopes correspondence show – but the risks and penalties of conception always framed heterosexuality in the past.

Over time, however, sexuality and fertility have become increasingly dis-tinct, and the economic and family constraints on sexual behaviour have changed. In the contemporary period, there has been an 'uncoupling' of sex, not simply from reproduction and child-bearing, but also from marriage (Hawkes, 1996). In the process, the *meaning* of 'sex' in personal life, and its implications for social relationships, has been transformed.

Questions for discussion

■ Emily Lennox lived an aristocratic, privileged life – but she had 22 chil-dren in 30 years. What would be the impact of this level of fertility on her personal daily life?

■ Think about how we have to reconstruct the personal and sexual lives of people in the past from what survives in the historical record. What sorts of things might be missed out from such historical sources? Will there be systematic omissions or distortions?

■ Post-industrial societies are currently said to be undergoing a 'second demographic transition'. Bearing in mind that big shifts in the *population* can emerge from smaller changes in the personal and sexual life of *indi-viduals*, how do you think this 'second demographic transition' will affect personal lives?

■ Think about current sexual practices – are there significant differences in how they are being documented and recorded, compared to past gen-erations? What picture of *our* sexual practices will survive for future generations?

Close Relationships and Personal Life

Carol Smart

4

Introduction

This chapter focuses on the cultural significance of forming close attachments to people outside one's family of origin and kinship network. It will explore heterosexual relationships because same-sex relationships will be covered in detail in Chapter 5. Here, we will consider what we can learn from the sociology of emotions, particularly relating to love, as a way of understanding contemporary personal life. We will then turn to specific forms of relationships such as cohabitation, marriage, divorce and separation, before addressing issues of living apart together and solo living and what these changing patterns of intimate living may mean for contemporary personal life.

Love and emotions

The study of emotions is now an important sub-field within sociology but, even so, emotions such as love are rarely addressed in most studies of relationships. This is a problem because sociology can offer an important way of understanding emotions which differs from common-sense approaches or the now popular psychological accounts which appear in magazines and self-help manuals. So, what follows is a brief outline of how to understand emotions sociologically.

Deborah Lupton (1998) has argued that emotions are socio-cultural constructs rather than innate feelings that we are born with. This means that what people feel and how they may express their feelings is not universal, nor unchanging. Different cultures, for example, have different repertoires of emotions and Western cultures have changed considerably over the last century in terms of what emotions can be expressed and who is allowed to express feelings in different contexts. This realization has led sociologists to understand how important culture is to emotions and, within this broad notion of culture, to focus on specific categories such as gender, class, religion, generation and so on. This means that women are likely to express emotions in different ways to men, upper-class men may express emotions differently to working-class men; people in their 70s are likely to express feelings differently to teenagers.

Arlie Hochschild (1983) introduced the concept of 'feeling rules' in which she relates the structure of society to how we express our emotions and also to the way in which we are meant to feel about things. For example, she argued that in Western culture women are expected to carry out 'emotion work' in both relationships and in the workplace. She carried out a study of female airline stewards in the USA and discovered that they were obliged to smile, to be compassionate and understanding, and to manage the distress (as well as inappropriate behaviour) of customers as part of their job. It was the women workers who had to contain their own feelings while being totally attentive to the feelings of others, but they also had to present themselves as happy, smiling and obliging at all times.

Lupton (1998) carried out focus groups with men and women in Australia in order to find out how they spoke about emotions. She discovered that they spoke quite differently about emotions; that they expected women to be more 'emotional' and more expressive; and that they also expected women to be more attentive to the feelings of their partners and their children. Lupton argued that men and women are not born with innate emotional differences but that as part of the socialization process men and women learn different emotion 'scripts', which means in turn that they take on board different ways of 'doing' emotion.

To understand this fully it is necessary to think about the ways in which the 'self' is constructed relationally. This is often referred to as the **'relational self'**. David Morgan discussed in Chapter 2 the distinction between the more internal self (the 'I') and the more social person (the 'Me'), the latter of which is the result of our interactions with others. So how others see us becomes a kind of mirror in which we can see ourselves (Burkitt, 2008; Griffiths, 1995). Hence, we adjust ourselves interactively, especially if the others concerned are people who are very important to us. It is not just that parents may *tell* a little boy not to cry or not to show his emotions; it is more than this because a young man's very sense of himself becomes imbued with the idea that he, as a gendered individual, does not do emotions in a demonstrable fashion. Hence, it becomes very hard to change how one does emotions because it requires a reshaping of the self. The two things go together.

Emotions, even though they are socially and culturally constructed, are nonetheless experienced as highly personal. This is why it is hard to understand, initially at least, that something as intimate and private as emotions of joy, desire, misery or shame can be both personal and social at the same time. This is because, sociologically speaking, emotional responses are understood to be influenced and even shaped by cultural and social factors. It follows from this that to understand close personal relationships we need to recognize that emotions such as love will play an important part in finding a partner, separating from a partner, deciding to become a parent and so on. But because 'love' and other emotions are understood slightly differently in different cultures, the part that they play in relationships will also vary, as we will see in the next section. Emotions give meaning(s) to personal relationships, but these very emotions are not 'extra-social' or beyond sociological understanding.

Marriage and cohabitation

In Western cultures there is a long tradition of basing marriage on romantic love (Giddens, 1992; Finch and Summerfield, 1991). Although there are exceptions to this (for example, arranged or introduced marriages in Jewish, Muslim and Hindu traditions; see Box 4.1) there is a normative assumption

---

Box 4.1 Arranged marriage

Western societies have, for at least a century or more, emphasized that their system of marriage should be based on 'free choice' and on romantic attachment or love. However, this was not always the case (for example, marriages between people of property or royalty). Moreover, as such cultures have become more multicultural, we now find many families living in Western societies who do not subscribe to these ideals. Orthodox Jewish families have long relied on the services of matchmakers to introduce young couples to each other, having vetted the families on each side. Many Pakistani and Hindu families also follow the traditions of arranged marriages. In Pakistani culture there is a system of cousin marriage in which it may be known from childhood who a boy or girl will marry on reaching adulthood.

The quotation below came from a Hindu man who was interviewed for a study on transnational families in the UK in the early 2000s (Smart and Shipman, 2004). His statement shows an appreciation of the tradition as well as emphasizing the extent to which a marriage is about the union of two families rather than just two individuals:

> Mrigendra: Well [it is a] nice system, what we call a vetted marriage not arranged marriage, vetted marriage. Somebody proposes or there is a girl from a certain family and my family enquire about them. The members of their family enquire about myself. Everything about this includes the family, their status in the society, and then after we meet once or twice ... If both sides go well then it's good.

It is helpful to understand these different forms of marriage in terms of a continuum rather than seeing 'love' marriages and 'arranged' marriages as the complete antithesis of each other. Few people who marry for love actually marry outside their class, ethnic or religious group, generational cohort and education level. In other words the tendency is to 'choose' from a very limited circle of potential partners. On the other hand, with vetted or arranged marriages couples are expected to like one another and to agree to the match. Although there are examples of forced marriages, these are not generally regarded as acceptable practices any longer. It is also sometimes argued that marriages that are vetted or arranged are more stable than those based on strong emotions or sexual desire; however, there is no real evidence for this since it is very hard to divorce or even separate from one's spouse in Muslim and Hindu cultures.

that close intimate and sexual relationships which result in marriage are usually based on romantic love. There is a whole industry surrounding weddings, including choosing romantic settings, selecting elaborate wedding attire, arranging exotic hen and stag nights and so on. There is also an extensive popular literature on falling in love, finding a partner, and planning to become a couple. It is hard to escape the expectation that one will marry and, of course, the whole process is presented as if it is entirely natural.

But if marriage is the inevitable outcome of being in love it would be hard to account for why, in most European countries and the USA, the marriage rate has been declining since the early 1970s unless fewer people now fall in love. For example, in England and Wales, the number of marriages registered in 2008 was the lowest since 1895 and there have been several fluctuations in the marriage rate in between these dates. Similar patterns can be found in most European countries, and Sweden now has the lowest rate of marriage in the world. In the USA the marriage rate per 1,000 of the population in 1950 was estimated as 11.1, by 1990 it had reduced to 9.8 and in 2008 it was 7.3 (http://www.infoplease.com/ipa/A0005044.html). It is clear that rates of marriage are subject to influence by factors such as wars, economic conditions, shifts in moral and cultural values, and legal changes. Thus, there is no automatic or 'natural' relationship between the emotion of love and the rate of marriage.

The age at which couples marry has also been subject to fluctuation, and an increased age at first marriage is a pattern that can be found in many European societies, the USA (Kiernan, 2002) and Australia. The graph below shows the changes occurring in Australia:

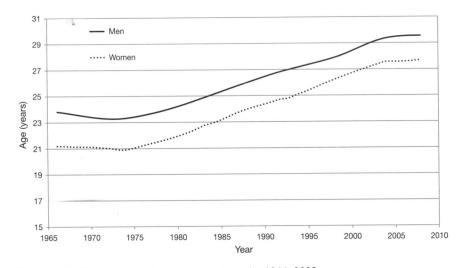

Figure 4.1   Median age at first marriage, Australia, 1966–2008

Source: Australian Institute of Family Studies, http://www.aifs.gov.au/institute/info/charts/marriage/median.html, data from ABS (various years) *Marriages and Divorces Australia*; ABS (various years) *Marriages Australia*; ABS (1997) *Austrailian Social Trends*.

In the UK, the Office for National Statistics has shown that in 1974 the average age of first marriage for men was 25 and for women it was 23. By 2004 it had risen to 31 years for men and 29 years for women. In the USA the situation is quite similar, with the median age of first marriage for men in 1950 being 22.8 years, while in 2007 it rose to 27.7 years. For women the median age in 1950 was 20.3 years and in 2007 it was 26 years (http://www.infoplease.com/ipa/A0005061.html). This is a substantial social variation and shows that couples are waiting considerably longer to get married. The presumption that prevailed in most Western countries in the 1950s and 1960s that a couple would meet while still living at home with their respective parents, then get engaged, then married and only then to start having children has become a much less dominant pattern of forming relationships. By 2010 it was not uncommon for young people to leave home first, then to cohabit and buy or rent a home; then they may decide to marry later, if they wanted children, have their children prior to marrying, or choose not to marry at all. In the early twenty-first century many heterosexual couples can make choices about the order in which they shape these life events. Such choices are not 'free' choices, however, but are made in the prevailing context of economic conditions, the cost of housing, the availability of employment and, of course, such things as state or family support for parenting.

Jane Lewis (2001) carried out a study of commitment in the UK in which she asked a younger generation of couples (mostly between the ages of 35–45) and their parents (the older generation aged 52–87) about their choices either to cohabit or to marry. She found that the older generation felt they had no choice at all about cohabiting – it was too socially scandalous – but they also had no real choice about marrying because it was such a strong social convention. Put simply, if they wanted a sexual relationship, children and/or to leave home, they had to get married. The younger generation by comparison felt they could choose whether to marry and/or cohabit and did not feel the same constraints about forming pre-marital sexual relationships.

Anthony Giddens (1992) has argued that heterosexual marriage has become little more than a lifestyle choice. This means that although many couples are still choosing to marry and even to have the full white wedding, it is no longer compulsory to do so. This shift in values as well as practices is causing concern to governments in both the UK and USA because there are strong morally based arguments that suggest that marriage provides a better and more stable form of relationship; especially if a couple have children (see Bengtson *et al.*, 2002, for the US evidence-based counter-argument). Sociologically speaking, there is insufficient evidence to suggest that marriage is better than cohabitation in terms of the stability it provides because these changes have not been occurring long enough to assess the effects reliably. Even more importantly, comparing statistics on relationship breakdown with those on divorce is incredibly difficult because there are no official records kept on cohabitation breakdown.

Comparing those who cohabit with those who marry is also notoriously difficult. For instance, those who marry are likely to be older than those who are starting to cohabit and, for many, cohabitation is a trial marriage so it is not surprising if it does not last. But we also know that, across the board, those people who cohabit are more likely to be socially and economically deprived and therefore able to command fewer economic and cultural resources (Kiernan *et al.*, 1998; Daly and Rake, 2003; Booth and Crouter, 2002). This then raises the question of whether it is poverty that causes unstable relationships or whether it is the decision not to marry.

A word of caution is necessary when trying to understand trends in relationships, especially when the changes in Western cultures since the 1950s have been dramatic and statistics on the decline in marriage, the rise of cohabitation and the increase in divorce can be combined to give the impression of chaos and instability. The first problem with over-interpreting change is that we have to choose our baseline carefully. For instance, if we take the baseline to be Britain or the USA in the 1950s then the change does seem very radical indeed. But the 1950s in Britain and the USA was far from a 'typical' decade. The popularity of marriage soared after the war and it coincided with a baby boom in both countries in 1946 and 1948. This baby boom produced a wave of young people who themselves were of marriageable age in the late 1960s and this in turn gave rise to another peak in the marriage rate. Again similar trends can be found in other Western societies. These fluctuating trends in intimate relationships can be understood to be quite normal if we take a long view of history and if we take account of the impact of changing social, economic, cultural and, of course, legal conditions (Brannen *et al.*, 2004; see also Wendy Bottero's chapter in the present volume for a discussion of historical changes). An excellent example of a study which puts the analysis of trends into context is provided by Bengtson and colleagues (2002) who carried out a major longitudinal study of family life in the USA over 30 years. Using survey data as well as interview data they come to the conclusion that, notwithstanding the trends in marriage and divorce, today's children are doing better than their parents' generation in terms of education and employment. They also argue that there is still a strong sense of solidarity across generations from grandparents to grandchildren.

It is important also to understand that not only are rates of marriage and cohabitation changing, but that the cultural meanings of marriage and cohabitation are changing too. So, for example, to be married in 1950 – whether in the USA, Australia or Europe – was rather different to the experience of being married today. Equally, to cohabit in 1950 was a totally different experience to cohabiting today. We know, for example, that there was very little 'prenuptial' cohabitation in many Western societies before the 1980s. If couples cohabited without marrying they often concealed the fact and the woman might take her partner's surname to hide the fact that she was not married. By the twenty-first century, however, cohabitation was not only commonplace but tended to occur most among younger couples, typically in their 20s. In the USA it has been estimated that in 1960 there were 500,000 cohabiting couples, but in 1997 that figure rose to 4,250,000 (Smock and Gupta, 2002). The

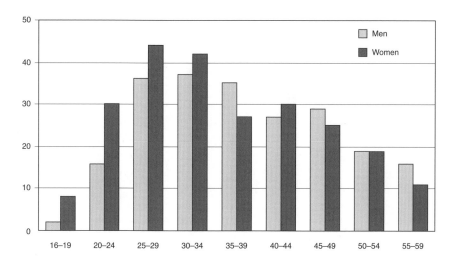

Figure 4.2 Non-married (including separated) people cohabiting, by sex and age, 2001/02 Great Britain, per cent

Source: National Statistics (2004) licensed under the Open Government Licence v.1.0.

Australian Institute of Family Studies has shown that couples who were cohabiting as a percentage of all couples in 1986 was 5.7 per cent, but by 2006 it had risen to 14.9 per cent (http://www.aifs.gov.au/institute/info/charts/cohabitation/allcouplesdata.html).

One other interesting change in cohabitation is that it appears to be growing in popularity among older couples, namely those in their 40s and even 50s (see Figure 4.2 for the example of the UK). There is evidence to suggest that older cohabitees are starting these relationships for the 'second time around' and so may be cautious about entering into another marriage, having experienced a possibly painful divorce already. This may be significant for couples who already have children because they are aware that a new marriage puts their children into a weaker position in relation to inheritance and next of kin status. So for this group of people cohabitation may seem particularly suitable, precisely because they can avoid some of the legal consequences of marriage.

We have noted above that the institution of marriage may be changing too, making marriage in the early 2000s very different to marriage in 1950. In the 1950s, in most Western societies, a woman getting married might have expected to give up her job in order to become a full-time housewife and look after her husband (Mansfield and Collard, 1988). Even if she did not do this immediately, she would do so on becoming pregnant because of social expectations and, in any case, she was likely to lose her job. This meant that marriage, and in particular motherhood, created a situation of economic dependence for wives upon their husbands. The married woman was not regarded as the legal equal of her husband; she had virtually no protection from domestic violence,

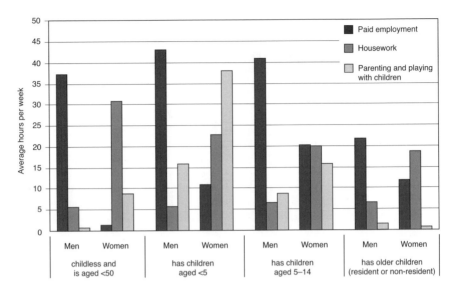

Figure 4.3   Family time and life cycle stage, Australia, 2004

Note: Housework includes preparing meals, washing dishes, cleaning the house, washing clothes and ironing. Parenting and playing with children includes playing with own children, helping them with personal care, teaching, coaching or actively supervising them, or getting them to child care, school and other activities.

Source: Australian Institute of Family Studies (2007) http://www.aifs.gov.au/institute/pubs/factssheets/ familytime.html. Data from Household, Income and Labour Dynamics in Australia (HILDA) survey (2004).

and could only get a divorce with great difficulty (Smart, *The Ties That Bind*, 1984).

These patterns of gendered responsibility and also gender inequality have not vanished from marriage altogether (Vogler *et al.*, 2006). There is evidence from countries like Canada, the USA, Australia and the UK to show that, on having children, women still become economically dependent upon their husbands because it is they who take time away from paid work to raise the children (Finnie, 1993; Smyth and Weston, 2000; Smock *et al.*, 1999). The graph above comes from a fact sheet produced by the Australian Institute of Family Studies in 2007 entitled 'A Snapshot of how Australian Families Spend Their Time'. It shows very clearly the impact on paid work once a couple have children; the gender differences are very striking.

As soon as women lose their independent earning power they become vulnerable to inequalities, especially if they go on to get divorced (see discussion below). So marriage and parenthood continue to have very different consequences for men and women. However, it would be false to imagine that there are no changes affecting men, particularly in their desire to become more active and involved as fathers. This is discussed in Box 4.2 below.

The idea that marriage is now a more equal relationship is, however, fiercely debated in the sociological literature on families. Giddens (1992), for example,

Box 4.2   Is fatherhood changing?

Fatherhood has become a really important topic of research in Western societies over the last decade or so. In the post-war years all the focus was on mothers and mother-hood because there was a strong desire in all these countries to improve child health and well-being and, as mothers were seen to be the 'natural' carers of children, their role was seen as particularly important. The good father in 1950 or 1960 was the man who was a reliable breadwinner and who put food on the table and provided a home in which mothers could care adequately for the children. There was a clear segregation of roles for mothers and fathers but this situation was challenged by the Women's movement in the 1970s, while also being undermined by changing social and economic conditions which meant that women were becoming better educated and increasingly attached to the labour market. So, as motherhood changed, fatherhood too began to be modified.

There are two important dimensions to understanding this change in fatherhood. The first is the change in men's *desire* to become more involved or 'hands-on' as fathers. The second is the change in men's *actual behaviour* in relation to their children. There is quite a lot of evidence for the former but less for the latter, so this requires careful explanation.

Studies that have explored men's desires to become more involved fathers show that this desire is often couched in a narrative, which explains that they saw little of their own fathers who were busy being breadwinners and that they want their own children to have a different kind of relationship with them (for example, see Dermott, 2008; Miller, 2010; Marsiglio, 1995; Lamb, 2010). They often say they want to 'be there' for their children. Moreover, the growth of divorce in all Western societies has alert-ed fathers to the fact that they may lose contact with their children unless they have formed good relationships with them before the break-up. But fathers face a dilemma because, except for rare countries like Sweden, it is exceptionally hard for men to reduce their working hours, especially at a time when their partners have left the workforce. Fathers are therefore caught in a difficult situation in which they may wish to be more involved but social and economic forces prevent them from doing much more than their fathers before them. This is a troubling contemporary problem for which, at present, there seems to be no solution.

argues that marriage is now based more on companionship and there is a greater democracy in gender relationships such that a husband can no longer presume to make unilateral decisions or to control all the couple's resources. But, against this, Lynn Jamieson (1998) argues that the empirical evidence for this new, democratic arrangement is partial. Studies of housework and child care do not show that men are taking an equal role in domestic matters or in caring responsibilities. It is important always to understand that personal life is not simply a matter of making individual choices and sticking to them. Relationships do not and cannot change simply as a matter of willpower, even if men and women want equality. For example, mothers may wish to remain in full-time work but find it impossible to do so because of the lack of child care, and the problem of managing children's illnesses or school hours which interrupt work. Thus, couples may make 'private' decisions about the shape of their relationships and how to share responsibilities, but they do so in a context of enduring gender inequality, a lack of structural support for child care and differing ideological demands made on mothers and fathers.

Divorce and separation

In all Western societies divorce rates have risen markedly since the end of World War II. These rises have been due to changes in divorce legislation, the improved economic position of women (largely due to an increase in women working outside the home), the decline in stigma associated with relationship breakdown and possibly also to increased life expectancy. But it is important to note that the rate of divorce in countries like the UK and USA is not still climbing, indeed in both countries it has levelled off. The fear that rising rates of divorce might bring about the end of family life now seems unfounded, and as both divorce and separation have become much more commonplace there is growing evidence that family life can adapt to these changes without disintegrating (Bengtson *et al.*, 2002). This means that whereas divorce was once interpreted as a worrying social problem, sociologists are now more inclined to understand it as one transition among others that occur during the life-course. In this sense, divorce and separation have become 'normalized'. However, this does not mean that these processes are without consequences for the couple, family members and wider society. In this sense, divorce and separation are both a personal and a social issue (Katz *et al.*, 2000).

The personal impact of divorce and separation tends to be felt differently by women, men and children. For women, especially those who have given up paid employment, divorce means financial hardship, often returning to poorly paid part-time work in order to accommodate child care, and not infrequently moving home. This is true for countries like the USA (Holden and Smock, 1991), Canada (Finnie, 1993), Australia (Smyth and Weston, 2000) and the UK (Douglas and Murch, 2000; Smart and Neale, 1999). For men it often entails seeing less of the children because mothers tend to remain primary carers. However, although there is a financial impact on men arising from child support payments and finding new accommodation, their situation in the labour market is not affected and they can regain their economic standing. Men are also more likely to go on to remarry while women, especially mothers of teenage children, are less likely to do so.

For children, divorce tends to mean that they cease to have daily contact with both parents and maintaining relationships with both mothers and fathers becomes subject to careful planning, weekend visits and sometimes even living in two homes in an equal-share arrangement (Smart *et al.*, 2001). This reshaping of families requires considerable personal adjustments which have to be dealt with at the same time as facing economic insecurity and emotional difficulties.

Notwithstanding these difficulties, there is evidence that couples are beginning to construct post-divorce family life according to more collaborative principles which are giving rise to new patterns of parenting across households (Hetherington and Kelly, 2002; Maclean and Eekelaar, 1997). Sociologically speaking this means that, while divorce may disrupt intimacy between adults, it becomes feasible for parent–child relationships to continue and even for relationships with all sets of grandparents to remain intact. In this way family life becomes more fluid while intergenerational bonds can remain supportive and strong (Bengtson *et al.*, 2002).

Solo living and 'living apart together' (LAT)

Living alone or having a 'steady' relationship but opting not to live together are both forms of living which are also attracting more sociological interest. At first glance both of these lifestyles might appear to be a rejection of family life, but the more research is carried out the more complex the picture becomes.

The first problem in this area is how to define 'solo living' and 'living apart together'. Looking first at solo living, it is clear that there are many routes into living alone. A young person may leave their parents' home to get a job and find a place to live on their own, an older person may get divorced or be widowed and similarly live alone. When we think of living alone we may conjure up the image of an elderly widow still living in her family home, or perhaps a never-married man who lives alone because he has not found a partner.[1] These cultural stereotypes tend to imply a disapproval of people who live alone. But the demographic make-up of people who live alone has started to change in Northern European countries and the USA, with more men and women in their 30s living alone, apparently by choice, often in urban centres.

These developments have led to more research and also a shift away from assuming that people who live alone do so out of necessity. Indeed, our whole understanding of the 'choices' people make about their relationships and how they live is starting to shift from the presumption that only living in a nuclear family based on marriage can be the proper way to live. This means that sociologically we are able to appreciate that living alone may bring benefits. Indeed, some research suggests that the longer people live alone, the less attracted they are to the idea of sharing their home with another person (Wasoff *et al.*, 2005). The experience of how a person comes to live alone is likely to have an impact on their experience of solo living and, in addition, the neighbourhood where one lives alone is also likely to be highly salient. In turn, these factors will be influenced by social class, age, gender and employment status.

A similarly complex picture emerges with 'living apart together' couples or LATs. This is a new area of study for sociologists, so there are few empirical studies of the phenomenon. Moreover, as Simon Duncan and Miranda Phillips (2009) have argued, it is very hard to define a LAT because it is a lifestyle

which is easily confused with the situation of simply going 'steady' while antic-
ipating living together sometime in the future. For this reason they refer to two
distinct groups of LATs: *dating LATs*, who are a steady couple who are planning to live together, and *partner LATs*, who have no immediate plans to move
in together. It is the latter group who have become sociologically interesting.
People may opt not to live with each other because they work in separate
cities, or they may both have acquired their own homes and do not wish to
give up their independence. Alternatively, one or both may be divorced and
may wish to keep their home life with their children separate from an intimate
relationship with a new partner. And of even greater significance can be the
responsibility for caring for an elderly relative which means that people post-
pone living together for an unknown amount of time.

There is, however, an uncertainty about whether LATs are a 'historically
new family form'. Some sociologists have argued that living in a *partnership
LAT* is a modern solution to the problem of keeping some independence and
separate resources, while still having a deep and meaningful permanent relationship. In other words, it results from 'choice'. But others see it more as a
necessity arising out of contemporary conditions of working and caring (for
example, the need for couples to work in separate cities in order to keep their
jobs or to get promotion). The debate is still ongoing (Levin, 2004; Roseneil
and Budgeon, 2004; Jamieson *et al.*, 2009).

Concluding remarks

This chapter has demonstrated how patterns of relationships and domestic living in Western democracies have been changing over the past 60 years. New
forms of relationships appear to have become feasible with changing economic and social conditions. Equally, changing social values mean that more people feel able to consider non-traditional forms of relationships without the
stigma and shame which may have been attached to them in previous times.
But it is important to think about the association between changing 'structures', changing 'values' and 'personal choices'. Although forming and ending
relationships is a very personal matter, indeed a core feature of personal life,
these processes cannot be separated from the social, economic and cultural
context in which they occur. It is, therefore, important to continue to think
about how all the changes described in this chapter may affect different social
groups, as well as different genders and generations.

Questions for discussion

■ Is getting married becoming more popular again? In discussing this proposition consider why marriage rates declined and the possible social reasons
for marriage regaining popularity.

- Considering all the emotional, social and economic consequences of divorce and separation, explain why rates of divorce remain so high.
- Living alone or in a LAT relationship is often seen as a response to a modern fear of commitment. What are the sociological arguments for and against this proposition?
- Draw on your parents' and grandparents' experiences of setting up their families and provide a sociological explanation for how and why family life may have changed across the generations.

'Marriage' and the Personal Life of Same-Sex Couples

Anna Einarsdottir

5

Introduction

In the previous chapter, Carol Smart examined recent shifts that have occurred in heterosexual intimate relationships in the context of changing **social norms** and legislation. This chapter explores these issues further by focusing on same-sex relationships, in particular, the legal recognition of same-sex relationships and what this has meant for the personal lives of non-heterosexual people. In the recent past, campaigns for LGBT (lesbian, gay, bisexual and transgender) rights have centred on the issue of 'marriage',[1] which was thought to contribute to the visibility and acceptance of non-heterosexual people. The examples drawn on in this chapter challenge this simplistic view and raise some fundamental questions about how freely people can express their sexualities in different places, settings and situations.

This chapter begins with a discussion of sexual identities and goes on to explain some of the key features of the debate about same-sex marriage. While academics have contributed to this debate on a theoretical level, real-life experiences have not been examined in much detail. For this reason the final section of this chapter explores the intersection of legislation and personal life by discussing how marital status affects same-sex couples in everyday situations.

Sexualities and heteronormativity

As has already been discussed by Carol Smart in Chapter 4, our sense of self or identity is relational. This means that our identities are double-sided, based on how we present ourselves and on how other people see us (Plummer, 2003). People may try to guess how old you are, pigeonhole you according to your gender and identify your 'race', but when it comes to your sexuality, things become a little more complicated given the absence of 'obvious' visual clues. You may have experienced this too. Take the cashier at your local supermarket, for example. You cannot tell whether or not she is a lesbian, and you have never been sure about that old classmate of yours either. He is probably gay. Then again we never seem to wonder whether the teacher is heterosexual or the bus driver straight. Why? Because heterosexuality is usually assumed and promoted as the norm. In scholarly debate, this is known as 'heteronormativity' (Nagle, 2003), a concept that will be discussed in more detail in relation to same-sex marriage later on in this chapter. In short, heteronormativity means that heterosexuality is taken as the norm, which explains why people 'come out' as lesbian, gay or bisexual (but not as straight).

In everyday life, people tend to explain their sexuality as a natural inborn drive. Even after a person has changed their sexual identity and practices, they can claim that they have always 'been' gay/lesbian/bisexual although they may not always have been consciously aware of this. In doing so, people draw on essentialist views about sexuality; that is, views that depict it as a 'natural' and fixed biological drive (Weeks, 2003). Yet, scholars have highlighted how fluid sexuality can be on the individual level, and how, on the social level, sexual practices and the meanings attached to them can vary over time or across cultures. This social constructionist view of sexuality underlines the subtle variations in sexual practices between cultures. For example, in different societies, the importance attached to sex varies and sex is regulated in different ways through social norms and legislation (for example, age of consent, access to reproductive clinics, and marriage) (Weeks, 2003).

This chapter now turns to examine one important social institution that is clearly heteronormative, and that has been the focus of much debate in recent years, namely marriage. First, we discuss how access to this traditionally heterosexual institution has been fought for in the campaign for 'partnership rights' for same-sex couples, before exploring in more detail some of the debates that have accompanied these campaigns.

Campaigning for 'partnership rights'

The drive for 'partnership rights' has been based on the principle that everyone, regardless of sexual orientation, should have the right to have their relationship officially recognized by the state and, consequently, access to all the benefits associated with marriage (such as tax relief, pension schemes, inheritance and property rights, and the status of next of kin). On the face of it, this appears to be a fairly straightforward argument about human rights, justice and equality, but it is also about the value of relationships and the way in which the state regulates our intimate lives (see Carol Smart's Chapter 4 on close relationships for a discussion of state regulation of heterosexual relationships).

The campaign for partnership rights has been a huge success in some parts of the world. Denmark was first to offer formal recognition of same-sex relationships in 1989. Since then, all the other Nordic countries, aside from the Faroe Islands, have followed suit, as well as large number of European countries. As of 2011, these include the United Kingdom, Ireland, Isle of Man, the

---

Box 5.1   A picture of same-sex marriages

Table 5.1 below shows the uptake of civil partnerships (same sex) and marriages (opposite sex) between 2005 and 2008 in the UK. As you see, the number of civil partnerships was low in 2005 and rose dramatically in 2006 before reaching a 'stable' figure between 7,000 and 8,000 per year. This can partly be explained by the fact that civil partnerships only became available in December of 2005, and also because a large number of people had been waiting for the opportunity to marry for some time, hence the high number of civil partnerships in 2006.

Table 5.1   Number of civil partnerships and marriages in the UK, 2005–08*

Year	Number of civil partnerships	Number of marriages
2005	1,953	247,805
2006	16,106	239,454
2007	8,728	235,367
2008	7,169	232,990

*The statistics on civil partnerships are based on figures from England, Wales, Scotland and Northern Ireland, whereas the statistics on marriages are based on figures from England and Wales only.
Source: Office for National Statistics (2010c, 2010d) licensed under the Open Goverment Licence v.1.0.

What we also see is that the number of civil partnerships is small relative to the number of opposite-sex marriages. This holds true also in other countries who offer same-sex couples formal recognition. In Norway, for instance, there is only one same-sex marriage for every 100 opposite-sex marriages (Noack et al., 2005). One interesting pattern is beginning to emerge in relation to same-sex marriages, namely that male couples tend to outnumber female couples initially, but with time, the gap between becomes smaller. This certainly holds true for the UK, as it does for most other countries. Figures from Denmark, Norway, Sweden, Iceland and the Netherlands, for instance, record a ratio of three to one male and female marriages (Waaldjik, 2001). Yet a different story can be told about the North American context. There figures show that female couples outnumber male couples in seven out of ten Canadian provinces (Rothblum, 2005) and in the US state of Vermont, twice as many women have had civil unions than men (Solomon et al., 2004).

We still know little about the background of those same-sex couples who marry or who are more likely to marry than others, but what we do know is this: only 10 per cent of same-sex marriages in Vermont were of ethnic minorities, indicating that same-sex marriage is more prevalent among the majority white population (Solomon et al., 2004). Same-sex partners tend to be older when they marry than opposite-sex partners. Statistics from the UK in 2008 show that the average age of civil partners was 40.9 years (41.8 for male couples and 40.0 for female couples), compared to the marriage age of 36.5 years for men and 33.8 years for women (Office for National Statistics, 2010c, 2010d).[2] Statistics from Norway further show that 20 per cent of the people who entered a same-sex marriage had been married to a person of the opposite sex in the past, and that 13 per cent of the men and 24 per cent of the women had at least one child prior to their same-sex marriage (Noack et al., 2005). This is a further illustration of the 'fluidity' of sexuality mentioned above.

Netherlands, Belgium, Luxembourg, Liechtenstein, France, Germany, the Czech Republic, Austria, Switzerland, Hungary, Slovenia, Croatia, Spain, Andorra and Portugal. A growing number of Latin American countries also offer same-sex couples formal recognition, including Argentina, Mexico, Ecuador, Uruguay, Brazil and Columbia. Elsewhere the situation is quite different. In North America, for instance, same-sex relationships are recognized in Canada, but only in six out of 50 states in the USA. The situation is similar in Oceania where same-sex relationships are nationally recognized in New Zealand but only in parts of Australia. In Africa and Asia, however, a formal recognition of same-sex relationships is limited to two countries, South Africa and Israel (ILGA, 2010).

As the above list suggests, some regional trends are starting to emerge concerning the legal status of same-sex relationships. These may be linked to different cultural attitudes to sex and sexual practices and the degree of state involvement in personal life. In some countries where same-sex couples are not legally recognized, homosexuality and homosexual acts are either totally absent from statutes or a criminal offence – but only between men, whereas women are not mentioned. This differentiation is interesting for two key reasons. First, because it suggests different attitudes towards gay men compared to lesbians and, second, because it illustrates how invisible female sexuality is and how little scope there is to define it outside of the heterosexual spectrum. In Box 5.1. we take a further look at the uptake of same-sex marriages from an international perspective.

The debates about same-sex marriage

Even though same-sex relationships are now widely recognized in many Western countries, the legislative process has not always been simple. On the whole, it can be said that same-sex marriage has generally been viewed as a necessary step in rectifying injustices between same- and opposite-sex couples. But there are also those who have expressed deep-rooted fears about the dissolution of family, marriage and even morality. Such views have mainly been voiced by religious groups. You may be familiar with some of their arguments that stress the exclusivity of marriage as a heterosexual institution ('marriage can only be between a man and a woman') and procreation as the fundamental purpose of marriage. From their perspective, same-sex couples simply fail to meet these key criteria for marriage and would undermine the institution of marriage with their allegedly immoral lifestyle choices. Views like these have found their way into mainstream media; however, what we examine here are the debates for and against same-sex marriage that have taken place within academia and the LGBT (lesbian, gay, bi and trans) community. As you will see, the opposition to same-sex marriage within these debates is based on very different reasons compared to the objections put forward by religious groups.

The bone of contention among academics seems to be the extent to which same- and opposite-sex couples are similar or different, and to what degree the institution of marriage would be transformed by opening it up to same-sex couples. This debate has been extremely polarized. Those who argue for same-sex marriage tend to emphasize the practical advantages of marriage and the economic rewards it can offer (Rothblum, 2005; Sullivan, 2004), but also, the social status that marriage provides (Wilkinson and Kitzinger, 2006; Weeks, 2007). While most scholars may question the desirability of marriage, many still argue that the option to marry should be available for lesbians and gay men (Weeks *et al.*, 2001) who they hope will, in turn, transform the institution of marriage and the way gender roles have traditionally played out within heterosexual marriage (Stoddard, 1997). The purported greater equality between spouses within same-sex marriage is hoped to influence opposite-sex marriages, which are characterized by gender inequality and gendered divisions of labour within the household (for example, the male breadwinner/female carer roles). We return to this issue below.

The strongest opposition to same-sex marriage has come from feminist and **queer** scholars, who have argued that calls for equality are based on the claim that same-sex couples are 'just like' heterosexual couples. They argue that this leaves virtually no room for a critical analysis of marriage as a patriarchal institution (that is, an institution where men have power over women) (Javors and Reimann, 2001), of heteronormativity, or of the way in which family relations are regulated by the state. The emphasis on the similarities between gay and straight couples is also believed to breach two of the main principles of gay liberation – that is, the affirmation of gay identity and the validation of alternative family forms. Feminist and queer scholars have further argued that same-sex marriage would reinforce relationship hierarchies, where heterosexual monogamous marriages are placed at the top and the relationships of non-heterosexuals, of those who do not marry, or of those who do not conform to monogamous relationships, at the bottom (Brandzel, 2005; Ettelbrick, 1997; Sycamore, 2004; Warner, 2000).

Although similar concerns have been raised within the LGBT community, only a handful of organizations or movements have actively campaigned against same-sex marriage. In the UK, for example, Outrage ran the strongest campaign by drawing on queer[3] politics and human rights arguments with the aim of liberating 'people of all sexualities'. They rejected same-sex marriage on the basis that it 'apes' heterosexual marriage and they argued for an Unmarried Partners Act that would have allowed all couples, same and opposite sex alike, to register their relationship. In the USA the movement LAGAI-Queer Insurrection (www.lagai.org), who base their politics on anti-authoritarian, anti-militarist, pro-feminist and anti-racist principles, similarly opposed marriage as a 'central institution of **patriarchy**'. Nevertheless, this considerable resistance to marriage within the LGBT community was kept in check, partly because of fears that a split community would have been less likely to run a successful rights-based campaign, but also because same-sex partnership recognition was seen as a more pragmatic option than challenging existing legal structures and the way in which benefits are tied to the couple relationship and marriage. Stonewall (www.stonewall.co.uk), the largest

LGBT organization within the UK, ran a tactical campaign and fully supported the Civil Partnership Act 2004, which came into effect in December 2005.

New forms of intimacies

Why have mainstream LGBT campaigners and some academics thought that
legal recognition of same-sex marriage might help to transform the heterosexual institution of marriage? The main reason for such confidence has been that
LGBT communities have already been at the forefront of the transformation
of intimacies and the way in which people do relationships. In Chapter 1, you
will have already read about the **individualization thesis** and in particular
about Giddens's (1992) claim that we have entered the age of the '**pure relationship**' that is based on romantic love and only survives for as long as it sat-
isfies both parties. He also argued that same-sex couples were in the vanguard
of this new way of relating in intimate romantic relationships.

Same-sex individuals have been viewed as trailblazers in other ways too,
especially in helping to change how people define family. While Giddens's theory assumes that people mainly seek intimacy within a couple relationship,
this has been challenged by the notion of '**families of choice**' that aims to de-
centre the dyadic couple relationship as primary, while emphasizing the role
that non-couple relationships can play in the lives of non-heterosexuals
(Jamieson, 2003; Weeks *et al.*, 2001; Weston, 1991). In addition, as discussed
in Chapter 1, Weeks and colleagues (2001) and Weston (1991) emphasized,
with their notion of families of choice, that 'family' is not necessarily restricted to blood relations, but can be created by choice. Further, these theorists
argue that families are not automatically fixed units defined by heterosexual
parameters; instead, they can be diverse and changeable.

We have so far discussed arguments for and against same-sex marriage, as
well as examining how families are changing and how opportunities have been
created for different ways of doing families, including same-sex families. The
next section turns to the notion of 'the closet' and explores how legal recognition of same-sex relationships has affected it.

The 'closet'

Eve Kosofsky Sedgwick (1991) maintained that Western culture is structured
around the 'epistemology of the closet', whereby knowing the truth is para-
mount and keeping secrets reflects weakness or possible corruption. Today
this means that it is considered better for non-heterosexuals to 'out' themselves rather than to stay in the 'closet' (at least in Western culture), because
staying in the 'closet' tends to be viewed as a deliberate attempt by lesbians
and gay men to hide their sexuality and to pass as heterosexual. On the one
hand, there is a pressure to reveal one's non-heterosexuality, but, on the other,

there is heteronormativity and outright homophobia in many situations and contexts. This means that some non-heterosexuals may prefer not to make their sexuality known but rather 'pass' as heterosexual. As we will see below, however, passing is not always deliberate, because non-heterosexuals are routinely assumed to be straight.

Under the epistemology of the closet, passing as heterosexual is not tolerated and strong moral pressure is put on people to come out of the 'closet'. The media often plays a crucial role in exposing 'secrets' about celebrities, including their homosexuality. George Michael, Anne Heche, Ellen Degeneres and Jodie Foster have all fallen victim to such exposure and were forced out of the closet after months or even years of speculation about their sexuality. They are now known as 'gay celebrities'. Not surprisingly, we do not talk of 'straight' or 'heterosexual' celebrities. In their case, they are simply 'celebrities' – yet another example of heteronormative practices and the silence that surrounds heterosexuality.

The issue of disclosure/non-disclosure takes an interesting turn when it concerns same-sex marriage. For a start, legal recognition of same-sex relationships was generally presented as an unambiguous move from the private domain of the 'closet' (whereby homosexuals were forced or expected to hide their sexuality) to a publicly recognized union. Marriage was believed to increase the visibility and acceptance of non-heterosexuals, and ultimately remove the 'need' to pass as heterosexual. It is worth noting here how much value is given to visibility alone. In the context of same-sex marriage, visibility was deemed to be not just automatic, but always positive. The next section explores whether this has been the case for married same-sex couples.

Being married

So far this chapter has focused on the debates around same-sex marriage and what may be gained or lost by such legal recognition. In these debates, same-sex marriage has been constructed as *in principle* good or bad, right or wrong, while the experiences of those who have taken the opportunity to marry have not been explored in much detail. This chapter now shifts the focus in order to explore the *practical impact* that being married may have on the lives of same-sex couples, by discussing two issues in particular. First, how marriage is understood in everyday conversation and, second, the extent to which same-sex marriage is a public relationship. In doing so, a new concept is introduced – the 'married closet' – in order to underline how private same-sex relationships can feel, not just to the couples themselves, but also to people they interact with, despite official recognition of such relationships.

The first issue the discussion raises is how the heteronormativity of marriage affects the various social interactions that same-sex couples engage in. The fact that heterosexual relationships are seen as the norm and marriage has traditionally been an heterosexual institution means that same-sex couples who are married bump up against this heteronormativity in their everyday interactions. In casual conversation with strangers or people you do not know very well, you may be asked whether you are married. If you reply with a simple 'yes', the next question is likely to concern your partner's occupation. In the ensuing conversation, it will generally be assumed that your partner is of the opposite sex. You may not pay attention to this if you are straight, but if you are not, you are left with two options: you can either go along with the idea, or challenge the assumption that your relationship is heterosexual. Correcting this kind of misunderstanding, however, can be both frustrating and tiring in the long run, as the example discussed in Box 5.2 illustrates.

Box 5.2   The 'married closet'

In a doctoral study exploring personal motivations for marriage and how marital status affects the everyday lives of same-sex couples in Iceland,[4] it was clear that a same-sex marriage was often mistaken for a heterosexual one, which left some of the women in a state of frustration. 'Educating' people about their relationship proved exhausting and, with time, some women came to automatically expect that they would be mistaken for a straight person, or that their same-sex relationship, when revealed, would give rise to negative reactions. This can lead to situations where a person becomes defensive even before any criticism of their relationship has been voiced.

Hulda, for example, recalls an incident at work when a carpenter was called in to fit shelves above her desk. During their conversation she realized that the carpenter had for some reason assumed that she was married to one of her male colleagues. She immediately responded:

> Hulda: 'No, no, no, I am not married to him' ... 'I am actually married to a woman.' 'Yes,' he said, and then I replied: 'Well, I don't care what you think about that,' – it just slipped out. 'It is entirely up to you how you handle it, it is your problem.' And he just said: 'Yes, yes, yes, yes, no problem.' It was a spontaneous reaction [on my part].

But the study also revealed how difficult it can be for straight people to show an interest in the private life non-heterosexuals, even in situations where they are perfectly aware of the fact that a relationship is between two people of the same sex. Some shy away from asking questions about the relationship, possibly because they are scared of posing the 'wrong' questions. They may also feel that the relationship is 'private' and that by asking questions they will be invading non-heterosexual privacy. This means that non-heterosexuals are normally the ones who have to 'break the ice' by broaching the subject of their relationship. This is because it can feel less challenging to 'invade' heterosexual space by talking about one's same-sex relationship than to disturb non-heterosexual privacy by asking questions about it.

What we may be witnessing here is the emergence of a new closet, the 'married' closet. Same-sex couples and the wider public equally contribute to its existence, the couples themselves for not revealing their marital status and the wider public for still assuming that marriage can only be between a husband and a wife.

The examples discussed in Box 5.2 suggest that lesbian and gay marriage has not transformed the institution of marriage as some hoped it would (Stoddard, 1997) or changed the 'normative meaning' of marriage – marriage remains heterosexual by default while same-sex marriage is still something that many straight people are uncomfortable encountering or talking about.

This raises a number of interesting questions relating to boundaries between public and private and the ways in which public spaces are heterosexual. It raises further questions about visibility, and how much control a person has over how she or he is seen. Equally, is visibility necessarily empowering? And more, how do people wish to be seen or recognized? It is this issue of visibility to which the next section now turns.

(In)visibility in heterosexualized spaces

As we have seen above, the epistemology of the closet means that there is pressure on non-heterosexuals to disclose their sexuality, while at the same time, heteronormativity means that disclosing such identities is not always necessarily an easy or comfortable thing to do. While most scholars agree that 'invisibility may be exhausting or painful', a few have demonstrated how 'risky or dangerous' visibility can feel for same-sex couples (Steinbugler, 2005, p. 429). In a study among lesbian couples in the UK, Johnston and Valentine (1995) argue:

> For many lesbian couples, the [public] expression of anything beyond 'friendship' is tantamount to 'flaunting it' and so they modify their behaviour to such an extent that their relationship is virtually invisible. (Johnston and Valentine, 1995, p. 102)

By modifying their behaviour in public spaces in this way, non-heterosexuals of course 'pass' as heterosexual, but such juggling of multiple identities can be taxing and raises questions about how freely homosexuality can be expressed. This has been given considerable attention within academia, often in relation to gay pride marches, but also in respect to the home (Valentine, 1993, 2002).

The home is usually understood as a private space where members of a family can live away from the scrutiny of others (Allan and Crow, 1989, p. 4). It is also generally understood as a space where people are 'offstage, free from surveillance' and where they 'feel they belong' (Saunders, 1989, p. 184). While the home may often be the only safe place to express non-heterosexuality (Valentine, 1993, 2002), this can be tricky for those who still live at home with their (straight) parents. Valentine (1993) explored this in detail among lesbians. The parents were not only heterosexual, but assumed that their daughters would inevitably be attracted to men. In such heterosexual family spaces, lesbians are not able to express their desires and the only option for them is to express their sexuality in 'public'. Although Valentine focused on women, we have no reason to believe that the circumstances would be different for gay men.

Heteronormativity is in no way isolated to the parental home, but extends also to most work places, open spaces and commercial environments. In these spaces, heterosexuals can openly display pictures of their partners or talk about dating or encounters with their in-laws (Valentine, 1993). It can safely be said that such expressions of heterosexual intimacy are so normalized that they warrant little attention. Heterosexuals also do not constantly have to ask themselves 'Is it OK to kiss or hold my partner's hand?' while out in public. For same-sex couples the situation can be quite different. In the first place, they are far more likely to think twice before showing affection in public, and then, if they do, it hardly ever goes unnoticed. In practice this means that same-sex couples hesitate to show affection in public. Without such expressions, however, same-sex relationships remain invisible (Valentine, 2002). In other words, by remaining invisible in public (heterosexual) spaces, non-heterosexuals 'pass' as heterosexual. It could be argued that whenever non-heterosexuals remain invisible in this way, the 'spatial supremacy of heterosexuality' (Valentine, 1993, p. 410) is left unchallenged.

The most obvious public presentation of homosexuality takes place during gay pride celebrations. Academics have given this form of organized visibility considerable attention. You may be surprised to learn that even at gay pride marches, homosexuality is deemed 'out of place'. Johnston (1997), for instance, explains that gay pride is fundamentally a performance of queer identities for a straight audience. Other scholars such as Brickell (2001) take this idea further. He claims that gay pride marches are accused of 'intruding' or 'invading' the public space of the street by 'flaunting' or even 'promoting' non-heterosexuality (Brickell, 2001, p. 164). This suggests that gay liberation disrupts the distinctions between public/private and personal/political (Brickell, 2001), an issue that is discussed further by Gemma Edwards in the present volume.

Visibility is clearly not a straightforward process. To start with, we have little or no control over how we are seen. How others see us is not necessarily how we would like to be seen and, furthermore, some spaces make it almost impossible for some people to be seen altogether. Yet for non-heterosexuals, passing is rarely viewed positively. Furthermore, same-sex marriage might in principle be a public institution but the above examples and Box 5.2 reveal how same-sex relationships upset the seemingly set boundaries between public and private. Taken as a whole this helps explain why same-sex relationships might feel private despite the official public recognition of marriage and why it can be difficult to establish conversations about such relationships. Marriage may be a comfortable line of conversation for heterosexual couples, but for same-sex couples this is often the point where a conversation comes to an end.

Concluding remarks

Becoming visible has generally been documented as a necessary and positive step in any form of rights-based campaigning for LGBT people, including the campaign for recognition of same-sex partnerships. While legal recognition was believed to mark the end of the 'closet' and the need to pass as heterosexual, non-heterosexuals were thought to be both ready for, and in control of, self-disclosure upon entering a public institution like marriage. Having reviewed the debates over same-sex marriage, it is clear that everyday life is far more complex than that. Many non-heterosexuals face the following paradox: they are expected to reveal their sexuality, while at the same time facing homophobia in public spaces and in a variety of social interactions. This can make it difficult for a non-heterosexual person to express her or his sexuality. We have also seen how marriage remains heterosexual by default. Together, these issues complicate everyday conversations about same-sex relationships as they can prevent heterosexuals from asking 'private' questions about non-heterosexual relationships and can stop non-heterosexuals from revealing their marital status. While legal recognition of this nature may be important, it by no means marks the end of the closet for non-heterosexuals. Instead, it has been transformed into a different closet, the 'married closet'.

Questions for discussion

- Why might it be important to some for some couples to marry, but not for others?
- Do you think that visibility may affect gay and lesbian couples differently? If so, how?
- What may restrain everyday conversation about same-sex relationships and marriage?
- Think of your own surroundings and discuss what makes different spaces heterosexual, gay or mixed.

What It Means to be Related

Jennifer Mason

Introduction

Is everyone always saying you look like your sister, or have you inherited a certain temperament from your grandfather? Do you feel a strong responsibility for your elderly parents, or a special relationship with a particular cousin? Do you love a family get together, or do you find relationships with your relatives difficult or oppressive? Do you sometimes struggle to decide whether and how you are related to people?

When we speak of 'relatives' we usually mean people who are related to each other beyond parents and their infant or dependent children, and the questions above point to some of the ways that such relationships can touch our personal lives. Sociologists and others have sometimes used the collective noun 'extended family' to refer to the people involved in these relationships, and the system of connection that they are involved in is often referred to as 'kinship'. In recent years, the term 'relatedness' has also been used to refer to and understand the way that kinship connects people. In focusing on what it means to be related, this chapter will explore sociological thinking and research on these matters.

Are relatives less important than they used to be?

In many Western societies there is a general sense of unease and sometimes moments of **moral panic**, expressed especially by the media and some politicians, that the extended family has lost its significance. Various 'causes' are asserted, including social, economic and demographic transformations of the late twentieth and early twenty-first centuries. These include high rates of divorce (which, it is suggested, leads to fragmented families), the increase in women's paid employment and women's greater independence (which is said to mean that fewer women are fully available to look after children and older generations), increased geographical mobility and a purported rising tide of 'individualism' (which has been interpreted as people selfishly putting their own interests before those of relatives). We shall see shortly that there is considerable sociological evidence to refute this pessimistic view, but first we shall examine two influential sociological theories of family and personal life that have appeared to support it.

Functionalism and the *individualization thesis*: the declining extended family?

Functionalism was a dominant theory of the 1950s, but its rhetorical influence lingers on in moral panics about supposedly out-of-control youth and the purported failure of families to care for their elderly. It was concerned with social cohesion and stability, and saw the family as central to achieving these, so that any potential breakdown in the family was problematic. Social and economic changes in industrialized societies were said to have produced a system of differentiation, so that functions previously performed by extended-family households were now provided by other agencies like schools, hospitals and factories.

Some mourned the 'loss of function' of the extended family. Others, notably Talcott Parsons, argued that the nuclear-family household had taken centre stage. He saw it as a specialist unit that was resourced primarily by the wages earned by the male 'head of household', and that performed the societal functions of reproduction, child care and the **socialization** of children and adults (that is, ensuring that children learn and adults live according to key **social norms**). In his essay on the 'American family', he argued that nuclear families had become 'isolated' from wider kin networks, both in terms of their living arrangements and in patterns of support (Parsons, 1955). For many social commentators then and since, this purported dislocation of nuclear families from wider kinship has been seen as a social problem.

Functionalism was strongly criticized for idealizing a 'golden age' of the past where several family generations apparently lived together in harmony, caring for each other in their old age. The demographic evidence is that prior to the twentieth century most people did not live long enough to be able to form multigenerational households or enjoy a lengthy old age, so the golden age is something of a myth (Finch, 1989). Functionalism also overestimated the prevalence and moral value of the nuclear family, failing to see the extent to which family diversity existed already in the 1950s, and glossing over the reality that nuclear families can involve exploitation and conflict. Its assumption that women could and should be available to provide unpaid labour was criticized by feminists and others on the grounds that it discriminated against women and was based on a white middle-class model of family life.

The **individualization thesis** emerged in the final decades of the twentieth century (see Chapter 1 for a fuller discussion). It starts from a view that Western societies are undergoing massive social, economic and cultural transformations involving 'de-traditionalization', which is a loosening of the grip of traditional 'institutions' like the family on the way personal lives are lived. Instead, it is argued, individuals negotiate and choose their own biographies, following their own 'projects of the self' (Giddens, 1991, 1992). This involves making decisions about all kinds of things (including their personal relationships) where, in the past, such choices would not have been possible or even contemplated. Extended families and kinship do not figure prominently or at all in the individualization thesis, thus it creates a sense of individuals floating free of family ties and commitments.

This perspective has been criticized by social theorists and empirical researchers who have shown that the assumption that people would be able and willing to dispense with their wider families should they so choose is very unrealistic (Jamieson, 1998; Mason, 'Managing Kinship Over Long Distances', 2004; Smart and Neale, 1999). A further criticism is that it reflects the orientations, experiences and privileges of white middle-class individuals and families, but not necessarily those of other groups in society (Smart and Shipman, 2004). But as with functionalism, the individualization thesis is echoed (and sometimes distorted) in populist and right-wing rhetoric where the argument is that people have selfishly left their families behind in the pursuit of their own interests.

Empirical research: the continuing significance of the extended family

The loss of function and individualization theses have been criticized for failing to attend to empirical evidence. If we look carefully at the research, there is a great deal of evidence to suggest that extended families play a very important role in people's personal lives, and that people do not 'float free' from kin. For example, a large-scale UK study found grandparents to be very involved with their grandchildren: 61 per cent of grandparents looked after grandchildren under the age of 15 during the day (Clarke and Roberts, 2004). Other UK research (Finch and Mason, 1993, 2000) found these 'filial' ties to be significant, but also that a wider range of kin was involved in providing and receiving support from each other. Robert Milardo (2010) shows that aunts and uncles in the USA can be very significant figures in the lives of parents and children (of all ages). Furthermore, studies of the specific kinship patterns and practices of Africans, Caribbeans and South Asians settled in the UK and North America show kin such as aunts, uncles and cousins to be particularly important in varying ways (Chamberlain, 1998; Shaw, 2000; Stack 1974). And there are increasing numbers of studies of siblings showing that these relationships are a significant part of people's lives (Edwards *et al.*, 2006).

These studies show that relationships between as well as within households can be very important, with significant resources and support – economic, emotional, practical – passing between relatives. But even though kinship is important, can we say whether it is *more or less* important than it was in the past? Many sociologists have argued that just because kinship is changing and diversifying to some extent, we should not assume that this means it is in

Box 6.1   Assessing the changing significance of the extended family – two studies using different methodological approaches

	Study One	Study Two
The study	Bengston *et al.* (2002) *How Families Still Matter.* A study of generational change and continuity in the US.	Charles *et al.* (2008) *Families in Transition.* A study of community life and kinship in South Wales
Questions driving the study	1. How different are today's youth from previous generations? Are they a generation 'at risk'? 2. How have changes in family structure and roles affective successive generations of youth? 3. Has there been a decline over generations in parents' influence on youth? 4. What are the gender differences in achievement orientations and family influence across generations?	How have families in a particular place been affected by massive social changes of recent decades? Has there been continuity as well as change?
Methods	Longitudinal methods involving sequential sweeps of data since 1970, gathered from a large sample of individuals (more than 2,000), representing 3 generations within over 300 families. A wide range of questions including those about attitudes, health, educational attainment, and relationships with family members 'up and down the generational ladder'. Also macro-level economic data and some analysis of socio-cultural trends.	A 'restudy' in 2002 of a community study conducted in 1960 (Rosser and Harris, 1965). Involved researching the same community, with the same or as similar as possible questions. Large surveys (around 2000 households in 1960, 1000 in 2002), supplemented by **qualitative research** in local areas
Logic of the Approach	Following individuals and families through time in 'real time' using standardized measures to observe changes and continuities in intergenerational relationships.	Revisiting a locality enables the exploration of kin relationships and change in the local socio-economic and cultural context.

	Study One	Study Two
Verdict on changing significance of extended family	Despite increased divorce and maternal employment (factors sometimes assumed to threaten the extended family): '[f]amilies are adapting by expanding support across generations. There is increasing interdependence and exchange across several generations of family members; this expansion has protected and enhanced the well-being of new generations of children' (Bengston *et al.*, 2002, p. 160)	Despite some major socio-economic changes, 'there is considerable continuity in family practices between 1960 and 2002 ... families are embedded in networks of kin and provide their members with substantial support over the life course; mothers and their adult daughters are at the heart of kinship networks and it is women who do the kin work ... The main difference between the two studies is that the frequency of contact between kin, particularly siblings, has fallen, although not nearly as much as might have been expected' (Charles *et al.*, 2008, pp. 224–5)

decline. Instead, as shown in Box 6.1, kin may matter just as much as they ever did, but in different ways. The enormous interest in Western societies in recent years in tracing one's own family history is one example suggesting that relatives, far from being an irrelevance, may have become significant in ways not contemplated by the functionalists of the 1950s (Lawler, 2008; Mason, 'Tangible Affinities and the Real Life Fascination of Kinship', 2008).

Asking whether extended families are more or less important poses methodological challenges for researchers because it is not usually appropriate to use the same measures for past and present. As Finch has argued in relation to using kin support as a 'measure':

> The amount and type of support which kin give each other varies with the particular historical circumstances within which family relationships are played out, so that looking at patterns of support at different points in time means that one is not comparing like with like in quite significant ways: there is variation both in people's need for support and in the capacity of relatives to provide it. (Finch, 1989, p. 81)

This means that how much support is provided, even if one could measure this retrospectively for previous historical eras, is not a reliable measure *by itself* of how important extended families are now or were in the past. Instead of asking whether kinship is more or less important, we should instead seek to understand the nature, meaning and significance of kinship at different times and in different contexts.

Who are our relatives?

Debates about the changing significance of kin tend to assume that we know and agree upon how to define and recognize our relatives – for example, as those related to us by blood or marriage. Yet recent research and new forms of theoretical thinking about kinship have suggested that these categories are not straightforward, nor are they constant across time and cultures.

A key element in this new thinking about relatedness is that it is better to understand kinship as connections, relationalities or configurations, rather than units with pre-defined membership, as may be implied in the 'nuclear family', the 'extended family', or the 'household' (Finch and Mason, 1993, 2000; Smart and Neale, 1999; Weeks *et al.*, 2001; Widmer and Jallinoja, 2008). From these perspectives, each person's kinship connections are conceptualized as personal to them: *you* are at the centre of *your own* network or set of relationalities. Thus, even your sister's kinship group will look rather different to yours, although it will involve some of the same people. This mode of 'reckoning' kinship also allows for the fact that you will, at one and the same time, be an *aunt* to your nephews, a *niece* to your uncle, a *sister* to your brother, a *daughter* to your mother, a *step daughter* to her partner, a *step granddaughter* to his or her mother and so on. We do not simply occupy one kin position in a fixed kin group even at any one time. Instead, the experience of being related involves different relational or kinship statuses simultaneously, some of which change over our lifetimes.

The different sets of relationships in your kin network will also be interlocking and contingent on each other, so that, for example, your relationship with your grandmother – how close you feel, how often you see her, what you do together or for each other – may be influenced by how she treats your kids, or how well you get on with her partner. And over time all of this changes, as people get older, and babies are born, people die, people form partnerships, break them and form others – as a consequence of these, new dynamics are set in train that influence not only those directly involved, but others through transforming the connections of kinship.

Understanding relatedness also involves questioning how the demarcation lines are drawn so that some relationships are seen as kinship, and others not. There is evidence from many studies of a great deal of complexity in kin relationships and in who people count as kin, not least because of increasing rates of cohabitation, same-sex 'marriage', divorce and repartnering, and childbirth outside marriage or civil unions. Research shows that people are sometimes uncertain about and often work quite hard to negotiate and decide upon their kin relationships in these 'new' (some are not so new) circumstances. What is more, there is not always a consensus in a family about it.

For example, if your brother has an ex-girlfriend with whom he had a child, you might conclude that you are that child's aunt or uncle if for no other reason than there is a blood relationship between you, via your brother. But if the ex-girlfriend already had another child by a different father, would you also be this child's aunt or uncle? And would you continue to be so after she and your brother split up? And then if she repartnered, would you still be related to her and her children, and how about her new partner? And would any of this be different if your brother were adopted, or a step brother, so there was actually no 'blood' or 'biological' relationship between you? And how far would the quality of relationship between the key people make a difference? For example, if you got on really well with your brother's ex, and regarded her 'like a sister'? Or if your parents thought of her as a daughter-in-law and had always treated her two children in the same way? Or alternatively, if you were estranged from your brother, or always hated his ex and thought her a malign influence on him and your other relatives?

This kind of complexity in kin relationships has been called the 'ordinary complexity of kinship' (Mason and Tipper, 'Being Related', 2008, p. 443), because it is an increasingly ordinary experience for people's families to involve these kinds of relationships. This means that many people get involved in the process of *working out* who they are related to, rather than being able always to take this for granted as a given. There are a number of principles and practices at play in the process of determining who relatives are.

Marriage

Marriage initially appears to be a clear-cut way in which relatedness is defined, because it confers relatedness on a couple, their children and their other relatives – bringing two families together. However, the picture is more complicated than this.

For a start, marriage is not a universal or unchanging phenomenon. In different cultures, ethnic groups and across time there have been different rules about what constitutes marriage; about whether people can or should marry their 'relatives', and which ones; about whether marriage is necessary to confer legitimacy and formal kinship recognition of offspring; about how many times people can marry (either sequentially or simultaneously) and whether divorce and remarriage are permissible; about whether marriage has to be heterosexual; and about whether cohabitation can confer the same rights, responsibilities and privileges as marriage. The way these questions are answered through the provisions of different legal and administrative arrangements influences who is and who is not, in a formal sense at least, recognized as a relative or kin by marriage, and whose kin groups are thought to be brought together (if any) when people partner or have children. Of course alongside the more formal or legal rules and judgements, are people's own understandings of these things, which may or may not concur.

Blood

Being related by blood seems on the face of it to be obvious, natural and uncomplicated as a way of determining who is related to whom. People usually are able to distinguish between blood kin, and other kin, and blood kin are nearly always recognized to be relatives (except sometimes in cases of extreme conflict or separation), although they are not automatically and always the 'closest' or considered to be 'my current family' (Finch, 2007).

Blood relatives also figure strongly in some of the ways that kinship is recognized formally – for example, legal provisions for 'intestacy' (when someone dies without making a will). When this happens, decisions have to be made about what to do with the deceased person's property, and who has a right to a share in what proportion. So, for example, in the countries of the UK and most states in the USA and Australia, intestacy provisions create a next of kin hierarchy of who will inherit first or in the largest share that runs something along the lines of: spouse, children, parents, siblings, grandparents, aunts/uncles, cousins (although there are differences and complexities in the rules and in the ordering of the categories). Significantly, unmarried partners or those not in a civil union do not usually make it into the hierarchy at all (though as a notable exception intestacy rules in Australian states tend to cover 'de facto relationships'), and 'children' usually include 'natural', 'illegimate' and adopted children, but not stepchildren. Friends are conspicuously absent too, as are in-laws (relatives of spouses). Thus there is a strong emphasis on blood and marriage as the constituents of kinship in intestacy provisions.

In England, Australia and most states in the USA, the principle of 'testamentary freedom' operates, which means that anyone can make a will to dispose of their property as they wish and this can involve 'disinheriting' close relatives. In England and Australia this testamentary freedom is however curbed somewhat so that if a person were to bequeath all their property to a charity, for example, certain family members can challenge this and courts have the discretion to depart from the original will. In most European countries inheritance is governed by a 'civil code' that requires specific categories of close relative to receive a certain share of the estate, thereby very strongly enforcing a particular version of kinship and family responsibility.

These kinds of provisions are important because they constitute a public statement or expression of a normative next-of-kin hierarchy. In this way, and for this purpose, they tell us who our relatives are, or who they are allowed to be. However, we know also that this is often at odds with people's own understandings of their own kinship or inheritance hierarchy (Finch and Mason, 2000).

Blood connection is becoming much less clear cut with the advent of assisted conception using gametes – that is, donated sperm or eggs. These technological and procedural innovations make possible new forms of 'biological' relationship between parents and children, so that a woman can give birth to a baby to whom neither she nor her sexual partner (the 'social' father of the child, or the 'non-birth mother' in lesbian parenting) is biogenetically related.

Anthropological research into these forms of parenting and kinship show that people's sense of relatedness may differ quite strongly from the scientific view of genetic origins (Franklin and McKinnon, 2001). Janet Carsten (2004) argues that such innovations bring about circumstances in which people can be highly creative and engaged in *making* their own kinship and in transforming how we think of biological relatedness. Jeannette Edwards (2000) argues that although assisted conception is still a minority experience, people more generally will readily engage their culturally developed 'kinship knowledge' to puzzle over and come to judgements about how new forms of relatedness should be understood.

Family resemblance

Another aspect of relatedness that has some connection with 'blood' and 'biology' but that is much less discussed in existing research and literature on relatedness, is the question of 'family resemblance'. Yet family resemblance can be a very important factor in people's everyday personal lives, and can be taken for granted or yearned for in its absence. Studies of 'adoption reunions' – meetings between people who were adopted and their birth families – have shown that 'meeting someone you look like' for the first time can be a 'highly charged issue' (Trinder *et al.*, 2005, p. 37). Resemblance seems to speak of or demonstrate kinship in a rather tangible way, for 'all to see', and can be a core element in people's personal identities (Lawler, 2008; Mason, 'Tangible Affinities and the Real Life Fascination of Kinship', 2008; Mason and Davies, 2009).

On the face of it, family resemblances seem to be straightforward manifestations of 'biological' kinship, but closer examination reveals them to be more complex. For example, not all 'biologically' related kin resemble each other to the same degree or at all. Moreover, resemblances can seem to 'skip a generation', and strong resemblances can exist between people who are not related in any biogenetic sense. Jennifer Mason and Katherine Davies (2009) argue that family resemblances are created at least in part through interactions and negotiations between people, and that their significance for kinship is established in this way (see also Mason, 'Tangible Affinities and the Real Life Fascination of Kinship', 2008). One interesting example of this comes from research into 'transnational adoption' in Spain and Norway. Here it has been shown that despite adoptive children coming from different ethnic origins to adoptive parents (and thereby having no genetic or 'racial' reason to resemble them), members of the 'receiving' families will look for, see, talk about and affirm resemblances between the children and their adoptive parents and families (Howell and Marre, 2006).

Family resemblance then is a way in which people identify and create kinship, but resemblances are not simply 'given' by 'nature' – they are made sense of, and sometimes actually *made*, in the context of relationships that people are defining as, and living as, kinship. Nevertheless, family resemblance is often perceived as a tangible, irrefutable outward sign of relatedness, and it can be a potent force in defining kinship.

Closeness

The quality of people's relationships with others can help to determine whether they see them as kin, and forms a basis on which they may differentiate among their relatives. Thus, people may count close friends as family (see Chapter 7 by Katherine Davies), or they may have a close relationship with one sister, a difficult one with another and have lost touch with another.

Kinship studies that have explored people's 'closeness' to their relatives have concluded that genealogical closeness (the supposed distance between formal kinship positions) is not the same as emotional closeness, and that kinship positions do not dictate or directly predict how close relationships will be, or which will be the most important (Finch and Mason, 1993). In the same way, frequency of contact or geographical proximity, although sometimes taken as an indicator of family solidarity, are not necessarily the same as a close relationship. While frequent contact may help close relationships to develop, it can also cause tensions and conflicts, or foster indifference. Similarly, geographical distance does not automatically lead to relationships that are less close. In an increasingly globalized world, many relatives are involved in 'transnational kinship', and use a range of strategies and forms of communication to 'do' kinship at a distance (Bryceson and Vuorela, 2002; Mason, 'Living Away from Relatives', 1999, 'Managing Kinship Over Long Distances', 2004).

Sometimes, people will include in their families others with whom they have no formal kinship connection because they nonetheless have a family-like relationship with them. The groundbreaking study by Kath Weston (1991), for example, of gay and lesbian couples in the USA, showed that networks of friends and lovers actively thought of themselves as relatives – or **families of choice** – and practised kinship through close emotional and practical support. Weeks and colleagues (2001) in the UK found that the gay and lesbian people in their study negotiated kinship groups that included others not connected by conventionally defined kinship ties. A study of children's kinship (Mason and Tipper, 'Being Related', 2008) found that some children created like-family relationships with non-relatives – for example, longstanding family friends who were considered to be aunts or uncles. The children effectively 'kinned' these relationships, by constructing a sense of lineage on the basis of the longevity of the family relationship (Mason and Tipper, 'Being Related', 2008). And as shown in Chapter 8, these 'others' do not have to be human, and if you ask adults or children who is in their family, many will include animals.

It is significant perhaps that in all of these examples, the notion of 'family' is used in a positive sense, so that incorporating the other into your family is a way of saying your relationship with them is highly valued. There is little evidence to suggest that people do the same thing with friends whom they dislike. This tendency for 'kinning' to only involve positive relationships suggests

---

Box 6.2   Kinship obligations and commitments

Do we feel a distinctive sense of obligation to our relatives? For example, are we duty bound to care for our elderly parents, or look after our grandchildren? Are we obliged to spend time with our 'extended' families on cultural and religious festivals like Eid, Diwali, Christmas, Thanksgiving and Hannukah? Certainly we know that extended families, conventionally defined, figure strongly in such celebrations and rituals. But who gets involved is a matter of negotiation, and the 'traditions' that they engage in are not simply 'followed' but are modified and created in families (Etzioni and Bloom, 2004).

Do people follow rules of family obligation based on kinship positions? For example, do you feel responsible for a relative *because* you are their daughter, or uncle, or grandchild? A UK study by Janet Finch and Jennifer Mason (1993) found that, although many people felt a strong sense of commitment to their relatives, this was 'negotiated' and developed over time rather than being an automatic outcome of their kinship position or of kinship rules. Negotiations sometimes took the form of explicit discussions, but very often commitments were developed in more complex and diffuse ways.

For example, this study found that women more often than men took on the responsibilities for caring for elderly or sick relatives (which has been noted widely in other studies), but that this is not straightforwardly explained by their gender. If it were, then we would expect all daughters in a family to be equally involved in caring, which is not the case. Instead, they argue that we should understand these patterns arising because of the history of the particular relationships involved, and the configuration of these women's other responsibilities (including child care and employment). These factors meant that, over time, some women became the obvious candidate in their family to provide care, and the least able to make 'legitimate excuses'. When commitments develop in this personal and negotiated way, people tend to feel them very strongly: more so than if they had been decreed on the basis of their gender or genealogical status alone. Indeed, we know that where the state has attempted to enforce family obligations between extended kin, this has not worked as well as expected (Finch, 1989, 2006).

---

that there is a greater degree of electivity in whether or not to recognize such people as kin than is possible with one's more conventionally defined relatives, who tend to be considered kin whether you like them or not. A study of children's kinship, for example, showed that although they could choose to define some conventional kin relationships as genealogically closer than they were (saying that a cousin was more like a sister, for example), they did not seem to be able to say that they were *not related to* a blood relative (Mason and Tipper, 'Being Related', 2008).

We have so far examined issues around who counts as kin, but said little about what this might mean in terms of the commitments that relatives might feel towards each other. This issue is discussed in more detail in Box 6.2.

Concluding remarks

To summarize, we can see that extended families have not 'lost their signifi-cance' but also that this is, in a sense, the wrong question to ask because kin-ship is a changing phenomenon and set of practices, and it needs to be under-stood in specific and changing socio-cultural, legal and historical contexts.

Similarly, we have seen that there is a complex and ambiguous interplay in how we determine who is a relative between conceptualizing kinship as 'natu-ral' or 'biological', on the one hand, and as created and negotiated, on the other. Indeed, the lines drawn between kinship as 'given' and kinship as 'made' are blurry, indistinct and subject to constant renegotiation (Carsten, 2004; Mason, 'Tangible Affinities and the Real Life Fascination of Kinship', 2008). Lawler puts it this way:

> Kinship appears to tie us firmly in to the biological and the natural, but, at the same time, it defies those categories. For one thing, it always takes work, both the work of recognizing kin and the work of producing iden-tities based on those kin. (Lawler, 2008, p. 53)

The idea that recognizing and defining one's kin takes 'work' extends from the theory, developed most clearly by David Morgan (*Family Connections*, 1996), that families are constituted through *practices*, and that people 'do' families and kinship, rather than simply inhabiting them. And in a context where many people are engaged in living the 'ordinary complexity of kinship', the need for public recognition of one's own kinship group and arrangements can become very important. We have seen that legal regulation has a role in defining who is and who is not kin, but that it is not always in tune with people's own understandings.

In this context, Janet Finch (2007) argues that *family display* is a vital way in which people establish that this is 'my current family', especially in ordinar-ily complex situations where this might not be obvious to the world at large. She says that this is done through family interactions that need to be not only *experienced*, but also *observed* by others, and these can be *narrated* as a way of making a public statement that this is 'my current family'. She gives the example of a family meal in a restaurant involving ex partners, new partners and step children, to show that in doing and displaying these activities and groupings as 'family-like', people are constituting their own kinship. This is an important line of argument, because Finch is suggesting that although people do have some capacity to negotiate, define and create their own kinship, they do not simply have a free choice about this. People cannot recognize just any-one as kin. Others have to go along with this, and some form of display and recognition needs to take place.

Questions for discussion

- Can you think of examples of 'family display' from your own personal life? Who was involved and what is it about these interactions that constitutes them as 'family display'?
- 'You can choose your friends but not your relatives.' How far is it true that relatives cannot be chosen?
- How would you go about producing a sociological answer to the question of whether kinship is becoming a lesser part of people's everyday lives?
- How might same-sex marriage transform people's wider kin relationships?

Friendship and Personal Life

Katherine Davies

7

Introduction

What does it mean to be a 'friend' in contemporary Western society? Images of friendship as a highly positive, desirable form of relationship abound in popular culture. Think of the lead characters in US hit television shows *Friends* or *Sex and the City* whose friendships are depicted as a supportive, life-affirming alternative to their – often less satisfactory – familial or romantic relationships. Similarly, popular clichés, such as the well known adage 'You can choose your friends but not your family', indicate that friendship is understood as a *chosen* relationship as opposed to a *given* tie and this is what seems to make it different from other relationships. But is friendship really so simply defined? Is it always such a distinctive sort of relationship and such a positive one?

This chapter considers the significance of friendship for personal life, and examines how a sociological exploration of friendship can highlight the complexities of relationships with friends, from defining the term 'friend' to addressing the position of friendship relationships in a changing social world and challenging the notion that friendships are always positive relationships, characterized by choice and fundamentally different from relationships with kin. Some of the questions we will consider are: has friendship become more significant than family in recent times? Has there been a decline in face-to-face friendship and are our friends really as freely chosen as we might think?

Defining friendship

What exactly is it that defines a friendship? It is a difficult concept to pin down because friendship can take so many different forms. Think about the 'types' of friends in your life. Do you have different relationships with friends you have known from your school days and those you met at university? Are your Facebook friends always 'real' friends? Do you do different things with different friends? It is likely that you have a number of diverse and complex friendship relationships in your life and that these relationships are themselves constantly shifting and evolving.

In their detailed empirical study into the meanings of friendships, Liz Spencer and Ray Pahl (2006) move beyond any simple definitions to explore the various practices and meanings associated with friendship. Because they find the term 'friend' rather limiting as a category of relationship, they favour the term 'personal community' to denote people's networks of friends and associates. Within such networks, the boundaries between different relationship categories such as 'friend', 'family member', 'colleague', 'neighbour' or 'acquaintance' are often blurred: after all, you can be friends with family members and friends can become 'like family'.

Spencer and Pahl found that the notion of a personal community got around the problem of applying definitive categories to relationships which often move between such boundaries and enabled them to think of friends in terms of a community of various social ties as opposed to a relational form existing between two individuals. Their study also highlighted how many people have numerous friends in their lives who fulfil different roles at different times. For example, they identified different 'repertoires' (Spencer and Pahl, 2006, p. 54) of friendship which show how there are differences in both the types of friend people have in their personal communities and the constellation of these friendships (the range of relationships which make up the personal community). Spencer and Pahl also suggest that people have 'friendship modes' (2006, p. 54) in that their friendships shift (are formed, lost or maintained) throughout the lifecourse.

Spencer and Pahl also found that there are different types of friendships, ranging from the very simple to the highly complex. Simple friendships might include 'associate' friends who share a single common activity (such as someone you sit next to in a particular lecture or play tennis with once a week) but where the friendship does not continue outside the parameters of this particular activity. Similarly 'fun friends' are more complex relationships than those with 'associates' but the friendship is still 'simple' because the relationship does not extend beyond fun forms of sociality. Complex friendships include 'comforter' friends who provide emotional support (which can be difficult or awkward to ask for in less complex relationships) and 'soulmates', the most complex and multistranded friendship of all, where friends confide, provide emotional support, help each other and have fun and so on.

New technologies of friendship

In thinking about what it means to be a 'friend' and what a 'personal community' might look like it is important to consider how developments in computer technology have affected how we conduct such relationships. Email and the advent of social networking and gaming websites (such as Facebook, Twitter,

Second Life and World of Warcraft) increase the possibilities for forming friendships with people without the necessity of face-to-face contact. On the surface, such technologies could be seen to be indicative of (or even responsible for) a demise in face-to-face ways of relating. However, there is little evidence to suggest this is the case. Although research is inevitably always a few steps behind the latest technological advancements, it appears as though new technologies of friendship are primarily used to enhance existing ties which still involve face-to-face contact. As Wellman and Hogan (2004) argue, the internet is embedded in everyday life, meaning that it primarily maps on to existing ties rather than replacing or transforming them:

> Rather than only connecting online, in-person or by telephone, many relationships are complex dances of serendipitous face-to-face encounters, scheduled meetings, telephone chats, email exchanges with one person or several others, and broader online discussions among those sharing interests. (Wellman and Hogan, 2004, p. 390)

It could be argued that new technologies, particularly social networking sites, are creating new ways of doing friendship which supplement existing practices of friendship. For example, the ubiquitous rise in popularity of the social networking site Facebook has been influential in shaping the ways people perceive and manage their personal networks. Although there is no telling whether Facebook will continue to be so central to future practices of friendship, in July 2010 over half a billion people were users of the site, indicating that regardless of its future longevity it has been a consequential factor in the development of the social meanings of friendship and friendship networks.

For example, in her blog about Facebook etiquette, Mariann Hardey identifies 'poking' (a Facebook function allowing users to give a friend a virtual 'poke' – making contact without actually typing a greeting – and which expanded to include all manner of other means of making contact including throwing virtual food or buying fish for a friend's virtual fish tank) as a new social practice existing in addition to face-to-face contact. Hardey writes:

> Social networking seems to be taking the lead with a 'new' kind of intimacy. Where face-to-face interactions had been a 'normal' state of affairs now individuals experience relationships across new media and broadcast to networks of very complex social links. Nothing says social networking at the present time more than being 'bitten' by a vampire, turned into a werewolf or zombie-fied; all 'new' twists on the old poking routine. Then there's 'super'poke'; c'est super non? (Hardey, 2007)

Thus, 'poking', along with other functions of social networking websites, can be understood as part of a new way of doing friendship which instead of replacing other forms of contact supplements them. Similarly, the various functions and practices involved with Facebook use requires the need for the development of new forms of etiquette surrounding how friendship is done, particularly concerning how to manage being contacted by old friends and how to deal with unwanted Facebook 'friends'.

Social change and the significance of friendship

Has friendship become more significant than family in recent times and has its role in our lives changed? Much of the sociological work on friendship has focused on differences between relationships with friends and those with family and kin. This is because, to some extent, the sociological interest in friendship has come about as a result of wider debates about whether – in light of social change – choice and reciprocity (commonly perceived preconditions for friendship) have become increasingly valued relationship characteristics in today's post-industrial society.

There have been many complex (and sometimes rather fiercely fought) debates in sociology about wider socio-cultural changes and their effect on our relationships. A number of social commentators (for example, Beck and Beck-Gernsheim, 1995; Putnam, 2000; Giddens, 1992) have concluded on the basis of the demographic changes in the patterning of contemporary relationships in Europe and the USA – such as the rise in divorce rates and the postponement of childbirth – that there has been a dramatic shift in the way people conduct their personal relationships (for a more detailed overview of these demographic changes please refer to Chapter 3 by Wendy Bottero and Chapter 4 by Carol Smart, this volume). It has been argued that the traditional 'nuclear' family is diminishing (yet see Bottero's, Smart's and Jennifer Mason's chapters for critiques of such views).

Anthony Giddens (1992), and Ulrich Beck and Elisabeth Beck-Gernsheim (1995), who are major proponents of the **individualization thesis** (also called the **de-traditionalization thesis**) introduced in Chapter 1, argue that in a society where set traditions and social rules are understood to be on the decline, and where even family relationships are no longer fully prescribed, the role of individual choice in the way we do relationships is increasingly significant. In this context of 'de-traditionalization', friendship has been heralded as an increasingly significant relationship form which best captures the zeitgeist (the spirit of the times). In a society where set traditions and social rules are understood to be on the decline, the role of individual choice in the way we do relationships is seen as increasingly significant.

In his discussion of the '**pure relationship**' (outlined in Chapter 1 of this volume), Giddens argues that friendship particularly captures the voluntarism and democracy of this concept. For Giddens, a friendship is a relational form 'unprompted by anything other than the rewards that the relationship provides' and is seen as distinctive from kin relationships in that 'one normally stays a friend of another only in so far as sentiments of closeness are reciprocated for their own sake' (1991, p. 90). Therefore, friendship is understood as typifying the 'pure relationship' because it survives only for so long as both parties derive enough satisfaction from it. Thus, although his concept refers largely to dyadic relationships (between two people) and is often used to discuss romantic couple relationships, it is arguably the ideals of friendship (choice, intimacy and personal disclosure) which are most truly highlighted in the pure relationship. Friendship therefore is seen as the ideal relationship form for post-industrialized society, in contrast to 'fixed' or 'given' relationships with kin and community which are seen as diminishing in significance.

Families of choice

In a study investigating friendships amongst non-heterosexual people, Jeffrey Weeks, Brian Heaphy and Catherine Donovan (2001) highlight how, in certain circumstances, friends can take on some of the functions traditionally performed by family members, providing an example of how chosen ties can be seen to be replacing given 'traditional' ties in certain specific contexts. Because of their exclusion from the then exclusively heterosexual institutions of 'family' and 'marriage' (many had been rejected by their own family of origin due to their sexuality), non-heterosexuals in the study often described their communities of friends as being 'family' relationships because it was in their friendships that they experienced the support traditionally seen as provided by families.

A great deal of importance was therefore placed upon *creating* networks of relationships that were conceived of as 'families' (in the sense of providing support, care and commitment) but that were *chosen*. The voluntaristic nature of these relationships leant them a heightened sense of ethics and morals; because they were chosen they were not taken for granted and instead required work and nourishment (Weeks *et al.*, 2001, p. 11). This is termed the 'friendship ethic' and means that there are particular features of friendship (choice for example, or the idea of being free to 'be yourself' in a society which often fails to approve of this self) which made such relationships especially valued in non-heterosexual communities at the time (Weeks *et al.*, 2001, pp. 51–2).

The study indicates the centrality of the concept of choice to these understandings of friendship and highlights how friendships can become heightened at times of particular need. This study might seem to support Giddens in that it depicts a situation where elective relationships are taking over from more traditional given ties. The empirical evidence of a 'friendship ethic' also indicates that individual choice can be understood as a highly virtuous and desirable relationship feature in particular contexts. Weeks and colleagues' study depicts friendship patterns in a particular context and as we will see in the following section, it is important not to overstate the significance of friendship compared to relationships with family.

Critiques of de-traditionalization and the 'pure relationship'

There are many persuasive criticisms of Giddens's work (see for example Smart's chapter in the present volume and Jamieson, 1998, 1999), and of the idea that society is becoming more individualistic in general. For example, despite Weeks and colleagues' (2001) findings that friends can take on the role of family in a context where 'traditional' familial ties are challenged, it would be inaccurate to understand friendship and kin relationships as generally oppositional with one clearly on the decline and the other increasing in importance. We have seen in Spencer and Pahl's work that such categories overlap in people's 'personal communities' and as we have seen in Mason's chapter in the present volume, empirical evidence indicates that the extended family remains significant.

Although it would appear that there is some evidence for Giddens's argument that de-traditionalization has resulted in an increased significance placed on the role of friendship (Pahl, 2000), his claim that 'pure relationships' based on choice and reciprocity are replacing more traditional ties with family seems less well supported by empirical evidence. Spencer and Pahl (2006), for example, whose study of personal communities we have already discussed, are careful to show that the categories of friend and family member are rarely mutually exclusive. They also show the various forms that friendship can take, with their definition of 'soulmate' friendships being the only friendship form identified in their study that is reminiscent of Giddens's dyadic 'pure relationship'. In addition, Pahl (2000) has argued that even friendship, the 'pure relationship' *par excellence* according to Giddens, is not something that can easily be discarded. This is because, in the context of the de-stabilization of 'traditional' relationships, having successful friendships that one sticks with is seen as a key way of ensuring a stable identity, as well as avoiding being viewed by others as fickle in one's relationships:

> Parents die, children leave home, couples dissolve and reunite; the emotional traumas of contemporary life take place in different places with different key actors. Sometimes the only continuity for increasingly reflexive people is provided by their friends. Unwilling to be perceived as social chameleons flitting from one job or partner to another, men and women may come to rely on their friends to provide support and confirmation of their enduring identities. (Pahl, 2000, p. 69)

The social patterning of friendship and the limits of choice

We have seen that what is often described as setting friendship apart from other relationships (particularly relationships with kin) in the sociological literature and in common parlance is the idea that it is the most voluntaristic of our social relationships. But are our friendships really such a free choice?

Graham Allan (1996) argues that friendships are in fact governed by social factors as well as personal choice. He stresses the need for social scientists to pay attention to the ways in which an individual's social environment structures and constrains the choices they make about their personal relationships:

> friendships are not just freely chosen. They are developed and sustained within the wider framework of people's lives. The choices people make, in other words, are constrained by aspects of social organization over which they have relatively little control. (Allan, 1996, p. 100)

Allan points to the various ways in which an individual's work situation, gender, domestic circumstances and existing friendships influence their friendship patterns. For example, domestic circumstances, such as having young children to care for, can influence forms of sociality with friends, constraining one's opportunities to make new friends or to maintain existing ties. Later in the lifecourse when children are older, many parents find they are able to socialize with friends more freely and in different ways.

There are a number of other empirical studies which have examined friendship ties at key moments in the lifecourse, such as Stephen Frosh, Ann Phoenix and Rob Pattman's (2002) study of male school friendships, Rachel Brooks's (2005) work on university friendships and Sarah Matthews's (1986) exploration of friendships in old age, indicating that practices and patterns of friendship are heavily influenced by factors such as age and stage in the lifecourse. For example, in her study of the significance of work friends in later life, Doris Francis (2000) traces patterns of friendship among a group of women who had worked together in a US city from the late 1930s until the mid-1970s. Francis found that these long-lasting friendships helped the women to adapt to changes and discontinuities in their lives as they got older: 'Through their shared dialogue, interaction and pooled memory, they enable each other to give coherent meaning and empowerment to the present and also to mark new directions for the future' (Francis, 2000, p. 176). Thus it is clear that the significance of our friendships ebb and flow through the lifecourse, becoming increasingly significant at particular junctures, and that our social environment enables and constrains our friendship choices in complex ways. Friendship therefore must be understood as embedded within wider social contexts rather than as based entirely on personal choice.

Another way in which the voluntaristic nature of friendship can be seen to be limited is that we tend to make friends with people who are socially similar to us. This idea that similarity breeds connection (McPherson *et al.*, 2001, p. 415) is termed '**homophily**' and describes how we tend to interact with people who are similar to ourselves in terms of social class, education, race/ethnicity, age, religion and so on. As Wendy Bottero writes:

Whilst we all have very complex *networks* of relations to a range of different people, social characteristics (class, gender, race etc.) are systematically embedded in these social networks, and the people closest to us also tend to be socially similar to us, along many dimensions of difference and inequality. (Bottero, *Stratification*, 2005, p. 166, emphasis in original)

Although it could be argued that homophily is in fact a reflection of our freedom to choose our friends (in that people actively choose to be friends with people like themselves), much of the research in the area shows how homophily is also caused by structural and social limits to our capacity to freely choose our friends.

Miller McPherson, Lynn Smith-Lovin and James Cook (2001) reviewed many studies of patterns of friendship in order to explore some of the key ways in which homophily in race/ethnicity, age, religion, education, occupation and gender limit our social worlds to differing degrees. They found that homophily is caused by a number of factors, including geographical distance, the organizations we belong to and occupational, family and informal roles.

Geographical distance was found to be a key cause of homophily because, despite the advent of new technologies of communication, we are still more likely to have closer ties with people who live in closer geographical proximity to us. This in turn influences our networks of friends in other ways; for example, living in a predominantly white middle-class area predisposes a person to have predominantly white middle-class friends. Similarly, many of our non-kin ties are formed through our membership of organizations such as school, work, or clubs. People who attend the same university, for example, are more likely to come from a similar background and to have shared values. Finally, our roles at work, in the family or elsewhere, influence how we form social ties. For example, people are more likely to strike up friendships at work with those who perform similar occupational roles. Also, we have already seen how being a parent can affect the way we form friendships and socialize with existing friends. This makes it more likely that parents will form friendships with other parents. Box 7.1 provides a detailed discussion of an empirical project investigating racial segregation of friendships in US schools.

So it seems that 'birds of a feather' do indeed 'flock together' (McPherson *et al.*, 2001, p. 415) and that the homogeneous nature of our networks of friends and associates (the fact that these networks often contain people with similar social characteristics) means that, rather than being an entirely free choice, the range of individuals with whom we associate is socially structured. Thus, we can see how both the forms of sociality we experience with friends (the various ways we interact with friends) and the types of people who comprise our networks of friends (or our 'personal communities' as Spencer and Pahl would put it) cannot be put down to individual choice alone but are also governed by social structures and contexts over which we have less control.

Box 7.1   Multiracial friendships and homophily

Lincoln Quillian and Mary E. Campbell (2003) used data from the US National Longitudinal Study of Adolescent Health to investigate the impact of the growing Asian and Hispanic population upon friendships among US school students. Students in the study were asked to name their five 'best' male and female friends and various statistical tests were used to determine the racial spread of these friendships. It is important to note that the nature of this question meant that the study could not pick up 'friendly' acquaintances (people who the students knew but did not think of as among their 'best' friends) or close friendships that did not figure in the student's top five friends.

The authors found that students' racial background had a strong influence upon their patterns of friendship, even among those whose family had been living in the USA for a number of generations. The more racially diverse the school, the more likely it was that students would form cross-race friendships. This finding supports the points made earlier about the significance of geographical proximity for homophily and is termed the 'propinquity effect', meaning that the more likely young people were to come into contact with fellow students from racial minority backgrounds the more likely they were to have friends from these minority groups. Significantly though, Quillian and Campbell also discovered that students who were members of small racial minority groups in their school were more likely to make friends with students from their own racial background. The authors state:

> We believe this to be because students desire several friends of their own racial group for reasons of social support and they alter their friend-making behaviour to achieve this goal when there are only a few same-race friends in their school. (Quillian and Campbell, 2003, p. 560)

These findings highlight some of the complexities of the homophily principle, indicating that the social structuring of our friendships can have numerous causal factors. The authors were also able to make a number of recommendations about the importance of maintaining balanced racial proportions of students in US schools in order to lessen homophily.

Friendship as the ideal relationship?

Friendship is often depicted (in academic research and in popular parlance) as a particularly positive relationship. Sociologists have often regarded friendship as a desirable, sometimes idealized, relationship. Giddens's (1992) 'pure relationship', with its emphasis on choice and reciprocity, is a good example of this. Also, Spencer and Pahl state that because their research focused on friendships that people consider to be important in their lives they did not find out much about 'the dark side of friendship, about unsatisfactory, competitive or destructive relationships, though this is undoubtedly an important theme' (2006, p. 2).

As well as this sociological bias towards focusing on positive implications of friendships, there is also a cultural tendency towards a rather glossy understanding of friendship. By this I mean that, culturally, friendship is understood as a largely positive, beneficial relationship. For example, describing a family member or partner as one's 'best friend' is a way of adding value to the relationship by drawing upon the ideas of voluntarism and intimacy denoted by the term 'friend' (at the same time, describing a friend as 'like family' fulfils a similar purpose by implying that the relationship is permanent). The key difference here is that the negative aspects of familial relationships (conflict, inequality, abuse) have been widely investigated in academia, whereas investigations into friendship have not veered far from an understanding of its positive qualities.

Television shows such as *Friends* and *Sex and the City* were also mentioned in the introduction to this chapter as examples of cultural representations of friendship as providing a preferable alternative system of support in the absence of satisfactory relationships with family or lovers (which is, of course, reminiscent of the conjecture that friendship is rising in significance as these more 'traditional' relationships lose their function). Indeed, popular culture is teeming with positive images of friendships. Think, for example, of television commercials depicting happy groups of friends enjoying a particular product, indicating that popularity 'sells'. These depictions serve to both represent and create cultural ideas about what friendship means and how it ought to be practised.

Due in no small part to such a positive cultural 'gloss' on the meanings of friendship in Western society, friendship also implicates our sense of self and we have already seen how Pahl (2000) and Spencer and Pahl (2006) identified friendship as ensuring a 'biographical anchor' and an enduring sense of identity. In a society where having rewarding friendships is highly valued, it could also be risky or damaging to be seen to be a person who does not have good friends. If we are free to choose our friends then it follows that we are responsible for these choices and the quality of the relationships that develop. We have also seen in Weeks and colleagues' (2001) study that to be a 'good' friend requires effort and work. Thus, if our friendships are failing it is often thought to be because we have not tried hard enough or behaved appropriately.

So it seems that there are a number of ways in which friendships can be understood as socially desirable relationships which are in turn bound up with our self-image. What we think of our friendships implies what we think of ourselves and, of course, the concept of homophily means that our friends are likely to be similar to us, providing a sort of mirror on ourselves (our achievements, failures and behaviour) (Pahl, 2000, p. 77). This connection complicates the idea of choice and voluntarism in friendship. Of course, it is *because* they are largely chosen ties that friendships are seen as socially desirable and as involving the self, but this link between sense of self and friendship challenges the presumption made by Giddens that people can drop relationships and walk away when they become unsatisfactory.

The darker side of friendship

Given that friendships are not so easily dropped if and when they become unsatisfactory, it follows that not all friendships will be positive, life-affirming, beneficial relationships. Like relationships with family members, sometimes friendships can be characterized by negative relational practices and can be

---

Box 7.2   Difficult friendships

In November 2008, a team of researchers from the University of Manchester[3] commissioned a Directive on the topic of 'The Ups and Downs of Friendship' from the Mass Observation Project (formerly known as the Mass Observation Archive). The Mass Observation Project has a panel of volunteers who write responses to numerous 'directives', or questions, which are posed about particular issues. In this case the researchers asked the panel to write about (among other things) 'difficult friendships' and friendships that had ended (Smart et al., 2010).

Many respondents to the directive said that they would drop a friend if the relationship became difficult. Although this may appear to support Giddens's (1992) claim that contemporary Western relationality is characterized by choice, most of the respondents described feeling 'bad' or 'guilty' about ending a friendship, indicating that walking away from troublesome friends is not taken lightly. As one woman wrote about a particular friend:

> I spent a lot of time supporting her emotionally but I ran out of stamina (or maybe compassion) after a few months and I just wanted the friendship to revert to its original balance. We are still friends but I don't see her as much, and I've cooled it a bit ... I'm loyal towards my friend – although I realize that it doesn't sound like it! This sounds awful, but I don't get a lot out of the friendship any more. (M4132, F., aged 42)

Some of those who stuck with difficult, irritating or boring friends drew on concepts such as length of the relationship or feelings of duty and responsibility to explain their reluctance to terminate the tie. These concepts are commonly used to understand relationships with family members but clearly also influence relations with friends:

> I have an ongoing friendship with a divorced man ... who is a good friend in many ways, but who can be very overbearing, loud and insensitive ... and he has an anxiety problem. I am sorry for him but find myself totally drained after a day in his company. It is not a peaceful or stimulating friendship, and can be quite boring but due to the length of time I have known him (15 years) and his problems, I do feel a certain 'responsibility' as he has a grown up family, but no other friend. (W2107, F., aged 68)

> Rather like family we do tend to rub one another up the wrong way from time to time ... but like family we have a lot invested in one another and the minor blips are soon forgotten and are really just that. (G4296, M., aged 31)

jealous, cloying, annoying or even toxic and damaging. As mentioned above, most sociological studies of friendship have focused primarily on their positive attributes (although Spencer and Pahl [2006], p. 42, do mention 'heart sink' ties whose company affords little pleasure), but it is also important to think about why we might stick with certain friendships despite a lack of those characteristics of equality or reciprocity which are often deemed fundamental to such chosen ties.

Perhaps the links between friendships and our sense of self mean we are often reluctant to contemplate being the sort of person who does not maintain friendships and work through difficulties in such relationships. Perhaps those friends who we have known for most of our lives and who therefore act as 'biographical anchors' (Spencer and Pahl, 2006, p. 56) no longer feel like entirely chosen associations but instead are people we feel we have a moral obligation or duty to maintain ties with. Box 7.2 provides a detailed discussion of an empirical investigation into the 'downsides' of friendship.

Concluding remarks

Previous sections of this chapter have indicated that sociological debates about the role of friendship in society are often tied up with those about the role of family and wider kin. We have also seen how such simplistic distinctions between 'friends' and 'family' may not be entirely accurate. So, is there any truth to the adage 'You can choose your friends but not your family'? On one hand, ideas put forward by theorists such as Giddens (1992) point to a rise in the importance of personal choice, equality and freedom in our personal relationships. Weeks and colleagues' (2001) study also shows how in the context of non-heterosexual associations, friendship can at key times replace the role of kin precisely because they are voluntary relationships. We have also seen how, culturally, friendship is heralded as an idealized relational form because it is understood as based on personal choice. However, on the other hand it seems that our freedom to choose our friendships may be overstated and numerous studies of homophily and the social patterning of friendship indicate that friendship is governed by social structures and inequalities as well as by personal choice. It is also clear that it is not always easy to leave friendships behind us if they become unsatisfactory.

Furthermore, it is important not to overstate or simplify the differences between relationships with friends and family. After all, 'friends' and 'family' relationships shift and evolve over time and are not discrete categories, but often overlap. It is also problematic to assume that the significance of friendship is set against a decline in the importance of family relationships – the empirical evidence indicates that family relationships are still central.

Questions for discussion

■ Think about the people in your own 'personal community'. To what extent do you see the homophily principle applying in your own life?

■ To what extent can friendship be understood as a relationship characterized by free choice? (Discuss with regards to the similarities/differences with kin relationships.)

■ Why do you think people might stick with friendships that are no longer wholly positive relationships?

■ Think about the claim that friendship has become more significant in contemporary Western society. Can you think of arguments both for and against this assertion?

Pets and Personal Life

Becky Tipper

8

Introduction

The chapters in this volume so far have examined relationships and various forms of relatedness between people. Not all of our personal relations, however, are with humans. Relationships with the pet animals who share our homes – nestled on the couch, curled in front of the fire, welcoming us home – can also be significant for many people. In fact, around half of households in most Western societies now have one or more pets and it seems that in the twenty-first century, pet-keeping has a distinctive character. Vast sums of money are spent on pet products and pets are often seen as part of the family, or even as 'substitute children'. This material and emotional investment sometimes leads to accusations that contemporary relationships with pets are frivolous or that pets are replacing people in our affections. Relationships with pets may also lead us to ask what kind of relationship it is possible to develop with an animal, and how we can understand close connections with other species. Pets, then, can be controversial and raise many questions. Yet, despite the predominance of pets in people's lives and the fascinating issues they raise, sociologists have only recently begun to study these relationships.

This chapter asks specifically how we might make sense of pets within a sociology of personal life and explores how the seemingly personal and private relationship with a pet can be viewed sociologically, examining how pet-keeping is related to **social structures** and **social change**. It will look at various theories which seek to account for the distinctive character of contemporary pet-keeping, asking how connections with pets might be understood in terms of other relationships, as well as how they can be understood as relationships in their own right.

Thinking about animals, humans and pets

In order to think about the issues raised specifically by pets (those animals whom we live with intimately), we need, first, to think more generally about how we understand animals and our relation to them. Although people may usually take for granted what it means to be a human or an animal, it can be argued that in Western societies, perceptions of animals reflect a very particular history. Western thinking is influenced by a Judeo-Christian worldview and shaped by particular philosophical traditions, where animals exist primarily to serve the purposes of human beings and where there is a clear dividing line between humans and animals. Consciousness, rationality and language are seen as being definitive of humanity: it is understood to be self-evident that while humans possess these attributes, animals do not (we will be examining critiques of this assumption below). This distinction has been central to Western philosophy. In the seventeenth century, the philosopher Descartes summed up prevailing thinking (and set the agenda for centuries to come) when he asserted that animals could not feel pain because they had no minds – they were merely bodies and therefore more like machines.

The impact of these enduring ideas about the categorical difference between humans and animals can be seen in everyday assumptions: whereas humans have inalienable rights, it is generally seen as legitimate and acceptable that animals can be owned, killed or eaten. Beliefs about the status of animals not only impact the treatment of animals – the oppression of certain groups of humans frequently also has been justified through comparisons with animals (Arluke and Sanders, 1996). Slavery, for instance, was legitimated in the eighteenth and nineteenth centuries through claims that non-white human beings were like animals and could therefore be treated like animals. This link between animals and the dynamics of human power is an issue this chapter will return to later.

Despite this dominant tradition of thinking about animals, an intriguing aspect of pets is that they appear to challenge a seemingly straightforward divide between humans and animals. In contrast to other animals in Western societies, pets are treated as individuals; loved and cared for; given names; live in their owners' houses and sometimes sleep in their beds; they are never eaten; and their deaths are often marked and mourned. Pets are provocative, since they seem to fall in between conventional categories of human and animal: they are recognized as animals, yet in some ways treated like humans. The notion that pets are a challenge to the 'animal–human boundary' (or 'animal–human divide') is a central issue which this chapter will examine in depth. But I want to ask first: if pets mark a fundamental shift in thinking about animals, how exactly did pet-keeping emerge?

Pets in social context

Pets, as they are currently understood in Western countries, are a rather recent invention. Although historically, some wealthy aristocrats may have had special bonds with particular animals, most people's relation to animals was more functional – animals provided food or worked by catching rats, hunting game, or pulling carts and ploughs. However, throughout the nineteenth century in Europe and North America, pets became a central part of newly emerging cultural images of an ideal home and a loving, intimate family life (see, for example, Grier, 2002). A number of factors converged to make this possible. Partly, increasing affluence meant that more people could afford to spend resources on feeding and caring for an animal who offered no economic benefit in return. Additionally, as historian Harriet Ritvo (1987) argues, animals had once symbolized the dangers presented by the natural world. Industrialization, technology and medical advances began to grant humans a sense of 'mastery over nature' so that it became possible to view animals as charming, loveable, potential pets, rather than as wild and threatening. Increasingly, pets became popular among a broad range of people rather than the preserve of a few rich individuals.

However, as Ritvo also notes, pet-keeping in nineteenth century societies remained entangled with the dynamics of social class. Pure-bred dogs, for example, were particularly desirable and were seen to reflect the status and 'breeding' of their owners, while mongrels were associated with the working class – both these dogs and their owners were seen to be similarly 'dangerous' and 'ill-bred'. This brief history of pet-keeping offers a background for understanding relationships with pets today, but also neatly illustrates some ways in which pets can be seen sociologically. We see how the meanings given to animals vary across time and place, as well as how relationships with pets may be linked to social class (either by affording status, or when powerful groups demean others with reference to their associations with pets). In other words, the intimate and personal relationship between a human and a pet can also be seen as inherently social.

Pets in the twenty-first century

In contemporary pet-keeping, pets may similarly afford status or be a way of constructing and expressing identity. There are many examples: unusual pets such as rats or snakes might be part of an 'alternative' identity; cats, poodles or Chihuahuas might be valued for their 'feminine' associations, whereas others may seek the 'masculine' image of dogs such as Alsatians; and British bulldogs, Yorkshire or Scottish terriers may express a regional or national identity (see, for example, Franklin, 1999).

However, associations with certain pets may also be linked to identity in more negative ways. In the UK, for instance, the Staffordshire bull terrier is associated with a British, working-class identity, but has also gained a reputation as aggressive and dangerous. In recent years, it has been labelled a 'chav dog'. Here, the use of 'chav' (to refer contemptuously to members of a poor underclass) seems to directly echo historical associations between undesirable, ill-bred dogs and their poor, allegedly dangerous and ill-bred owners. Similarly, other images in the popular media show how particular associations with pets can be used to demean certain groups. The character of the 'Crazy Cat Lady' in *The Simpsons* TV show (who hurls her numerous cats at unsuspecting visitors to her home) embodies a familiar cultural stereotype where a childless older woman living with many pet cats is inevitably seen as misanthropic, anti-social, and even mentally ill. We can also note how some groups are denigrated if they have different practices regarding animals usually perceived as 'pets'. For instance, Westerners often view the eating of dogs as evidence that other cultures are uncivilized, cruel and barbaric (while selectively ignoring their own society's practices, such as factory farming, which might equally be regarded as cruel) (Elder *et al.*, 1998).

Such examples show how connections with pets can speak to wider issues of class, gender and ethnic or cultural identity, both in ways that people choose for themselves and in the ways that others view those connections. Judging people on the basis of their relations with pet animals can be one way in which divisions of race, ethnicity, gender or class are reinforced.

Although some aspects of pet-keeping are as relevant today as in the past, contemporary pet-keeping seems also to have a particularly distinctive character. Throughout the twentieth century, pets became deeply embedded in people's personal lives. As noted in the introduction, around half of households in Western industrialized nations have pets: 62 per cent of households in the USA; 47 per cent in the UK; 63 per cent in Australia; and 56 per cent in Canada.[1] Such figures only account for households which currently live with a pet, so we can assume that at *some point* in their life, many more people will have shared their home with a pet animal or will at least be acquainted with their friends' or relatives' pets. There seems to be huge emotional investment in pets – many people consider them to be part of the family and can experience profound grief when a pet dies. In these distinctively 21st-century pet relationships, new media even play a part – just as Facebook and MySpace have today become integral to the practice of human relationships, there also exist many online social networking sites for dogs, where pet owners can set up a page on behalf of their dog and interact with other dogs. Alongside this investment of time and emotional resources in pets, there is increasing financial investment in a rapidly expanding market for pet products. How, then, might we make sense of the changing place of pets in personal life?

Pets in a consumer society?

One striking aspect of contemporary pet-keeping is the amount of money spent on pets (see Chapter 10 by Dale Southerton for an account of how also other aspects of our lives have been affected by **consumer culture**). In 2009, $45.5 billion was spent on pet products in the USA, while around £4 billion was spent in the UK.[2] This includes staples such as food and cat litter, but it is also possible to buy clothing, jewellery and furniture especially for pets, or to check into hotels which offer luxury facilities for pets. In 2008, a new airline

---

Box 8.1   Pets and consumerism

Here I examine Heidi Nast's (2006) analysis of contemporary relations with pets. Nast is deeply critical of pet-related consumer trends in the USA and other industrialized nations and provides many examples to illustrate the growth of this consumer market. She discusses, for instance, the popularity of various leisure pursuits for pets (including dog yoga, or 'Doga') and the case of the people who paid US$32,000 (at 2005 prices) to have their dead cat cloned.

Nast contends that, despite such investment, pets are themselves expendable and are simply disposed of when we no longer want them. She highlights how around 4 million unwanted pets are euthanized (put down) in the USA each year (similarly, in the UK, the number of animals abandoned to the Royal Society for the Prevention of Cruelty to Animals rose to over 11,000 in 2008).[3] Nast argues that such engagements with pets reflect a contemporary culture of 'narcissistic consumption' (2006, p. 304), where pets are fetishized and commodified. In other words, we spend vast amounts of money on unnecessary commodities *for* pets and simultaneously treat these animals *as* disposable commodities.

For Nast, one particularly harmful aspect of pet-related consumerism is the possibility that it might serve as a distraction from pressing issues of human inequality and poverty. Instead of addressing enduring global inequalities between humans, people channel vast emotional and financial resources into pet animals. She suggests that there is a racial dimension to this, since such investment is largely the preserve of affluent, white pet owners. Nast also notes how enormous sums of money are donated to charities which help people in low-income communities to get their pets neutered or obtain veterinary treatment and care (Nast, 2006, pp. 313–14). It might be seen as ironic that there is no equivalent investment in the human members of these communities, who may even lack access to medical care themselves.

---

called Pet Airways was launched in the USA – dedicated to treating pets not as cargo, but as 'pawsengers'.

As Joanna Swabe (2005) observes, pet owners can now spend large sums on increasingly sophisticated healthcare for their pets. Deceased pets can be interred and memorialized in specialist pet cemeteries. It may seem that pets are (at least in the media) also taking on the role of 'fashion accessories' – for example, in the trend for female celebrities to carry small 'teacup' dogs. In fact, Paris Hilton's teacup dog – Tinkerbell, the Chihuahua – has become a celebrity in her own right and Paris Hilton has even launched a range of clothes, shoes, bikinis and jewellery for dogs. In Box 8.1 we examine in more detail Nast's (2006) critique of the consumerism that now surrounds pets.

Pets replacing people?

Nast's analysis focuses largely on how twenty-first-century pet relations can be understood in light of contemporary consumerism. Alongside this emphasis on consumerism, other dominant explanations for the place of pets in contemporary life have focused on the changing nature of personal relationships. It can be argued that personal life has undergone profound changes in our late modern society, where people delay having children or choose not to have children at all; where jobs and romantic relationships are no longer guaranteed for life, but are instead fluid and contingent; and where relationships with family and kin may be weaker as people become more geographically mobile. These ideas are key to Anthony Giddens's influential theories about '**de-traditionalization**' and '**individualization**' (please refer to Chapter 1 for an in-depth discussion of this thesis).

In such a society, then, it may seem that *pets* play a particular role. Sociologist Adrian Franklin draws on Giddens's ideas to explore relationships with pets, particularly the notion that, in the face of contemporary uncertainty and risk, people lack 'ontological security', that is 'knowing, almost without having to think about it, that key areas of one's life are stable, predictable and taken for granted' (Franklin, 1999, p. 85). Franklin argues that pets provide unconditional affection, reliability and a sense of 'ontological security' which is otherwise absent in contemporary human relationships. Another (often contentious) aspect of this argument is the claim that contemporary pets specifically function as 'substitute children' for adults without children of their own. Certainly, there may be some truth in this. As Patricia Anderson (2003) found in her research with people who kept parrots, many people saw their pet as child-like and had even coined the term 'fids' to refer to their 'feathered kids'. Similarly, in an ethnographic study of visitors to 'Fido's Barkery' – a café for dogs and their owners in the USA – Jessica Greenebaum (2004) found that most of these dog owners saw their pets as children, or 'fur babies'.

This idea that pets replace what is lacking in human relationships in our lives has been called the 'deficiency argument' (Irvine, 2004, p. 18), and has a great deal of currency in both social theory and media discussions of pets. Although it is not the case in Franklin's analysis, the deficiency argument tends to present the increased importance of pets in negative terms. The idea that animals replace missing human connections can be seen as a sad indictment on contemporary society, where pets are the recipients of care and affection which ought to be directed towards people (for example, Rollin and Rollin, 2003). Many writers are especially critical of humans who treat their pets as substitute children. Nast (2006) argues that pets provide the perfect child substitute in contemporary consumer societies characterized by narcissism (that is, selfishness or self-involvement) – pets can be indulged and showered with affection but, unlike children, require little commitment and can be easily abandoned if owners grow tired of them. Others argue that seeing pets simply as 'furry babies' means that owners may fail to care appropriately for their pets, since animals' needs (for social interaction, stimulation, exercise and food) can be very different to those of humans (see, for example, Haraway, 2003; Swabe, 2005).

Evaluating arguments about contemporary relations with pets

The 'deficiency argument' and what we might think of as the 'consumer society argument' assert that contemporary relationships with pets can be explained with reference to changes in personal life, namely the growth of consumerism and individualization. However, we need to be cautious about assuming that such arguments can entirely explain contemporary pet relationships.

First, we might ask how widely we can generalize from these points. Although some people consider their pets to be 'children', pet owners are diverse and may have different attitudes towards their pets – even childless pet owners do not necessarily view their pets as 'children' (see, for example, Swabe, 2005). Similarly, although it is possible to cite extreme examples of consumerism (such as cloning a dead pet), we might question whether these are typical of most people's ordinary relationships with their pets.

Second, the 'deficiency argument' (where pets fill the place of missing human connections), is based on the view of people in contemporary societies as highly individualized and isolated. Claims for such a dramatically fragmented society may be overstated in the first place, but we might also ask how far contemporary pets do replace human relationships. In fact, several studies have shown that single and childless people *do not* have more pets than other groups and that most pets actually live in families with children (for example, Irvine, 2004). This implies that sweeping claims about pets serving primarily as replacements for human relationships or as substitute children should be viewed with some hesitation.

Third, we might also look closer at the argument that investing emotional and financial resources in pets is indicative of an excessive 'consumer society'. Pet owners themselves may have very different interpretations. For instance, Greenebaum (2004) notes that the dog owners at Fido's Barkery viewed their spending on their dogs as an act of *love and care* for their 'fur baby' rather than a frivolous waste of time and resources. This might lead us to ask whether there is an alternative interpretation of contemporary relationships with pets, where emotional and financial investment in pets is not necessarily viewed as inherently misguided. It is this question which the next section will address.

Rethinking the animal–human boundary?

We have examined some persuasive and popular arguments about relationships with pets. We turn now to look at a very different approach to the questions posed by contemporary pet-keeping. Some writers now argue that, in contemporary pet-keeping, people are in fact *renegotiating* the animal–human boundary. In other words, what is distinctive about these relationships is that they challenge the ideas which have traditionally dominated Western thinking about animals (that is, the perspective which draws a clear line between humans and animals, epitomized by Descartes's claim that animals were mindless machines, to be used for food or work and where humans are the only species capable of thought and emotion). As we noted earlier, pets might always be seen to present a challenge to the animal–human divide. However, Franklin argues that in **late modernity** relations with pets are part of a growing tendency to question traditional attitudes towards animals, and that 'the categorical boundary between humans and animals, [previously] so fiercely defended … has been seriously challenged, if not dismantled in places' (1999, p. 3).

One aspect of this change in thinking is that, in contrast to claims that pets are treated as fashion accessories or status symbols, it might be argued that people increasingly view their pet animals as *companions* rather than 'things' (Franklin, 1999). Interestingly, this seems to be reflected in changing terminology around pet-keeping. Many people (particularly in the USA) now use the terms 'caretaker' or 'guardian' instead of 'owner', and prefer the term 'companion animal' to 'pet' because these express a more mutual relationship where animals are seen as valued individuals rather than belongings. This means that different sociological accounts of pets are also possible: rather than seeing pets as replacements for humans, commodities, or a waste of money, what might be distinctive about pets in the twenty-first century is that people are articulating and practising *new* sorts of relationships with and understandings of animals.

Leslie Irvine (2004, 2007) has looked in depth at the interactions between pets and people, arguing that owners recognize their animals as thinking, feeling, interactive individuals. Irvine's argument is that it is important to look at animals from a **symbolic interactionist** perspective – that is, saying that we can have meaningful interactions with animals as well as with people. Of course, animals do not use language, but Irvine argues that animals interact and express themselves effectively through their bodies and actions. She discusses how animals have unique personality traits; can show emotions (including happiness, fear and sadness); can remember past events and people; and can act intentionally (that is, they do not mindlessly follow their 'instinct' but can also have a goal in mind and consciously pursue it). Pet animals interact *with* us; they initiate contact or play; sometimes predict our behaviour; or seem to know when we need comfort. Irvine argues that these factors together indicate that animals have a sense of 'self' and that this is one of the things we value in interactions with pets – they are unique 'selves' with whom we develop meaningful relationships. Living with and getting to know a pet animal, then, often means challenging a simple categorization of animals as inferior and incapable of interaction, feeling and thought.

In contemporary pet-keeping, such views of animal minds and selves do seem to be gaining currency. Additionally, although sociologists have long ignored people's relationships with animals, Irvine's work (and that of others, such as Alger and Alger, 1997) asserts that interactions between humans and animals are worthy of serious study. Both the understandings of pet owners *and* the approaches of some sociologists can thus be seen to reflect a contemporary challenge to older views of humans and animals.

Claims about the mental capacities of pets might be dismissed as 'anthropomorphism' (that is, the projection of human qualities and abilities on to animals). However, it can be argued that the idea of 'anthropomorphism' depends on the prior assumption that only humans can think and feel in complex ways and that animals have no mental lives. For instance, to see claims for animal emotion as merely 'anthropomorphic' relies on the idea of a traditional, clear boundary between animals and humans, where only humans have the capacity for sophisticated emotions. Instead, as Irvine (2004, 2007) argues, we might better understand the differences between human and animal minds as a matter of *degree* – recognizing that animals have certain capacities for thinking and interacting, that they are not exactly like humans but neither are they empty-headed 'machines'.

In fact, much of the pleasure of relationships with pets may come from the fact that they are *not* like us: they do not speak, and their bodies and 'ways of being' are radically different from our own (Irvine, 2004). Relating to a pet, then, involves forming a mutual relationship with a thinking individual but also interacting with a creature who is quite unlike oneself. Some recent studies of pets underline this: Julie Smith (2003) argues that many people who keep house rabbits as pets do indeed view their pets as individual cohabitants but are also aware of the rabbits' distinctive and species-specific needs. Rebekah Fox (2006), in her study of pet owners, also found that people saw their pets as capable of sophisticated emotions and thought, but that they did not simply think of them as 'like humans' – they were also conscious of their pets' instinctive and 'animal' behaviours. Both Smith and Fox argue that pet-keeping requires us to question the animal–human boundary by seeing both similarities and differences between humans and animals.

In summary, it might be argued that contemporary pet-keeping reflects a changing orientation towards animals: where animals are treated as individuals who engage in complex interactions, who can be respected, known and cared for; where differences between humans and animals are not as categorical as once thought; and where being non-human does not necessarily mean being inferior. Through intimate relationships with pets, the possibility is opened up that the boundary between animals and humans is not as clear and definitive as it might seem.

This perspective also offers an alternative orientation to the question of whether pets replace relationships with people. As Irvine suggests, owners experience their connections with their pets as relationships with unique individuals – your dog is not just the same as any other dog. Rather than assuming that pets provide a poor substitute for 'real' relationships lacking in contemporary lives, this perspective emphasizes instead that relationships with animals might themselves be seen as meaningful connections, no less 'real' because they are with animals rather than with humans.

Another question emerges if we begin to take claims about animal minds seriously. If we accept that pet animals can be 'selves' with emotional and cognitive capacities, we might also come to question how Western societies treat other animals, such as those that are farmed and eaten (Irvine, 2004, 2007). Closely examining relationships with pets may thus raise challenging questions about how people relate to animals in other ways.

Pets as 'part of the family'

This chapter has looked at some arguments about how changing personal lives might be seen to impact people's connections with pets, and how views of close relationships with animals might also be changing. In this last section, let us draw some of these ideas together and look in more detail at pets within the context of families and kinship.

In one study of family life, Nickie Charles and Charlotte Davies (2008) found that, although they did not ask specifically about pets, 24 per cent of the interviewees mentioned pets as they talked about their families and kin networks (see Box 8.2 for a closer look at this study). This was even more striking in another project which used qualitative interviews to explore children's perspectives on their family and kin relationship, where 90 per cent of the children spoke about animals and frequently considered their own pets (as well as their friends' and relatives' pets) to be important relationships or 'part of the family' (Tipper, ' "A Dog Who I Know Quite Well" ', 2011). Unlike the visitors to Fido's Barkery in Greenebaum's research, the interviewees in these two studies were not passionate pet owners, but were simply participants in more general studies about family and kinship – nevertheless, pets mattered to them.

We have seen earlier how pets are sometimes considered to be 'substitute children' for childless adults, but the findings of Charles and Davies (2008) and Becky Tipper (' "A Dog Who I Know Quite Well" ', 2011) show how a wide range of people might consider pets to be part of their family. Both studies found that pets could be considered to be 'part of the family' because (like humans) they were individuals who were loved and valued and who in turn provided love and support. As we have seen in Jennifer Mason's chapter in this volume, people are often creative and actively engaged in defining 'family' or what it means to be 'related' – in this case, even including animals in such definitions. When people choose to include *pets* within their definition of family, they are bringing animals into a sphere usually reserved for humans. As such, this can be seen as another way in which relating to pets presents a challenge to the animal–human divide.

Interestingly, both the above studies found that it was not only people's own pets who mattered, but that pets were entangled in kinship and relationships more generally. For instance, pets helped to foster connections between people (for example, when people cared for a relative's or friend's cat if they went on holiday), but pets could also sometimes hinder relationships (for example, when people avoided visiting a relative whose dog was annoying or aggressive). Pets, then, could play a role in developing relationships between humans. Additionally, sometimes people also developed close, personal bonds with the individual pet animals who lived with their relatives or friends. This highlights how individual animals may be important in the context of personal life, even for people who do not own pets.

Charles and Davies's discussion in Box 8.2 of their interviewees' embarrassment (when expressing love for pets) highlights that, although, in some ways, contemporary relationships with pets *do* seem to challenge traditional views of animals, at the same time, there is a persistent sense that it is not right to care for or value animals in the same way as for humans. It may be that such

---

Box 8.2   Pets as kin

This box examines more closely findings reported by Charles and Davies (2008), drawing on data they collected as part of a wider study into changes in family life in South Wales. In their qualitative interviews, they asked people about their ties with family and kin, and who counted as 'family'. Of their 193 interviewees, 46 spoke about pets who were embedded in kin networks and sometimes considered to be 'family'. Charles and Davies argue that:

> family and kinship are socially constructed and different rationales are used to justify the choices made [about who counts as family] … what we are suggesting also is that this construction may ignore the species barrier, thereby recognising the possibility of kinship between humans and other animals. (2008, 9.3)

The authors argue that the way people spoke about their relationships with pets 'suggests that the boundaries between human and non-human animals are not fixed and they can be transgressed; this is particularly clear when pets are constructed as children' (Charles and Davies, 2008, 8.2). For instance, here is what one woman, who was expecting a baby, said about her relationship with her dog:

> We've had him two years now, he's been the baby, see, because I wasn't going to have more children, and I don't know how he's going to react when this baby comes. He was terrible with the budgie. (Interviewer says to dog: You are going to be jealous.) Yeah, because I did baby him quite a bit, but tried not to since I found out I was pregnant, I've tried to, not to distance myself, but to, just tell him who is boss, type of thing, so he started to realize he is a dog not a child. (Laughs.) So we'll see when the baby comes anyway. (Charles and Davies, 2008, 8.2)

Interestingly, Charles and Davies also note that most of their interviewees who spoke about pets did so tentatively and with self-conscious laughter. They suggest that this is due to the 'ambivalence with which animals are regarded within western culture … There is … a sense in which close, intimate relations with pets are seen as an indication of inadequacy and an inability to form appropriate relations with other humans' (Charles and Davies, 2008, 9.4).

ambivalence is central to understanding pets: engaging with pets involves challenging boundaries, but the legacy of traditional thinking about the animal–human divide still seems to exert a powerful influence.

Concluding remarks

This chapter has explored various approaches to explaining the place of pets in personal lives. Relationships with pets can be seen as deeply entwined with the social: meanings of animals vary across time and place, and between different groups of people. In seeking to account for the particularly distinctive nature of contemporary pet-keeping, some writers have suggested that current relationships with pets reflect a 'consumer society' characterized by excessive indulgence towards pet animals, who are also treated as expendable commodities. Other theorists emphasize the importance of changing personal relationships, suggesting that pets provide affection lacking in human connections in contemporary individualized societies (or the 'deficiency' argument). An alternative position is that contemporary pet relationships can be seen to reflect (and contribute to) a re-evaluation of traditional ideas about humans and animals. This argument emphasizes that in interactions with pet animals, people critically examine the possibility of relating to another species, engage in thinking about what it means to be human, and perhaps come to question traditional ideas about the animal–human boundary.

These perspectives offer different insights into what may be distinctive about contemporary pet-keeping. However, it seems that no one approach offers a complete account. The argument that contemporary pet-keeping reflects a fundamental rethinking of the animal–human divide is compelling, but the very popularity of the 'consumer society' and 'deficiency' arguments underlines that close relationships with pets are still widely regarded as dubious or misguided. We also see that although many pets are loved and valued, many others are unwanted and abandoned. As Charles and Davies (2008) note, even pet owners themselves can be ambivalent about expressing affection for animals. As such, it seems that relationships with pets in contemporary society cannot be easily characterized: pets may be seen as family, belongings, children, things, individuals, companions and commodities. Sweeping generalizations offering only *one* explanation for the nature of contemporary pets may therefore miss much of the complexity and variety of these relationships.

Until recently, sociologists have paid little attention to animals and our relationships to them. However, as we have seen, the questions raised by pets offer fertile ground for sociologists interested in contemporary personal life. Examining relationships with pets can lead us to look in new ways at social relationships, to ask fundamental questions about how we relate to other species and to reflect on what it means to be human.

Questions for discussion

■ Western nations spend billions each year on products for pets. What kinds of products and services do you think it is reasonable to buy for pets? Are there some things which you consider to be 'excessive' (for example, cloning a dead pet; or extended and expensive medical care for an ill pet)? Why?

■ Think about the pets you have known (either those you have lived with or those living with family members or friends). In what ways are these animals treated as 'members of the family'? In what ways are they not? What do you think of people who consider their pet to be a 'substitute child'?

■ From your own experience with pet animals, what sorts of emotional and psychological capacities do you think they have? Did they have distinctive personalities? Did they seem to show emotions? Were there times when they seemed to know what you were thinking or feeling?

■ Discuss arguments both for and against the claim that investing more (both financially and emotionally) in pets mean we care less about people. If we did not give so much money, affection and time to pets, would such resources otherwise be spent on humans? Why/why not?

Children's Personal Lives

Carol Smart

9

Introduction

In the mid-1990s sociology underwent a small revolution. This revolution became known as the 'new' sociology of childhood and was pioneered by a group of researchers who were determined that sociology should take children and their experiences more seriously as the focus of both research and theorising. As a consequence of this intellectual challenge it began to be appreciated that children, including young children, have personal lives and that these lives merit inclusion into the sociological canon in the way that the lives of women, or minority ethnic groups, or sexual minorities have been embraced. This chapter outlines this shift in thinking about childhood and children and will explain what the challenge has done to alter sociological thinking. A selection of empirical studies of children's lives will then be presented in order to explore the approach and to give substance to the claim that children are people too.

Sociology and childhood

> [Childhood is] a period of growth, that is to say, the period in which the individual, in both the physical and moral sense, does not yet exist, the period in which he [sic] is made, develops and is formed ... In everything, the child is characterized by the very instability of his nature, which is the law of growth. The educationalist is presented not with a person wholly formed – not a complete work or a finished product – but with a *becoming*, an incipient being, a person in the process of formation. (Durkheim, 1979[1911], p. 150, emphasis in original)

This quotation from Emile Durkheim, published in a book which originally appeared in 1911, presents the classical sociological approach to understanding children and childhood. Childhood was seen as a stage on the way to adulthood and, while this approach is clearly correct in one way, the unfortunate consequence of this view was that children were regarded as significant only in so much as they were adults-in-the-making. So the views of actual children, or their everyday experiences during the course of their childhoods, were dismissed as unimportant because they were merely expressions of a phase of development which would soon be left behind. In this model only the adult mattered sociologically. This view of children and childhood fitted perfectly with a period in history (the early twentieth century) in Western societies when children had virtually no legal rights, when child-rearing practices were highly authoritarian compared with today, and when childhood was actually quite short since the majority of children left school in order to earn a living at around 12 years of age, if not earlier.

This prevailing framework for understanding childhood gave rise to two strands of sociological work. The first strand of sociological enquiry has been to focus on the **socialization** of children (that is, the process whereby children learn the **social norms** and customs of their society). This stems directly from the Durkheimian approach noted above because sociology, in seeing the child as essentially an adult-in-the-making, focused attention on the 'making' side of the concept. So socialization theories became very significant because these processes were seen virtually to determine the type of adult that would emerge and that, in turn, was seen as central to sociological interests (Denzin, 1977). In this model the child is always located in 'the family' or in the education system and the real focus becomes how the parents socialize the child or how the education system educates the child. In this respect the child is present only in as much as he or she becomes a successful project. In fact, early studies of 'the family' rarely mentioned the child except as a passive entity to be moulded by parents. As long as the parents were seen as doing a proper job, the child him or herself was not particularly interesting.

This is not to say that children, or at least young people, made no appearance in the literature. But this was usually when they were deemed to have failed to be properly socialized. So there is a huge literature on delinquent boys or children who fail in the education system. Some of these studies of delinquency did break the mould to some extent because researchers sometimes used to 'hang out' with gangs or drug users, while others spent time trying to understand the young person's perspective as they struggled through the education system or became involved with youth cultures (Willis, 1978). But these studies, excellent though they were, usually focused on young people (that is, aged 14+ years) and rarely on children of around six or seven years of age. They also tended to focus mainly on young working-class men. An unfortunate by-product of this approach tended to be that children only ever came into focus if they were deemed to be a social problem. There was little on ordinary everyday life from a child's perspective.

The second strand is the structuralist approach, which concentrates on how childhood has been shaped by larger social and cultural forces (Pinchbeck and Hewitt, 1973; Hendrick, 1997). Such studies compare, in very broad terms, how childhood is differently constructed in feudal/agrarian times, or during the industrialization process, or in the modern moment. Such studies look for explanations of forms of, or changes in, childhood in terms of such forces as the demands of capitalism (for cheap labour in factories), colonialization (the involuntary migration of poor or abandoned children to countries like Australia or Canada), or the influence of religion (for example, corporal punishment of children to inculcate religious beliefs).

These kinds of studies are still important because they reveal how cultural ideas of childhood are malleable and changing (see, for example, Wendy Bottero's chapter in this volume for a discussion of how ideas of childhood changed during the nineteenth century). They also point to ideas about growing 'child-centredness', particularly with the growth of welfare states in Western societies, which increasingly seek to protect childhood and define it in opposition to adulthood. And they also point to other developments such as the expansion of education, which means that childhood is now stretched as far as the age of 18 years or even 21 years, when young people leave higher education and enter the labour market.

These structuralist approaches have been vital for bringing a sociological imagination to understanding childhood such that we no longer see it as an inevitable and unchanging 'phase' of life, but as a period which can take many different forms and shapes and hence can be experienced very differently by different groups of children.

These two dominant approaches within sociology do still provide valuable insights into contemporary childhood. However, the study of childhood was from an adult perspective and children were rarely treated as equals in the research process with views which might be as valid as the views of their parents or educators, let alone treated as really valuable to sociological analysis. It was this rather top-down approach that the 'new' sociology of childhood turned on its head.

The 'new' sociology of childhood

The authors who are largely credited with bringing the new approach into the field of childhood are Allison James and Alan Prout (1990) with a collection of essays about childhood in the UK, the USA, South America and the Nordic countries. Their book *Constructing and Reconstructing Childhood* is seen as the turning point in studies of childhood but it is fair to say that others were simultaneously experimenting with the new approach, particularly in Nordic countries (see Alanen, 1992; Brannen and O'Brien, 1996; Mayall, 1994; Qvortrup, 1993). The challenge of this new approach was twofold in that it required a different theoretical framework, which shifted the core understanding of childhood away from the idea that the child is simply in a process of transition and hence only of interest once he or she has arrived at adulthood, and a different empirical approach in which children were seen as active participants in the research process with voices which should demand the same kind of treatment and respect as adult voices.

This dual approach gave rise to a host of new studies on children. The idea was not to suggest that only children's voices mattered, but that for a better understanding of childhood it was essential to include the views and experiences of children themselves while they were living through childhood. It was deemed inappropriate, for example, only to ask adults what they remembered about being children; equally it was deemed inadequate to understand the workings of schools or families by simply amassing figures on exam passes or delinquency rates.

One important consequence of this development was the realization that there are multiple childhoods even within single cultures and during the same eras. The traditional idea of childhood as a stage that everyone goes through in order to achieve adulthood gives the impression that childhood is a determined process governed by biology (for example, the ageing process, puberty) and psychological or cognitive development (such as reaching a stage of understanding or of moral competence). However, the new sociological approach quintessentially recognized that there are many different childhoods if the experiences and standpoints of the children are taken as a starting point. Hence, there may be, in a Western society such as the UK or the USA, disabled childhoods, Chinese childhoods, girls' childhoods, the childhoods of adopted children, poor childhoods and so on.

In what follows, this chapter gives some examples of this new approach to understanding childhood by exploring studies of children's relationships with family and kin, minority ethnic childhoods and, finally, children's use of public space. I have selected these to show the diversity of research that has been carried out, but there are a great many other topics which have now been approached from the point of view of children which are equally relevant. The point to bear in mind when reading about these is that the starting point of the research is the assumption that children have their own personal lives and that their perspectives on their own lives are immensely valuable.

Children's families and kinship

Children are born into sets of relationships and/or families and as a consequence it is easy to imagine that they slot into a pre-existing system of kinship through which they are 'given' their bonds and ties of affection by adults. In other words, we have tended to assume that children have little choice when it comes to kinship. However, Jennifer Mason and Becky Tipper ('Being Related', 2008) interviewed 49 children from very mixed backgrounds in the UK, aged between seven and 12 years old, about how they saw the relationships that mattered (in a good and bad way) to them. They found that children were well aware of 'proper' forms of genealogical relatedness (that is, mother, sister, cousin, aunt) but they would include in their circles of who mattered a more flexible array of kin than formal definitions allow. Hence, a grandmother's new partner might be called a grandfather even though there was no genetic link, or a half sibling and even step sibling might simply be known as brother and sister. Mason and Tipper also found that, with changing patterns of households, conventional nomenclatures of kinship did not adequately describe these 'new' relationships, while the term 'friend' was not suitable either. So, for example, it was unclear to children what to call the former partner of a half-brother who is still linked to their family through the child that the couple had together.

From this study Mason and Tipper were able to see what changing family structures looked like from children's perspectives and they discovered that what mattered to the children was their sense of closeness to those people they invited into their own circle of kin, rather than simply the formal, genealogical principles of a 'proper' aunt, cousin or grandparent. They also found that just because someone was 'proper' kin, it did not mean that the children would automatically feel affection for them (see Chapter 6 by Jennifer Mason for an in-depth discussion of relatedness).

Taking seriously these understandings of kinship and discovering the flexibility of children in how they will include or exclude people from their circle of kin, throws a different light on changing family structures and how they may impact upon childhood. It also shows that children are not passive in relation to kinship, and although they do not have choice about who is genetically related to them (or related by marriage), they can exercise choice in terms of selecting who matters to them and who they feel close to. A key event in life in relation to which children might exercise such choice is parental divorce, as discussed in Box 9.1.

The 'new' sociology of childhood has been keen to hear children's own views on their parents' divorce. One such study was conducted by Carol Smart, Bren Neale and Amanda Wade (2001), who sought to find out what children felt about living in post-divorce families. They interviewed 117 children, 103 of whom were under 16 years old, with the majority of them being between eight and 11 years. The study was designed to discover how children managed the everyday experiences of living with one parent and seeing the other occasionally, or even living half their time with their mothers and half with their fathers. They explored what it was like for children to pack a bag on Sunday nights to go off to the other parent, what it was like for them if their parents were hostile to each other, what it meant if in one home they lived alone with a parent while in the other there was a step parent and step sibling and even a new half sibling. While most previous studies of children and divorce focused on measuring the effect of divorce in terms of children's exam results or their later sexual behaviour, this work simply wanted to uncover what life was like *during* childhood and to see what strategies the children developed and whether they reported themselves to be happy, miserable or just content.

The research found that children had some very clear views about the quality

---

Box 9.1   Childhood and divorce

One of the most important changes to childhood in Western societies in the last 50 years has been the rise in the numbers of children experiencing their parents' divorce. In Australia in 2005 there were 52,399 divorces and this affected the lives of 49,358 children under the age of 18 (http://www.aifs.gov.au/institute/info/charts/divorce/divorcechildren.html). In England and Wales in 2005 there were 141,750 divorces involving 136,332 children under the age of 16 (Office for National Statistics, 2006, p. 96). Although the divorce rate in countries like the USA, the UK and Australia is declining slightly, the possibility that parents will divorce or separate during a child's childhood is something that most children will inevitably contemplate. It is likely that in all schools (except those of strict religious observance) children will know other children whose parents have separated and so the possibility of divorce becomes real for everyone.

This fact changes the landscape of contemporary childhood considerably and it means that thousands of children each year have to adjust to transformations in parenting, possibly living in new homes, accommodating to new step parents and step or half siblings, and possibly seeing much less of one parent, especially if they move away. The possible harms of divorce have been the focus of much research, but this focus is giving way to a new understanding of how children can adapt to change in families.

The shift in thinking about children and divorce is based on a recognition of children's resilience and this is, in part, a result of studies of childhood which have allowed children's own voices to be heard. But it is also due to changes in the legal systems of all Western societies which now take account of the United Nations Convention on the Rights of the Child (ratified in 1989 with the exception of the USA). The Convention is an international human rights treaty that grants all children and young people (aged 17 and under) a comprehensive set of rights, which includes a right to be consulted and a right to family life. This means that parents are not able to make decisions when they divorce which go against the welfare needs and rights of their children. To some extent this allows children to become proper legal citizens and so it is an unintended consequence of divorce that children have acquired more rights within the **private sphere** of the family.

---

of their lives and their relationships with parents, new partners and new step siblings. Most importantly the study showed how much children wanted a voice in decisions about their lives and how they could cope with change if they were kept informed and involved. These conclusions have also been found in research in the USA (Kelly, 2003; Hetherington, 2003), in Norway (Moxnes, 2003) and New Zealand (Smith et al., 2003). But Smart and colleagues also found that children went a long way to be caring towards their parents, being attentive to their loneliness, recognizing that the divorce meant a lower standard of living for everyone, and also helping more because they knew that parents could be stressed. So far from being the passive victims of divorce, the study showed that children actively engaged with the situation they were in and could try hard to make the situation better for everyone.

Minority ethnic childhoods

We noted above that sociologists now recognize that there can be multiple childhoods which mean that children can experience very different childhoods even if they live in close proximity. An important part of this difference is related to ethnicity because a young African Caribbean boy living in a poor inner-city housing estate will have a very different childhood compared to a white girl living in the suburbs, and also a very different childhood to a Pakistani Muslim child living in a provincial town (Shaw, 2000). Intersecting identities of ethnicity, gender, class and religion make experiences of childhood quite unlike each other.

Children from minority ethnic backgrounds have tended to be understood as living problematic lives. That is to say they have been seen as more likely to engage in crime (if they are African Caribbean), or poor/lacking in **social capital** (if they are refugees or recent migrants with unskilled parents), or segregated by religion (if their faith requires special kinds of observances, such as wearing the veil). However, more recent studies have sought to avoid these stereotypes by researching the children's own worldviews and perspectives on their ethnic identities. This has transformed research away from seeing children from minority ethnic backgrounds as culturally deprived to seeing them as agents in their own lives where they are actively engaged in constructing their own realities and meanings.

Tracey Reynolds (2010), for example, has argued that, for African Caribbean young people, being part of a transnational family can actually be a powerful resource (Goulbourne, 1999). By a transnational family she means that migrants from the Caribbean to the UK have retained links with kin who stayed behind. This kinship network then becomes a resource for second-generation migrants allowing young people to be more globally mobile, to develop skills in one country which they can put to use 'back home', or by activating a network of support when necessary. The ability to remain in touch with a wide transnational kinship has developed considerably over the last two decades with technologies such as Skype, cheaper air fares and even a more global labour market (Bryceson and Vuorela, 2002). This means that for second- or third-generation migrant children, their transnational family networks can act as a resource (or positive social capital) which might help off-set some of the disadvantages (or negative social capital) they may experience in terms of poverty, discrimination or even racism in their country of residence.

Other studies have also explored children's sense of cultural identity (Ackroyd and Pilkington, 1999; Moinian, 2009) as a way of questioning the assumption that migrant or minority ethnic children have troubled or confused identities as a consequence of living in a predominantly 'white' or secular society such as Britain, Northern Europe or the Nordic countries. One such study conducted by Farzaneh Moinian is detailed in Box 9.2.

The argument put forward by Moinian that children's identities can be complex is one that is shared also by other researchers. For example Judith

---

Box 9.2   Children's hybrid identities

Farzaneh Moinian's (2009) study was based on multiple interviews with five children born in Sweden of Iranian parents. She also visited the children's homes and met their families over the course of several months. Although this was a small study it is important for the ideas she develops because she explores ideas about hybrid identities. Her argument is that children in situations where they are part of different, often quite diverse, cultures actively create a new, distinct identity. By using the term 'hybrid identity', she challenges the idea that people have just one identity and she argues that we achieve different identities as we progress through life, never becoming static but always open to degrees of flexibility depending on circumstances and experiences. In this way she rejects a 'fixedness' of both identity and culture and sees them as always open to change.

Importantly, hybridity also refers to the situation where identity may be formed by very different elements which are usually assumed to remain separate. Hence, the children in her study were both Iranian and Swedish; they were imbued with the culture of their parents and some understanding of their parents' homeland, but also imbued with values from the Swedish education system. They would have had both Iranian and Swedish (and probably other) friends. In some instances children in this situation may speak more than one language (Farsi at home and Swedish at school) and might also become 'fluent' in several religious teachings as well as knowing about secularism. Moinian therefore argues that these children can develop a 'third space' which is neither Iranian nor Swedish but their own creation. For example, one child said to her that he liked salami, pizza and spaghetti more than either Iranian or Swedish food and, laughing, asked if this made him Italian. The children were also well aware of not fitting exactly into either culture. In particular, being of Iranian heritage they had brown eyes and dark hair, while most native-born Swedes had fair hair, pale eyes and complexions. So the children were constantly aware of their particular position in the culture into which they had been born.

Moinian was able to understand how children can produce complex notions of the self and identity which do not simply fit with how adults may perceive their situation. The findings from her study can be applied to other children of migrant parents too, so that we begin to understand the intricate interplay between cultural heritage, place and a sense of self.

Ackroyd and Andrew Pilkington (1999) argue against the dominant, but rather simplistic, idea that migrant children must have a right to 'a cultural identity'. They argue that the imposition of a static notion of cultural identity which children must have instilled in them runs counter to the ways in which children themselves construct their own (hybrid) cultural identities. In this way both Moinian, and Ackroyd and Pilkington argue that by engaging with children themselves it is possible to gain a much better understanding of how fluid cultural identities are and that it becomes possible to see minority ethnic children as actively engaged in the production of their own identities, rather than seeing them as recipients of a socialization process that passes on a fixed cultural heritage.

Children and public space

As suggested above, there has been a tendency in sociological thinking to include children within the confines of family life or school. Hence the idea that the ways in which children use and perceive public space might be of sociological interest is a new one (for an in-depth discussion of personal life in public spaces, see Vanessa May's Chapter 10). Yet Margaret O'Brien and colleagues (2000) have argued that it is important to look at public space, particularly urban space in the context of the idea of the 'just' city. This means that the city should be fair to children and allow them as much free movement as possible. At present they argue that children in inner cities face a hostile urban environment which limits their ability to participate alongside other citizens.

One of the reasons why children experience public space in a different way to adults is because of perceived and actual risks. As O'Brien and her colleagues argue, the city environment has changed particularly with the increase in traffic, which presents real risks to young children getting around independently. There are also perceived risks of 'stranger danger' (Scott *et al.*, 1998) which may be exaggerated but which nonetheless influence both parents and children in how they use public space. As a consequence of these real and perceived risks it is suggested that children are offered a reduced kind of citizenship in which their movements are increasingly restricted and that they rarely have the opportunity for independent exploration of their environments. This, in turn, is thought to be giving rise to generations of obese and unfit children who will have both physical and intellectual impairments as a result. Against this backcloth sociologists and geographers have sought to find out what it is like being a child who uses public spaces and whether childhoods are being diminished in some way by modern forms of urban living.

A key study was carried out by O'Brien and colleagues (2000) to find out the experiences of children living in the inner-city areas and more suburban neighbourhoods of London and also in one 'new town' just outside London. The areas were ethnically mixed and many were quite deprived, and the researchers carried out a survey of children and parents through schools. In addition they carried out focus groups, 20 in-depth interviews with ten and 11 year olds and also accompanied children on 'walkabouts'. This was a very innovative study which followed the principles of the new sociology of childhood in that it placed children and their experiences in the centre of the research. They found that children's use of public space was most restricted in the inner-city areas and that, in particular, girls from minority ethnic families were the most limited in their ability to use public spaces (for example, going to parks or riding bicycles). However, they also found that children themselves shared some of the fears of their parents about being safe from risks and not all of them objected to being accompanied and organized by their parents. O'Brien and colleagues also suggest that, rather than seeing the home as a place of entrapment, children may now find it to be a stimulating environment. This was particularly true for children of higher-income families who had good play spaces and access to technologies which kept them in touch with friends and the 'outside' world.

Similar studies have been carried out in other cities. For example, Lia Karsten (2002) carried out a study of children's spaces in Amsterdam. She found that urban planners give little thought to children's use of public space and that there was ongoing a progressive exclusion of children from such spaces. Where there were initiatives that gave consideration to children, they were often segregated and did not allow children to participate fully in the life of the city. James Spilsbury (2002) carried out a study of children in Cleveland (Ohio, USA), focusing specifically on children's sense of safety in public spaces. His argument is that personal violence (and fear of violence) has seriously eroded children's environments in many cities in the USA. He suggests that children have to learn to negotiate danger in their neighbourhoods and, through an ethnographic study with 60 children aged between seven and 11 years, he sought to understand how they cope with the violence they encounter in their localities. Spilsbury used a walking and talking methodology which allowed the children to take the lead in the study. His results showed, like many of the studies mentioned above, that children were actively engaged in managing their own lives, in this case by discovering how to keep safe and learning who they could rely upon if faced with danger.

Concluding remarks

This chapter has outlined the importance of the new sociology of childhood and in particular has explored the kinds of research questions and findings that have resulted from this new approach which appreciates the extent to which children have their own personal lives. It explored three fields of study, namely family relationships, ethnicity and public space. However, it is important to recognize that for all the new insights this approach has brought, more traditional sociological approaches, namely socialization and structuralist theories, should not simply be abandoned. These two approaches ask different questions and so have a different focus. It remains necessary to keep structuralist approaches because it is vital to understand issues of power which are embedded in generational differences and also to understand how different structures (of class, gender, religion and so on) shape childhood(s). Equally we should not forget that, as well as being persons in their own right, children are also in the process of becoming adults, so they will not stay the same and they are capable of quite rapid change as they grow and develop. The next task for the sociology of childhood is therefore to bring all these perspectives together.

Questions for discussion

■ It has been claimed that the new sociology of childhood has improved our understanding of contemporary children's lives. Do you agree with the claim? Why/why not?

■ If the new sociology of childhood is correct, then there are many different childhoods. Taking either ethnicity, gender, social class or nationality as your focus, consider how social difference might influence the childhood a child would experience in the place where you grew up.

■ Compare your childhood with that of your parents and grandparents. Thinking sociologically, what are the main differences and similarities?

■ How could cities be made more child-friendly? Is this necessary? Why/why not?

Personal Life in Public Spaces

Vanessa May

Introduction

So far the chapters in this book have focused on close relationships between couples, family, kin and friends. The remaining chapters broaden the scope by focusing on 'public' issues and how these intersect with personal life. The present chapter focuses on personal life in public spaces with the aim of questioning the taken-for-granted boundary between 'public' and 'private'. Personal life tends to be understood, both by 'lay' people and by sociologists, as something that happens within close relationships and in private spaces such as the home. Yet as this chapter discusses, close relationships are also conducted in public spaces, and the seemingly impersonal contact we have with acquaintances and strangers in public space are important in shaping our personal lives. The chapter concludes with a brief discussion of the consequences that such a view of public space as somewhere where important relationships and interactions take place has for how sociologists understand 'society'. But first the chapter offers a brief discussion of what constitutes 'public' space and who has access to it.

What is 'public' space and whose is it?

Space and our use of it tend to be divided into 'public' and 'private'. This distinction is often taken for granted, and it is assumed that people 'just know' what distinguishes the two. Public space is generally understood to be open and accessible to all – think, for example, of streets, parks and shops. In contrast, access to private space (for example, the home) tends to be restricted to specific people such as friends and family. In practice, however, this distinction is not so clear-cut. For example, public space is not equally accessible to all groups in society (as will be discussed below), while the private space of home can be infiltrated by the **public sphere** – for example, in the form of state intervention in family life through family policy. The public/private distinction is also based

109

on the assumption that, whereas many public spaces such as shops and bars are commercialized, private spaces are not. This assumption is, however, also problematic. As Dale Southerton points out in Chapter 12, no aspect of our personal lives, even our identity, remains untouched by **consumer culture**.

Although these classifications may seem straightforward, they are not 'natural' or fixed. Notions of what is 'public' and what is 'private' space and understandings of what constitutes 'appropriate' use of them change over time and vary across cultures (in other words, they are socially constructed). For example, viewing the home as a purely private space is a relatively new phenomenon, brought about by **industrialization** and the resulting division of domestic and commercial activities into the separate spheres of home and factory. But what is more, these different spheres became 'gendered'. In other words, because men were in most Western industrialized societies considered to be the breadwinners of their families, they were more active in the public sphere of work and politics. Consequently, men gained more access to and control over public spaces. Public spaces came to be seen as men's spaces, while the home became the province of women (please see Gemma Edwards's chapter in this volume for an in-depth discussion of the development of such 'separate spheres' thinking). A 'respectable' woman needed a legitimate reason to be out in public without the company of a man, particularly after dark, lest she be thought to be a prostitute (Baldwin, 2002, p. 594). Things changed dramatically during the twentieth century, when women began increasingly to work outside the home and to frequent many other public spaces such as dance halls, movie theatres and restaurants.

Although women's access to public space is, in Western countries, now in principle equal to men's, these historical developments can still be seen reflected in the differences between how men and women use and perceive public space. Studies have found that women tend to feel less safe in public spaces than men do, especially at night (Day, 2001; Carro *et al.*, 2010; Warr, 1984). This is partly due to the harassment (often of a sexual nature) that many women experience while out in public – in a survey conducted in the USA, Kimberly Fairchild and Laurie Rudman (2008) found that over 40 per cent of the women surveyed experience sexual harassment such as catcalls every few days or so, while over a quarter of the women reported experiencing unwanted physical contact such as grabbing at least once a month. As a consequence, many women limit their use of public space for fear of being harassed, attacked or raped. For example, they may avoid being in public spaces alone, or stick to indoor public spaces like cafés rather than venture outdoors (Green and Singleton, 2006). There is, however, some debate over whether this perception of public spaces as especially dangerous to women reflects an actual risk or whether it is the product of widespread notions of femininity that portray women as more vulnerable than men.

A person's sense that they have access to public space (and that they can openly express their identity once there) can also be limited by sexuality (as we have already seen in Anna Einarsdottir's Chapter 5 in this volume), disability

(Kitchin, 1998; Freund, 2001), age, or 'race' and ethnicity. We will here focus on the latter two by discussing the differences in how people of different ages perceive and behave in public space, as well as racial segregation of residential areas. As Carol Smart has already discussed in Chapter 9, children, similarly to women, comprise a group that is defined as somewhat 'vulnerable' and therefore 'at risk'. Consequently, children's use of public space is restricted. For example, some towns in the USA and in New Zealand have set curfews for children under a certain age (Collins and Kearns, 2000). Public space is, in other words, largely controlled by (working-age) adults.

But we can also see that as people age, their relationship to public space can change. Studies conducted in different countries and at different times indicate that older people are more afraid of 'victimization', that is, they fear they will be the victims of crime, especially in public spaces. Mark Warr (1984) surveyed 331 people living in Seattle in the USA, asking them, for example, how worried they were about being threatened by a knife, club or gun, or about being beaten up by a stranger. He found that those over 66 years of age were more afraid than younger people of being the victims of crime in public spaces. More recently, Carro and colleagues (2010) conducted a survey among 358 people living in Barcelona in Spain, asking them how dangerous they experienced public spaces to be, and about their experiences of crime or other dangerous incidents in public space. Similarly to Warr, they found that as people age, they tend to feel increasingly insecure in public spaces.

There are also different expectations of how people of different ages should behave in public, or social norms relating to public behaviour. For example, a study of older women in the USA found that they felt marginalized and stigmatized in public spaces because of their age (Stalp *et al.*, 2009). One form of such ageism encountered by these women was the expectation that they behave according to the stereotype of an ageing woman who is not 'loud and noticeable' in public. The women who took part in Stalp and colleagues' study wanted to actively challenge such ageist thinking by being more visible in public spaces – for example, by wearing striking clothing such as red hats.

Apart from gender and age, also 'race' or ethnicity can determine a person's right to use public space. For example, up until the 1960s most public spaces such as public transport and schools were racially segregated in the United States and, more recently, one aspect of Apartheid in South Africa was that the government enforced a policy of racial segregation that affected most aspects of life (Gaule, 2005).

Given that public space is unequally accessible to different groups, it is perhaps not surprising that conflicts can emerge over the use of public space (Smets, 2005). Groups that are marginalized or excluded from public spaces also have the ability to resist such exclusion. Sometimes this resistance builds into an organized collective movement with the aim of ensuring a groups' right to access public space. For example, disability rights groups have in many countries successfully fought for legislation that requires any public building to provide wheelchair access (Ben-Moshe and Powell, 2007). During the 1950s and 1960s, the Civil Rights movement in the USA successfully challenged laws that allowed racial segregation of residential areas and public spaces (such as schools and public transport) (Gotham, 2000; Gadsden, 2010, Cassanello, 2008). Desegregation of public space has, however, not been fully realized in practice in Western countries. For example, people from different racial or ethnic groups tend to live in different areas (Wacquant, 2008; Samara, 2010).

This continuing (unofficial) residential segregation is partly the result of racial inequalities in socio-economic status. In other words, in many Western countries, racial and ethnic minorities are, on average, poorer than the majority white population, and tend, therefore, to live in more disadvantaged neighbourhoods separate from whites. But contemporary racial segregation can also be the result of discrimination experienced by ethnic and racial minorities. For example, black people entering an area that is mostly populated by whites can encounter suspicion or even outright hostility, thus reducing the likelihood that they would move to such an area (Anderson, 1990; Wacquant, 2008). Box 10.1 discusses a study that explored some of the reasons behind residential segregation in the USA.

Box 10.1   Why is racial segregation of residential areas continuing in the USA?

This box focuses on a study by Casey Dawkins (2005) who wanted to find explanations for why black–white residential segregation continues in the USA half a century after the abolishment of legislation that allowed the segregation of public spaces and over 30 years after legislation that made racial discrimination in housing illegal. Dawkins used data from the Panel Study of Income Dynamics (PSID) to explore how the racial composition of a person's childhood neighbourhood and the degree of interracial contact a person experiences as a child impacts what kind of area they want to live in as an adult (please refer to Chapter 14 for an explanation of what a panel study is). Dawkins found that people tend to choose to live in areas that, in their racial composition, resemble the area where they grew up. In other words, if a white person grew up in a predominantly white area, it is likely that they will live in such an area as an adult as well. This wish to live in an area where other residents are of the same race seems to be strongest among whites, even among those who were exposed to interracial contact in their childhood. This is in clear contrast to those African Americans whose parents had contact with whites: they are more likely to end up living in more racially integrated neighbourhoods. Dawkins concludes that 'Interracial contact has a more significant impact on reducing levels of Black prejudice than on reducing levels of White prejudice' (Dawkins, 2005, p. 554). Dawkins proposes that the persistence of black–white segregation is probably partly explained by continued racial discrimination. Such discrimination appears, for example, in the form of hostility expressed by white residents towards African Americans who are planning to or who have moved to their area, or of estate agents who discourage African Americans from moving into a white area.

What goes on in public space?

How people use public space depends also partly on how such spaces are built and designed (Brownlow, 2006; see also Box 10.2). For example 'night life' – that is, socializing in public spaces after dark – is a relatively new phenomenon made possible by street lighting. In the nineteenth century, cities such as London and Paris began lighting their streets with small gas lamps (Baldwin, 2002). Even this dim lighting enabled people to move about more easily in public spaces after dark, which also meant that the meanings attached to people doing so changed. Whereas before, any person who was out after dark could easily be considered as potentially morally dubious (a prostitute or a thief, for example), street lighting began to change this as increasing numbers of people took to the streets in the evenings and at night. Of course, since then the quality of street lighting has improved significantly, and the range of activities available to urban dwellers after dark has expanded, further blurring the boundary between day-time and night-time activities.

Another technological development that has changed how people use public space is the invention of modern modes of transport such as trains, cars and aeroplanes (Urry, 2007). Many people now travel regularly on public transport, especially those who live in cities. This is largely the result of the separation of work and education into public spaces such as offices, factories, schools and universities, which requires commuting to work or school, sometimes across long distances. This means not only that many people spend the majority of their waking hours either commuting to or at their place of work or study, but also that they regularly interact with people who are personally unknown to them. Indeed, public spaces are characterized by the fact that we are likely to come across strangers and acquaintances in them (see Dale Southerton's discussion of Simmel's essay 'Metropolis and the Mental Life', 1970 [1903] in Chapter 12).

These interactions or relationships between strangers or acquaintances differ from those between family members and friends in that they tend to be less intimate and shorter in duration. But there are also different types of stranger and acquaintance relationship, as identified by Lyn Lofland (1998, pp. 53–9). Interactions between strangers tend to be fleeting and to involve no significant emotional investment. Think, for example, of two strangers negotiating their way past each other on a crowded bus, or a customer in a shop interacting with the cashier. These exchanges generally last only a few seconds or minutes, and do not usually involve the two parties discussing any intimate details about their lives. Relationships between acquaintances (who, for example, frequent the same swimming pool or club) last longer, for weeks, months or even years. They also involve slightly more knowledge about the other person than relationships between strangers do, though even acquaintances do not know each other intimately. We might for example only know their name, occupation or where they live (Morgan, *Acquaintances*, 2009).

The distinction between public and private seems, thus, to render public space somehow outside the 'personal' because of the assumption that we only interact with people we barely know and, therefore, few meaningful personal relationships take place there. In other words, our experiences in public spaces are not generally considered as part of our personal life. But there are four arguments that can be made against this assumption. First, our interactions with strangers and acquaintances are an important aspect of our personal lives. Second, the unwritten rules of interaction in public are significant because they not only help make us feel 'at home' in the world, but also offer a way for us to present ourselves as acceptable members of society. Third, we also conduct aspects of our close personal relationships in public. Fourth, it is partly through these myriad interactions that we give meaning to space – that is, create places which play a part in our sense of collective and personal identity. Each of these points is examined below.

The importance of strangers and acquaintances

If we think about it, as David Morgan (*Acquaintances*, 2009) urges us to do, acquaintances are everywhere: fellow students who we might see on a weekly basis yet know little about apart from the fact that they are studying the same subject as we are; people we see regularly at work but only know their role in the company; or neighbours whose names and occupations we might know but little else. With such people we might start exchanging nods or a few words of greeting, perhaps even a few pleasantries, but we rarely engage in any conversation that would reveal our more private thoughts or intimate aspects of our biography.

As already discussed in previous chapters of this book, there is generally a tendency to think of relationships in a hierarchical manner, with family relationships as the most important, followed by friendships, and acquaintances and strangers as the least significant people in our lives. In some senses this might be the case. For example, family members might be able to rely on each other to feel a certain sense of obligation in terms of offering care or support that cannot be expected from a stranger or even a friend (Finch and Mason, 1993). However, contrary to the perhaps widespread notion that our relationships with strangers and acquaintances are not important because they are not long in duration or high in emotional content, Lofland (1973) has argued that this kind of anonymous sociability is significant, especially in contemporary urban life where we can expect to interact with large numbers of strangers and acquaintances on a daily basis.

For one, public spaces gain their identity and ambience partly through the people who populate them (Lofland, 1973, p. 83): for example, the bankers who work in the City of London give it a business-like air, while the clubbers who frequent the bars and clubs of Manchester's Gay Village lend it an atmosphere of hedonism. This general character of a place, as well as the nature of the interactions we have there with strangers and acquaintances, will have an impact on whether this setting feels 'friendly' or 'hostile'. Lofland (1998, p. 69) therefore argues that it is time for sociologists to discard the widely held notion that our 'primary' relationships with family and friends are automatically more important than these other relationships. This sentiment is echoed by David Morgan (2009) in his work, *Acquaintances*. In talking about the significance of the 'fleeting encounter', he argues that our relationships with acquaintances are important in and of themselves. Given how much of people's daily lives are spent in (semi-) public settings interacting with strangers and acquaintances, these interactions help make up the fabric of everyday life and to a degree determine the quality of people's personal life.

The importance of knowing how to (inter)act

This chapter now turns to examine the unwritten social rules that our interactions in public spaces seem to follow. These not only help to ensure '**social order**' – that is, the smooth running of daily life according to predictable patterns (as will be examined below) – but are also significant for people's sense of self. We need certain skills in order to cope in the world of strangers, such as skills of interpreting and 'coding' people, locations and behaviour. We also have to learn how to dress and behave appropriately, depending on where we are and who we are interacting with. Mastering these skills means that we can signal to others that we are an acceptable member of society who knows the unwritten rules of conduct and follows them. Being able to do this is important because our selves are relational, that is, our sense of self is to an extent based on how we think others view us (see David Morgan's discussion of Mead's relational theory of the self in Chapter 2). Knowing how to act in any given situation is, in other words, not merely a question of 'presenting' an acceptable self to others, but is also an integral part of building a sense of self as a moral human being (Garfinkel, 1967).

One of the most famous sociologists to have studied interactions in public spaces is Erving Goffman, who argued that ordinary face-to-face interactions between people tend to follow certain patterns. Goffman (1963) proposed that our dealings with each other seem to universally become subject to (unwritten) ground rules of co-mingling – that is, rules regarding appropriate face-to-face behaviour. In other words, how we interact with others is to some degree scripted, something that we may not be consciously aware of. It is impossible to imagine a society without such a complex set of ground rules, concerning, for example, how to greet people or the appropriate use of eye contact. As anyone who has been abroad will know, these vary from society to society (in other words, they are socially constructed).

Individuals in turn tend to develop 'patterned adaptations' to these rules by either conforming to, by-passing, or deviating from them. It is these patterned adaptations that, according to Goffman, form the 'social order' (please see Box 10.2 for an example of how social order is created in shopping malls). A very basic example of such social order is pedestrian traffic on city streets, which usually runs relatively smoothly, according to some common pattern or order. Next time you are walking along a busy road, stop for a while to look at how people manage to navigate their way past each other in a more or less orderly manner.

One key rule of co-mingling identified by Goffman is that of 'civil inattention', which concerns how we behave in relation to others in public spaces such as lifts and buses. When entering such a space, people tend to scan it with their eyes to signal that they are aware of other people's presence (civil), but do not then proceed to stare at others, engage them unnecessarily in conversation or openly eavesdrop on their conversations (inattention). By practising such civil inattention people are signalling to others (and to themselves) that they are aware of shared rules and abide by them – that is, that they are morally accountable and socially acceptable persons.

Some spaces, such as bars, however, are designed for public sociability, where it is perfectly acceptable for strangers and acquaintances to initiate at least a brief social interaction with each other. One such space studied by Irenee Beattie and colleagues (2005) is the 'singles dance' to which single adults come in order to meet and dance with other singles. Beattie and colleagues found that the relationships between the dancers tended to be fleeting, mostly lasting for only one or two dances, and rarely extending outside the event of the singles dance itself. In addition, these encounters were to a large extent non-verbal, with the participants communicating with each other with subtle nods and hand gestures to indicate their willingness to dance. Taking their cue from Goffman, Beattie and colleagues draw the conclusion that these dances are played out by the participants as though scripted according to the unwritten rule that 'predatory' behaviour is unacceptable and risks stigmatization. They argue that the fleeting and superficial nature of these relationships offers the participants something in itself: a form of safe and familiar fun that will not become serious.

It is such knowledge of the shared rules of interaction in public spaces that allows us to interact with strangers and acquaintances in relatively predictable ways. Breaches of these rules can feel upsetting or intimidating – for example, if a stranger approached us with the intent to divulge 'private' troubles or to ask for considerable help that would require substantial time and effort on our part. It is the fact that most public interactions run smoothly in a patterned way that makes us feel at home and safe in public spaces. In fact, many of us probably go about our everyday lives interacting with strangers and acquaintances without giving these interactions a second thought – they are part of the taken-for-granted fabric of our personal lives, and perhaps only noticed when they do not run according to plan. The rules that govern these interactions, however, play a fundamental part in our personal lives: they allow us to make sense of other people (and ourselves) in terms of some collectively shared social rules and norms.

Public interactions with friends and family

One further aspect of the porous nature of the boundary between 'public' and 'private' is that we not only interact with strangers and acquaintances in public spaces, but we also conduct aspects of our close relationships there (although the most intimate moments of our 'private' personal lives, such as having sex or arguing, are expected to and do mostly take place in the private space of the home).

Just as with our interactions with strangers, there are also some basic rules attached to how we interact with intimates in public and how others respect the 'private' nature of these interactions. One way of signalling that such an interaction is 'private' is by maintaining group boundaries. For example, people in a group might sit or stand facing each other and lean into one another as they speak (Manzo, 2005, p. 93). In her study of how American families create such quasi-private spaces in the public space of a zoo, Marjorie DeVault (2000) found that family groups would usually walk through the zoo in close proximity to each other and maintain 'groupness' through eye contact and talk. While parents sauntered along slowly and their children ran around, they kept each other within eye-sight and regularly called out to one another.

Other people are then expected to respect the 'privacy' of the group by engaging in civil inattention and by not breaching the (invisible) group boundary. For example, DeVault found that family groups tended to also be aware of other groups and to respect their boundaries – for example, by placing themselves at a distance from them. Parents were heard to instruct their children to stand in 'open areas', and would admonish those children who 'trespassed' on the territory of another group. Consequently, collisions between groups rarely happened. In Box 10.2 we take a closer look at a study that explored how social order is created in shopping malls.

Box 10.2 Creating social order in shopping malls

John Manzo (2005) conducted a study of four shopping malls in the USA and Canada, focusing on how social order is established through the design and surveillance of public space, as well as 'informally' between the patrons. The key aim of mall design is to ensure a steady stream of customers (and thereby profit) – for example, by creating 'welcoming' spaces where people are happy to spend time and through 'the regulation of human behaviours in ways that are beneficial to the flow of pedestrian traffic' (Manzo, 2005, p. 86). For example patterns on the floor indicate 'corridors' that people are expected to move along, and the design of food courts discourages lengthy stays. People are encouraged to 'eat and go' by not providing intimate spaces for private meals, or large tables for family or group gatherings, thus ensuring a steady stream of new paying customers.

But the orderly behaviour of people is not simply the result of the social control efforts of the malls. Patrons interact with the design of a space also in non-intended ways in order to make the space to some extent their 'own'. In addition to this, they are engaged in social control of each other's behaviour. Manzo observed, for example, groups of older men congregating in cafés and food courts, creating private spaces for themselves. They did so by spreading their things across several tables as a way of demarcating 'their' space. They also used high-volume talk and talking across tables to each other as a way of signalling that their corner of the establishment was out of bounds to those not included in the group. These group boundaries tended to be respected by other customers, who rarely encroached on the men's space.

Manzo found that customers in the food courts could use also other, perhaps more subtle, ways of signalling to others that their conversations were private – for example, by facing or leaning into each other. Those around them respected this privacy through 'civil inattention'. People would also claim tables as 'theirs' by placing their things on them, and anyone attempting to 'breach' this space by sitting there was told 'we're sitting here'. Manzo says that never once were such claims for space challenged. It is partly through the following of such unwritten rules of interaction that social order is maintained.

The meaning of place

We do not, however, interact with only people in public spaces – we also interact, and develop a relationship and an emotional connection, with the spaces themselves. By doing so, we attribute meaning to space and this is how we create place – that is, a space that means something to us. Lofland (1998, pp. 65–70) distinguishes between three types of person-to-place connections. First, memorialized locales are those places where significant events such as battles have taken place, or where such events are remembered with the help of a memorial such as a statue or plaque. Such places can come to symbolize a sense of collective identity such as nationality. The second type of connection is formed with familiarized locales through which our routine, often daily, paths traverse. Such places become familiar to us and we can develop a deep attachment to them, to the point that their loss is experienced as significant. Lofland (1998, p. 67), for example, details the profound emotional impact that the closure of a local supermarket had on many of the regular customers. The mere existence of such familiarized locales is important in itself and, even though we may not visit them that often, they symbolize to us our 'home range'. Hang-outs and home territories comprise the third type of place to which people form a connection. These are places that feel like 'home', such as a clubhouse or a bar, where we feel we can behave in a slightly less guarded fashion than we would 'out in public', despite the fact that these places are technically open to people who are strangers to us.

As already discussed above, there are some unwritten rules for public interactions, what could also be called 'street etiquette'. This is likely to vary from one place to another, and having local knowledge as to how to behave in a place can be a deciding factor in whether or not we feel at home somewhere. For example, Elijah Anderson (1990) found that people living in an area of inner-city Chicago developed a particular 'streetwise' attitude in order to navigate the at times dangerous public spaces. Being 'streetwise' allows a person not only to conduct rapid assessments as to the likelihood that a passer-by poses a threat and to act on this appraisal so as to defuse a potentially threatening situation, but also to indicate to others that they are not 'vulnerable' and should be allowed to pass un-harassed. Such streetwise behaviour enables residents to go about their business and makes the public spaces a more comfortable environment for them – and, it could be argued, contributes to a sense of belonging to that place.

A place that we have a sense of belonging to is also likely to have significance for our sense of self. We create a sense of belonging to places which we feel reflect who we are and thus create a sense of self 'through place' (Tilley, 1994, p. 26; Savage *et al.*, 2005). Charles Tilley (1994) proposes that our collective and personal identities are partly based on place because we understand ourselves as people from a particular place. For example, residents of New York City can come to feel that the energy and vibrancy of the city reflects their own personality and, as in most cities and regions, the residents also develop some sense of collective identity as New Yorkers.

Concluding remarks

By drawing a distinction between 'private' and 'public' spheres and by mainly focusing on interactions with intimates, many sociologists studying personal life have ignored a rich and meaningful aspect of our everyday lives: the interactions we have in public both with our friends and family, but also with acquaintances and strangers, as well as the sense of belonging that we can feel to certain places. Indeed, the fabric of our personal lives is partly fashioned from these elements. In addition, without necessarily being consciously aware of it, we are well versed in complex sets of rules about how to behave in such public spaces. This knowledge helps us feel at home and makes us feel a part of a community, as well as offering us an (acceptable) sense of self. In these ways, what goes on in public spaces is of significant importance to our personal lives.

Questions for discussion

■ What do you understand by 'private' and 'public' space? What differentiates the two? Are there any similarities between them?
■ Consider two technological inventions such as street lighting and the mobile phone. How do you think that these have changed the use of public space – for example, the rules of social interaction in public spaces?

- Next time you are at the student cafeteria, pay attention to who decides to sit where, whether there are larger groups who take up a lot of space, how they demarcate 'their' space and how they signal to others their group boundaries, and how others react to this.
- Are there any public spaces you are aware of that have restricted access to certain groups of people? Why do you think that is? How are these restrictions made known? Are there any public spaces you feel you might not have access to?

Are We Running Out of Time?

Dale Southerton

11

Introduction

Lewis Carroll's White Rabbit from *Alice in Wonderland* – the white rabbit who frantically dashes around holding a clock claiming 'I'm late, I'm late, for a very important date' – is symbolic of contemporary perceptions that the pace of daily life is accelerating and that there is an increasing shortage of time. Such time pressures are held either directly or indirectly responsible for a huge range of contemporary social 'problems'. Families are thought to be torn asunder because couples, parents and children do not have the time available to spend with one another. Finding time to spend with friends, and for idle chat with neighbours, becomes increasingly difficult and, without time to participate in public activities, community life is eroded leading to the fragmentation of public life and political disinterestedness (Putnam, 2000). This chapter explores the time squeeze by considering how meanings and values attached to time have changed as a result of **industrialization**, examines whether people are suffering a time shortage, and discusses the implications of these for contemporary experiences of personal life.

The *rationalization* of time

Daily life has not always been so regimented by time or, at least, by 'clock time', as it tends to be nowadays. Historical archives that document the canonization process (an inquiry into whether a deceased person was to be made a saint), provide a rich source of data on 'time reckoning' in medieval times. Around 1290, William Cragh was hung outside the walls of Swansea, only to be revived by the Bishop of Hereford, Thomas de Cantilupe. In 1307 the now dead Bishop was to be considered for canonization on account of his miracle revival of William Cragh. What is interesting about the archives for our present purposes is not whether this was actually a miracle, but the evidence provided by nine witnesses that William was indeed dead before being revived by the good Bishop. When asked how long he hung on the gallows for, the witnesses gave answers such as 'for the space of time that a man would have gone a quarter mile at an ordinary pace'. The witnesses also found it difficult to pinpoint how many years ago the 'miracle' happened with estimates ranging from 15 to 18 years (Bartlett, 2005).

Contrasting such forms of time reckoning with the precise calibration of the clock and daily life in the contemporary period (symbolized by Lewis Carroll's White Rabbit) raises the question as to how and why time reckoning was so radically transformed. Young and Schuller (1988) argue that, before the dominance of the clock, time reckoning was based on 'natural rhythms', dictated by the difference between night and day, seasons, being awake versus being asleep and so on. There was no agreed standardized unit of measurement – hence time being measured according to how long it would take a man to walk quarter of a mile at an ordinary pace. The shift to clock time has, however, imposed a whole range of taken-for-granted time scales on everyday life, including eating breakfast, lunch and dinner at set times of the day as opposed to eating when hungry, or measuring human life in stages – from infant to toddler to 'tween' to teenager to young adult all the way to retirement – rather than it being defined in relation to a person's individual physical development or life experiences (Gillis, 1997). Every aspect of contemporary everyday life has become subject to time measurement and planning: time has become rationalized (subjected to the principles of rational and efficient measurement and calculation) and commodified (a resource or object exchanged for money).

This shift is captured in E. P. Thompson's (1967) classic account 'Time, Work-Discipline and Industrial Capitalism'. Thompson argues that a key distinction between pre-industrial and industrial societies is the shift from task-oriented to time-oriented action. Task orientation can be associated with a form of natural time where work in pre-industrial societies followed natural imperatives – fence-mending occurred only when a fence needed mending, and when a basket was needed one appropriate for the task at hand was produced, rather than hundreds of baskets roughly suitable for a range of potential tasks (O'Malley, 1992).

To understand time-oriented action it is necessary to consider in more detail the emergence of rationalized time reckoning which, according to Thompson, has its roots in religion. Protestantism emphasized pre-destination and a compulsion to work hard. This mapped neatly on to an emerging idea that societies, and thus individuals, should not waste, but save, time. Time, like anything else, was subject to Protestant ideas of thrift – that it was a sin to waste the resources that God has provided. Work, and the time it takes to do it, thus came to be treated with diligence and frugality. In other words, work was to be conducted efficiently, thus avoiding wasting time.

It was, however, the onset of mass industrial society that transformed everyday experiences of time. As industrialization developed, it became increasingly necessary to regulate time so that social and economic activity could be synchronized. In the past, the way that people knew it was time to go to church or that the market was about to close was through the ringing of bells (Glennie and Thrift, 1996). However, to get people to work at the same time – so that machines could be started up and workers work together, without wasting time waiting for those who had not heard the bells or followed the same urgency in heeding them – required more sophisticated forms of synchronization. Clock time presented the answer. At first, public clocks served the purpose, but as the eighteenth and nineteenth centuries progressed, time-pieces in the form of household clocks and then watches became widespread. Such time-pieces had the effect of not only ensuring that workers arrived at the factory, took breaks and finished at the same time, but also coordinated exchange between factories, such that raw materials were delivered at appropriate times (Landes, 1983). The whole factory system began to be regulated by clock time.

According to Thompson (1967), for capitalism to continue its expansion, time orientation needed to move beyond worker compliance with clock time towards workers' acquiring time discipline. In addition to learning that they needed to arrive and leave at particular times, workers also needed to learn to want to work shorter hours, that is, to internalize time efficiency. Ticking, ringing and striking clocks were all employed as devices that made workers aware of the passing of time.

Gradually, time discipline became so crucial to economic and work organization that, by the early twentieth century, industrialists began employing scientists to maximize economic productivity. F. W. Taylor's (1911) time and motion studies were particularly influential. Taylor monitored how workers worked, and noticed that much time was wasted between tasks. As a result, he championed the introduction of a number of efficiency measures. Each task in the production process came to be understood and managed as much in relation to clock time as money. Work came to be paid by the hour, week or month; labour costs began to be counted in 'man hours'; over-time and time out through illness, holidays and strikes came to be understood as extra or lost time. Time was no longer understood in terms of the natural passage of time but as having an abstract exchange value, that is, having a monetary value (Adam, 1995). This is also termed the '**commodification**' of time, whereby it comes to be viewed as a commodity to be exchanged for money.

Thompson's (1967) account can be criticized for simplifying and romanticizing 'task-oriented' societies characterized by a hand-to-mouth existence in harmony with nature. To return to the above example of mending fences and making baskets, as O'Malley (1992, p. 345) shows, fences were improved even when they were not broken, and new baskets were made even if the old ones had not yet worn out. There also existed already many forms of time discipline, including the regulation of market trading times by the ringing of bells so that wholesalers and stall-owners, and stall-owners and customers, could be kept separate. If they were not, then customers would attempt to buy direct from wholesalers and the system of trade would collapse (Glennie and Thrift, 1996).

As with any broad social history dealing with change over a period of hundreds of years, Thompson's theory smoothes over variations and nuances in the ways that time is, or was, organized. But his overall argument identifies a process of critical importance for understanding time in daily life. The significant distinction between the White Rabbit and the witness accounts of William Cragh's miracle revival is the emergence of a dominant understanding that time is a resource to be saved, accumulated, bartered and spent. Only once time has become rationalized and commodified can it be understood as a scarce resource that is subject to being over- or under-used and as something that we do not have enough of. But are contemporary notions of time shortage justified?

Are we running out of time?

There are four interrelated ways of addressing the question 'are we running out of time?' The first is to consider whether people are 'doing more'. The second is to examine whether there has been an intensification of particular types or combinations of activities; the third, to consider whether daily life has become fragmented and de-routinized; the fourth, to examine subjective experiences of time and the challenge of coordinating moments of 'togetherness'. Each of these is discussed in turn below.

Doing more

In her book *The Overworked American*, Juliet Schor (1992) points to a simple paradox: Americans were working longer hours at the end of the twentieth century despite having become more productive. Using estimates of hours spent in paid and unpaid work between 1969 and 1987, Schor demonstrates the steady increase of work time. This contrasts with productivity measures (which calculate the goods and services that result from each hour of work), which show that American productivity had increased such that in 1990 the USA produced in six months the same volume of goods and services that it did in the whole of 1948. Rather than take such productive gains as 'leisure time', the average American has instead increased their consumption, owning and consuming more than double the consumer goods and services of the average American in 1948.

Schor identifies two fundamental processes to explain these trajectories. The first is the logic of production in capitalist economics. It is financially more advantageous for firms to train a limited number of employees who work long hours as opposed to a large number of employees who work limited hours. This would partly explain why Americans continue to work long hours. Second is the emergence of **consumer culture** and its capacity, through the media and marketing, to increase people's expectations and their perceived needs and wants. Premised on the basis that people compare their consumption to that of other people and that a global consumer culture places the lifestyles of the most affluent as the ideal against which they should measure their consumption, then 'the average individual needs to earn more money' in order to fund consumer lifestyles (Schor, 1998, p. 123; see also Chapter 12 in this volume, where consumer culture is discussed in more detail). The overall consequence is that people work more to consume more, which squeezes the time available for leisure and personal life.

Schor presents a provocative commentary on American consumer culture and its capacity to generate time pressure – that is, to generate pervasive feelings of time famine. The main weakness of her argument is the empirical basis for claiming that people work more. Robinson and Godbey (1997) show that the amount of time Americans spent working has declined over the same time period as Schor claimed it had increased. Paradoxically, their data also reveal that Americans felt more time pressured in 1987 than they did in 1969 (see Box 11.1 for a comparison of US and UK time diary data).

Box 11.1 Changes over time: a glancing comparison of UK and US time use

Table 11.1 Mean minutes spent on activities within a 24-hour day, UK and USA between 1975 and 2000, respondents aged 20–59*

	UK			USA		
	1975	2000	Change	1975	1998	Change
Paid work	289	266	−23	248	298	50
Unpaid work	205	223	18	176	176	0
Total non-work (includes sleep)	946	951	5	1016	966	−50
Eat at home	79	54	−25	42	52**	10
Eating out	11	25	14	30	28**	−2
Leisure travel	15	31	16	21	20	−1
Playing sport	5	11	6	4	20	16
Television	122	129	7	132	109	−23
Other non-work	714	701	−13	787	737	−50
Total	1440	1440	–	1440	1440	–

* Data derived from the Multi-National Time Use Survey, Oxford University, UK.
** In 1998 US time diary data categorized 'eating' as a singular category and the figures reported here represent estimates based on a combination of time diary data and US food expenditure data (see Warde *et al.*, 2007, for further details).

Table 11.1 above presents a very basic analysis of the average amount of time spent in different categories of primary activity per day in the UK and the USA at two points in time.

These data are quite crude (they only contain information for a relatively narrow age range) and are not perfectly comparable (because different countries can interpret activities such as 'unpaid work' differently). Nevertheless, they are revealing about cultural differences across societies. Table 11.1 suggests that Americans do indeed spend significantly more time in paid work than they did in the 1970s, while the British spend much less – leading to the average American now working longer hours than their British counterparts. This is somewhat compensated for by an increase in the average amount of time Britons spend in unpaid work (including personal care). The net result is that Britons have more non-work time in 2000 than they did in 1975, while Americans have seen their total amount of non-work time decline by 50 minutes per day. Despite this, Americans have more non-work time per day than do the British.

When a closer look is taken at some non-work activities, it seems that eating habits in the UK have shifted away from eating at home towards eating out, although the British still spend more time eating at home than do Americans. Perhaps more surprising is the relatively large increase in UK leisure travel when compared with the USA, and that Americans have significantly increased the amount of time they spend participating in sport, while Britons have overtaken the Americans with respect to the average amount of time spent watching television.

While crude, such an exercise in comparative time use analysis demonstrates that significant variations across societies in the way that people spend their time persist. It also places in context claims that Americans spend more time in paid work and Europeans less – the data above suggests that this is true, but this does not necessarily mean that Americans have more or less leisurely lives or that they suffer time pressure disproportionately to people living in other societies.

In the case of European societies, there is greater consistency of evidence that there has been a decline in time spent working, which is primarily the result of legislation that has set maximum weekly working hours. Debate in Europe has, instead, focused on whether the entry of more women into paid employment has reduced traditional inequalities in the domestic division of labour whereby women have taken care of more housework and child care than men have. Table 11.2 presents the mean minutes devoted to paid and unpaid work (that is, domestic chores, taking care of children and so on) for men and women in the UK in 1961 and 2001, and reveals the residual 'non-work' time that remains. While men still spend more time in paid work than women, the gap has narrowed. The pattern is reversed for unpaid work; men have increased the amount of time they devote to unpaid work in the home by over an hour and women have seen theirs reduce by almost half an hour. Taken together, both men and women have reduced their total work time (both paid and unpaid work) and increased their non-work (leisure) time, although men's non-work time has increased more than women's has.

While Table 11.2 shows that inequalities still exist between women and men in terms of the amount of unpaid work they perform in the home, the trajectories could also be read as a narrowing of this gendered division of labour. Jonathan Gershuny, Michael Godwin and Sally Jones (1994) describe this as 'lagged adaptation'. They argue that as women enter paid work men slowly

Table 11.2 Change in total minutes per day devoted to paid and unpaid work among UK adults aged 20–60, 1961–2001

		1961	*2001*	*Change between 1961 and 2001*
Paid work	**Men**	434	323	–111
	Women	183	203	+23
	All	307	262	–45
Unpaid work	**Men**	83	146	+63
	Women	303	277	–26
	All	193	213	+20
Total work (paid and unpaid work)	**Men**	517	469	–48
	Women	486	480	–6
	All	500	475	–25
Non-work time	**Men**	923	971	+48
	Women	954	959	+5
	All	939	965	+26

Source: Adapted from Gershuny, 2005.

adjust to take on more unpaid work. This is not simply a process of acquiring new competence in performing unfamiliar domestic tasks such as cooking or ironing, it is also a process where traditional masculine and feminine identities are challenged and remade. This adaptation process leads to a 'time-lag' between women entering paid work and men taking over their fair share of domestic tasks. Data such as those presented in Table 11.2 indicate a continuing process towards gender equality that has not yet reached maturity.

Critics of the lagged adaptation theory challenge the notion that mean minutes of time spent in generic categories of activity represent a robust measure of how men and women experience time. When combinations of primary and secondary activities – primary being the activity recorded as the main activity, secondary being activities performed simultaneously (see Southerton, 'Changing Times', 2009a, for a full discussion) – are taken into account, the picture changes. Michael Bittman and Judy Wajcman (2000) demonstrate that, even though the amount of leisure time enjoyed by men and women in all OECD countries has become equal, this does not result in similar experiences. When secondary activities are included in the analysis, men appear to enjoy consolidated periods, of say two hours, of leisure, while a principal feature of women's leisure is that it is punctuated by unpaid work, especially child care. For example, men tended to participate more in activities such as playing and watching sport while women's leisure activities, which often involved socializing with other women, were conducted simultaneously with caring for their children. Oriel Sullivan (1997), using data from the UK in 1987, also shows that married women multi-task to a much greater extent than do men.

The evidence for the argument that we are 'doing more' in daily life is somewhat thin, and seems to suggest that people are in fact working less, particularly in Europe. It would also seem that, while differences between men and women in terms of the time devoted to paid and unpaid work are narrowing, women's experience of time is qualitatively different from men's.

Intensification of activities

Sullivan's evidence of multi-tasking implies that women may suffer from a dual burden, in which they experience an intensification of the volume of activities to be managed on a day-to-day basis. In other words, women are doing more activities in the same amount of time. This is illustrated through Craig Thompson's (1996) study of how American women 'juggle' work and home. He provides examples of children eating their breakfast during the car journey to school as mothers attempted to juggle getting their children dressed, fed, to school on time and then themselves to work. The mothers justified such juggling by saying that they were trying to provide a life for their children that they themselves never had – such as having the opportunity to play a musical instrument, try out different sports and to have the consumer goods they themselves were denied as children. These mothers felt an obligation to work in order to provide a basic consumer lifestyle acceptable to themselves and their children. In this sense there are similarities with Schor's 'work more to consume more' argument. However, many of the women interviewed employed others to do housework and, therefore, while their hours of paid work increased their hours of unpaid work declined. They had more non-work time, but that time was experienced as an intensification of activities necessary to juggle not only work and home, but also the increase in children's activities.

The argument over intensification of activities and its effect on people's sense of (running out of) time can also be applied to leisure and consumption activities. According to Staffan Linder (1970), leisure has become an important source of personal identity and a marker of social status. A person can display his or her social status by the range of leisure activities s/he takes part in. To display status through leisure in this way requires the consumption of more and more leisure-related activities and products, a process which in turn renders leisure less leisurely as people attempt to cram more of it into their daily lives. This argument has been developed further by Eric Darier (1998), who suggests that being busy has become symbolic of a 'full' and 'valued' life. The cultural pressures to try new and varied leisure experiences together with the knowledge that one is ageing and has only limited time in which to experience all that consumer culture has to offer, leads to anxieties and a sense of obligation to oneself to experience as many cultural activities, cuisines, tourist destinations and so on, as possible. And for Jonathan Gershuny (2005), being busy at work has become a 'badge of honour' and a marker of social status. Even though Europeans (and perhaps also Americans) do not seem to be doing more in terms of the total time spent on work and non-work, it does appear that both work and leisure activities have intensified so that people are trying to cram more activities into the same amount of time.

Fragmentation and de-routinization

Accounts of temporal fragmentation and de-routinization suggest that how time is organized and experienced has changed in ways that make us feel more time pressured. The most profound change in terms of how time is organized has been a shift towards flexible working and the emergence of a 24/7 society in which services (such as banking and retail) are available 24 hours, seven days a week. Both can offer individuals greater discretion over the times at which they conduct particular activities, as well as economic and logistical benefits for firms and employers. Not everyone experiences flexible working hours in the same manner, however. A critical distinction needs, therefore, to be made between 'flexibility for' workers and 'flexibility of' workers. In the first, flexibility works for the employee because it gives greater control over their personal schedules. In the latter, the flexibility of the worker is primarily for the employers' benefit because it allows them to manage peaks and troughs in demand more effectively and to provide 24/7 services. As Koen Breedveld (1998) demonstrates, those workers who enjoy 'flexibility for' tend to be the professional middle classes, while 'flexibility of' employment is largely the experience of lower socio-economic groups.

Distinguishing between flexibility for and of employees is important because it illustrates that experiences of time vary in terms of how it is organized. This is a theme considered in detail by Lucia Reisch (2001), who identifies four dimensions of 'time wealth': (a) the chronometric dimension (having the right *amount* of time); (b) the chronologic dimension (having time at the *right* time of the day, week or season); (c) the personal time autonomy/sovereignty dimension (having *control* over time); and (d) the synchronization dimension (where one's own time rhythm *fits* with that of family and friends). If we consider these four dimensions in relation to Breedveld's distinction between the professional middle classes who experience 'flexibility for' but who are also, according to Gershuny (2005), the group who work comparatively longer hours, and lower socio-economic status groups who work comparatively fewer hours but experience 'flexibility of' employment, then a clear difference emerges. Those in lower-paid jobs may have more leisure time measured in hours, but they do not have the right quality of time because they have little control over when their leisure times occurs; while the professional middle classes may not have as much leisure time because they work comparatively long hours, but they do have greater control and autonomy over how they organize their leisure and work times.

There is a further dimension to flexible working that warrants attention, and that is the impact it can have on the quality of relationships. As Kerry Daly (1996) reports, studies consistently reveal that couples who state they are satisfied with their relationships are those who spend leisure time together. As a consequence, flexible working, often regarded as something that can help people improve their work–life balance, may have the effect of reducing the time spent together by couples. Couples who experience flexibility for occupations tend to work longer hours, while those with flexibility of occupations are likely to work at different times of the day (Warren, 2003).

Further evidence of how the changing organization of time may produce negative outcomes for personal life is presented by Arlie Hochschild's (1997) study of a major American corporation. She argued that as hours of paid work increase (what she calls the first shift), time for domestic matters (the second shift) becomes squeezed, and time devoted to close relationships begins to be experienced as a 'third shift'. In addition, domestic life has arguably gone through a process of rationalization according to the principles of Taylorization, whereby tasks are fragmented or broken down into their component parts and resequenced so as to maximize temporal efficiency. Washing clothes, for example, is collapsed into components of washing, drying and ironing, each component being separate from the others. According to Hochschild, even time spent with family and friends comes to be experienced as a 'third shift' subject to rationalization – that is, the calculated planning of when to spend time with loved ones which corrodes the quality of the time spent together.

Coordinating daily life

A problem with approaches that attempt to explain contemporary feelings of time scarcity is the lack of historical empirical evidence. Box 11.2 reports on analysis of UK Mass Observation Project 'day in the life of' diaries completed by volunteers in 1937 (Southerton, 'Temporal Rhythms', 2009b; please see Katherine Davies's chapter, in this volume, on friendship for a further example of use of Mass Observation Project data). This analysis was part of a larger study that compared historical and contemporary data on how people experience time. While by no means representing a definitive representation of temporal experiences in the 1930s, the diaries do provide an indication of some key social changes that have occurred in people's daily lives. This is particularly the case when compared with contemporary experiences of time revealed by analysis of the UK Health and Lifestyles Survey (HALs) from 1985 and 1992 (Southerton and Tomlinson, 2005) and in-depth household interviews conducted in 2000 (Southerton, ' "Squeezing Time" ', 2003). Please see Box 11.2 for a discussion of some of the key differences found.

The respondents interviewed in 2000 unanimously agreed that time was more pressured today than in the past, and were quick to offer explanations as to why this is the case: pressures that result from consumption, workplace competition, juggling work and family life, and a fear of wasting time (Southerton, ' "Squeezing Time" ', 2003). However, when it came to discussing time pressures in their own lives respondents were ambivalent. To not be time pressured was in some way regarded as not leading a full life. To be too time

---

Box 11.2   Comparing British daily life in 1937 and 2000

This box examines a study conducted comparing 'day in the life of' diaries from 1937 with household interviews about experiences of time in 2000 (Southerton, 'Temporal Rhythms', 2009b). One of the most important differences that this study highlighted concerned how women's days were structured. Whereas the people interviewed in 2000 talked about having some control over how they organized their days, the 1937 diarists depict days that are clearly structured around fixed mealtimes, as well as according to the demands of work.

Another difference between 1937 and 2000 that the study highlighted was that, in 1937, the week was more clearly structured so that household tasks were done on specific days of the week. This was partially due to practical reasons. Monday was 'wash day' because the 'kitchen stove' (oven) needed to be lit for a long duration on Mondays in order to make a stew out of the 'leftovers' from Sunday lunch. It made sense to use the stove to heat water for washing clothes and also for taking the weekly bath, with the added benefit that the kitchen was warm so that clothes could be dried indoors should it be raining outside.

In contrast, in 2000, there were no such fixed schedules to follow, and one of the main issues facing the people I interviewed for this study was the difficulty in coordinating the timetables of different family members. For example, an issue mentioned by people in 2000 but not in 1937 was the difficulty of getting family members to be present at a meal. In addition, people in 2000 were greatly concerned about being able to spend leisure time with their spouses – something that the 1937 diarists seemed to take for granted. Partly this has to do with contemporary ideals about intimate relationships as requiring the 'making' of quality time for each other, but also with the fact that people's lives are less routine now than they were in 1937.

From these examples we can see that temporal rhythms and interpersonal relationships influence each other. In 1937, the rigid temporal rhythms meant that family members routinely spent time together. In contrast, by 2000, people have more individual control over how they spend their time, but families must actively schedule their times of togetherness.

---

pressured was held as an admission that they did not make enough time to spend with the people most important to them.

In negotiating this ambivalence interview respondents described their daily lives as a roller-coaster ride with moments of harriedness and calm; of 'hot spots' and 'cold spots'. Hot spots are periods within the day or week with a high density and intensity of activities; cold spots the opposite. The challenge as described by respondents was to coordinate within their networks of friends and family so that their cold spots (often described as 'quality time') were collectively aligned. To achieve this, hot spots were necessary. For example, respondents reported cramming Saturday mornings with domestic chores so that they could have 'quality time' in the afternoon with their partner, children or friends. Hot spots of harriedness were thus the response to the difficulty of coordinating one's activities with those of friends and family. Quality time, in this sense, represents the rationalized and calculated use of time in personal life that Hochschild (1997) described in her study of American families, and failure to achieve it was met with a sense of personal failure in managing personal relationships.

Analysis of the HALs data, which contained a question on the extent to which respondents felt pressed for time, helped to sharpen and generalize the findings from the household interviews. Interestingly, the groups who felt more 'pressed for time' were: women, who reported feeling more pressed for time than men did; those who worked flexible hours as opposed to shifts; and, those who frequently socialized with friends by arrangement (as opposed to without arrangement). Perhaps somewhat counter-intuitively, those who reported feeling most pressed for time were *not* those who worked the longest hours, but those whose social lives required greater coordination.

While there is evidence of the intensification of activities, of in some cases people appearing to 'do more' and of activities in daily life having become fragmented and de-routinized, it is the challenge of coordinating daily lives within social networks that leads to feelings of time pressure. Interview respondents went to great, and sometimes elaborate, lengths to create 'family' or 'quality time', which judging by their absence in the 1937 diaries are truly modern concepts, ranging from evening meals to family days out and romantic overseas weekend breaks for frazzled couples. The fear and anxiety about running out of time to spend with loved ones has resulted not from a lack of time, but from elaborate needs to coordinate and schedule time to spend together.

Fears have been expressed concerning the corrosive impact that such harriedness is having on personal relationships. In the face of clock-time rationalization, of workplace pressures and the impending need to juggle lifestyles, personal relationships remain intact, albeit with greater anxiety about creating quality time for being together. Whether that time amounts to quality time is open to debate. Thompson's (1996) and Hochschild's (1997) accounts of American life suggest that achieving quality time is becoming more and more difficult as working mothers find themselves increasingly juggling the demands of work and career, personal leisure time and family, while at the same time managing and coordinating their own and their family members' social activities . And it does seem that women, more so than men, take on the task of coordinating, scheduling and managing the family's 'quality time'. This is a form of being pushed for time that does not show up on any measure of how many minutes people spend working or have available for leisure (Southerton, 'Time Pressure, Technology and Gender', 2007). Yet, despite the fragmentation and de-routinization of daily life that results from processes such as flexible working – and the challenge of coordinating personal schedules – couples, families and friends continue to strive for moments of togetherness. Time pressures in the form of harried hot spots represent not the undermining of personal life but the conditions for preserving it.

Concluding remarks

Contemporary society is often characterized as being time pressured, despite time diary studies in Europe showing that people have more free time (non-work time) than in the past (while different data in the USA conflict on this matter). According to many accounts, the principal cause of time pressure is that people are trying to cram an increasing number of activities into their daily lives. Other accounts focus on the changing temporal organization of daily life. The emergence of flexible working hours and availability of services 24 hours a day are generally thought to have fragmented and de-routinized the collective rhythms of daily life. Such processes place greater responsibility on individuals to manage their time and present the complex challenge of coordinating personal schedules with those of others (who share equally complex personal schedules). Rather than necessarily undermining personal life, the resilience of desires to maintain times of togetherness through the scheduling of hot and cold spots serves to highlight the continued significance of personal relationships. The remaining question is less whether personal life is undermined by time pressure but how it evolves in relation to the changing temporal organization of daily life.

Questions for discussion

- What is meant by the terms 'rationalization' and 'commodification' of time? Can you think of some concrete examples to illustrate these?
- In what ways might flexible working hours and 24/7 services help families achieve a work–life balance?
- Make a list of the ways that you manage your personal time schedules; to what extent do your schedules require coordination with others?
- What is 'quality time' and what are the main challenges for achieving it?

Consumer Culture and Personal Life

Dale Southerton

Introduction

'Consumer society', 'consumerism', 'commercialization' and 'materialism' are all popular phrases used to describe contemporary societies; societies in which consumption has become a critical feature of everyday life. The term '**consumer culture**' captures and encompasses all of these phrases by emphasizing that consumption has become embedded in cultural ways of life: 'Consumer culture [is] a social arrangement in which the relation between lived culture and social resources, between meaningful ways of life and the symbolic and material resources on which they depend, is mediated through markets' (Slater, 1997, p. 8). The emphasis on markets reflects the significant growth of one particular way in which goods and services are provisioned in society. Other modes of provisioning goods and services are through the state (such as healthcare, education and waste collection) and interpersonal networks (for example, friends and family who often provide goods and services whether through informal help, giving gifts or cooking meals). More generally, consumer culture can be understood as referring to a condition in which consumption is argued to influence most, if not all, aspects of everyday life. Theories of consumer culture share the central tenet that consumption replaces production as the principle source of our identities, in terms of how we relate to one another, and how we understand, interpret and relate to the world we live in.

Following a brief outline of the emergence of consumer culture, this chapter considers different theories regarding the effects that consumer culture has had on personal life. First, it examines claims that it produces self-oriented, narcissistic and self-promoting individuals. This is contrasted with theories which suggest that consumer culture permits playful lifestyles that offer individuals greater freedom of self-expression. The former arguments present personal life as corroded by consumption, the latter proposes that consumer culture has led to new forms of social groupings and personal associations. Finally, the chapter considers whether consumption reproduces social distinctions between class-based groups.

134

The emergence of consumer culture

The origins of consumer culture can be found in the rapid social changes that followed urbanization and **industrialization** in the nineteenth century, although contemporary forms of consumer culture really only took shape in the latter third of the twentieth century. Industrialization, which increased the volume of goods and services available for consumption, went hand-in-hand with urbanization as people sought employment in the factories of cities. Moving from rural communities to urban centres meant a significant change in people's everyday lives. In his classic essay 'The Metropolis and Mental Life', Georg Simmel (1970[1903]) examined how people responded to living in cities. For Simmel, life in modern cities was characterized by frequent interactions with strangers, and individuals were little more than one person in a crowd. Being in the crowd had its advantages: it meant that individuals could effectively hide among the throng of people and observe modern life going on around them. The down-side of such anonymity was that because people no longer knew personally the majority of the individuals that they saw or interacted with in their everyday lives; other people become faceless and social interaction impersonal.

Simmel proposed that, within this large anonymous urban environment, the only way to 'stand out' of the crowd and reassert any sense of individuality was through consumption. This required a delicate balance of imitating others (in order not to stand out too much) but without simply copying what those others in the crowd were doing (which would provide for no sense of individuality at all). The way to achieve this was through the pursuit of fashion, which provided some guidance of what to wear but offered enough variety for a sense of individuality (Gronow, 1997). Thus, it could be argued that it was urbanization that led to consumption becoming a means of expressing, to oneself and to others, a sense of individuality.

Drawing from Simmel's account of urban life, Thorstein Veblen (1925[1899]) considered the growing significance of consumption in expressing one's social status. Discussing the American nouveaux riche at the turn of the twentieth century, he argued that a key mechanism for displaying wealth and status was to consume that which others could not afford. Expensive clothing, modes of transport, art, homes and so on all became ways of conspicuously displaying wealth. For Veblen such **'conspicuous consumption'** (that is, consumption that is highly visible to others, and has the aim of impressing upon others that one is wealthy) became the principal way to express social status. Furthermore, if trying to move up to a higher social status, those in lower status groups began to imitate those with a higher status, who in turn responded by seeking new forms of conspicuous consumption to maintain their social distance. This endless cycle of consumer competition not only rendered consumption more important in people's daily lives but also meant that consumption became critical to the way that people perceived and related to others.

The process of industrialization also had profound implications for the ways in which people related to the goods that comprise the material world which surrounded them. For Karl Marx (1976[1867]), industrial society transformed the meaning of goods. In pre-industrial societies, where goods were made by hand, the meaning of those goods was tied to their production. The value of a table, for example, was determined by the amount of time it would take to make it, the quality of the materials used and by its usefulness – what Marx called 'use value'. However, industrial production made it difficult to have any sense of the labour involved in producing goods. This created the space for goods to take on new meaning, meanings not associated with the conditions in which a good was produced. As a result, the meanings of goods came to be less associated with their 'use value', but instead they took on a 'symbolic value'. This means that the value of a table, for example, is no longer determined by what went into producing it or how useful it is, but rather it is valued for the symbolic meaning it might have, such as being an antique, a designer table or a fashion item.

From the 1950s onwards the emergence of mass production resulted in mass consumption on unprecedented scales. As the consumption of high-status goods became available to more members of Western societies, symbolic value became an increasingly important way to distinguish between goods. Advertising and marketing developed to convince consumers that the various goods being offered by producers differed from each other (for example, that there is a significant difference between two brands of toothpaste), and consumers sought to create their personal styles of consumption that differed from that of the masses. Indeed, by the 1960s, youth cultures began to take mass-produced goods and give them new symbolic meanings in order to create their own collective styles of consumption (a lifestyle). For example, in his study of 1960s Mod culture, Dick Hebdige (1979) found that the moped (originally designed for women), Italian suits, and soul and rhythm and blues music were combined to produce a distinctive subcultural style.

The acceleration of such processes in the latter third of the twentieth century led Scott Lash and John Urry (1987) to argue that societies were no longer organized around the circulation and exchange of goods (production), but around the circulation and exchange of the signs and symbols that could be associated with them (consumption). In what they call 'dis-organized capitalism', what is significant is no longer the exchange and circulation of goods but that of signs and images.

While somewhat simplified, the story of consumer culture is one of the emerging symbolic significance of goods for expressing individuality, identity and status. Consumption became a source of social competition and of displaying social status. No longer was clothing understood only as a way of keeping warm and dry, but as a way of symbolically expressing identity, social aspirations and difference (from other social groups). These processes reached a new level of maturity at the end of the twentieth century. Fuelled by the increasing range of consumer goods (thanks to mass production), the capacity for groups or subcultures to mould those goods so that they expressed a particular lifestyle, and the rise of advertising that seeks to symbolically differentiate goods, a consumer culture in which style and image comes to dominate over the function and use of commodities had emerged.

Consumer culture: the corrosion of personal life

The emergence of consumer culture has had profound, although hotly contested, implications for contemporary personal lives. Some accounts are less optimistic in their prognoses than others. One such set of accounts suggest that consumer culture has a corrosive affect on the quality of interpersonal relationships, where authenticity, how people relate to others, senses of self-identity and feelings of belonging are undermined by the symbolic allure of goods and the pervasiveness of consumption.

For Jean Baudrillard (1988), the kinds of processes where the meanings of goods get detached from their use value take a sinister turn in what he terms 'post-modern' consumer cultures. Baudrillard argues that the meaning of goods today can *only* be found in their symbolic value. He argues that the continual advertising of products removes goods from their use value such that consumer goods represent nothing more than a simulation. In other words, goods no longer refer to reality but simulate it. Baudrillard calls this hyperreality, where goods refer to a hyper-real world. Baudrillard used Las Vegas as an example: a place where nothing is real, everything is a replica. For example, the 'Egyptian pyramids' and 'Parisian landmarks' that can be found in Las Vegas represent a pastiche of the originals that are taken out of context and given new meanings as they are placed among a whole range of replicas that simulate other cultures.

Shopping malls are also a good example of such simulation. Take the Trafford Centre in Manchester, England, as an illustration. Having walked around the huge range of multinational and British chain stores, one can walk into the food gallery and stroll through the French cafés and the Japanese, Italian, traditional British and American fast food sectors and sit down in the main concourse, which is modelled on the deck of the *Titanic*. For Baudrillard, all this simulation of other cultures continues to the point where the simulations appear more real than that which is being simulated, such that when one actually goes to the real Paris it appears a poor copy of the Paris symbolized in movies, films and 'French cafés' found in shopping malls the world over. Baudrillard also argues that the consequence of such post-modern consumer culture is that it does not simply reduce culture to a culture of commodity symbols, but it actually obliterates all connections between people. This is because people can only relate to the world and to others, or even understand who they themselves are, through the hyper-real and simulated images found within consumer culture.

Andrew Wernick (1991), building on Baudrillard, argues that consumer culture and the dominance of commodities sold through marketing and advertising has deep-seated implications for how people view themselves and for personal life. He emphasizes the central role that advertising and marketing play in circulating the hyper-real meanings of goods. He calls this 'promotional culture', where pop records, political candidates, art galleries, philosophical texts, news magazines and sporting events are all intensively advertised and promoted. In consumer culture *everything* is up for promotion.

For Wernick, promotional culture has profound effects on people's sense of self and how people relate to one another. He states that people develop a hardened scepticism because they know that everything is effectively about promotion. The only way of resisting this is through cynicism and mass apathy, which, according to Wernick, explains, for example, why fewer and fewer people vote at political elections in the UK and the USA. At the same time, everyone plays a part in promotional culture. Not only do many people actually work in 'promotion industries' such as advertising, but also everyone engages in self-promotion. Wernick (1991, p. 192) states that 'from dating and clothes shopping to attending a job interview, virtually everyone is involved in self-promotion'. And even when a person is not promoting himself or herself, other people interpret their actions as if they are. In this context of endless promotion and scepticism of others, a crisis of authenticity emerges, where people can no longer believe that others are behaving in an authentic manner. This leads Wernick to ask: 'If social survival, let alone competitive success, depends on continual, audience-oriented, self-staging, what are we behind the mask?'

An answer to this question is provided by Christopher Lasch (1979) in his book *The Culture of Narcissism*, an account which pre-dates the works of Baudrillard and Wernick. Lasch suggests that consumer culture, where social differences can only be expressed through symbols of material wealth and hedonistic lifestyles, breeds a narcissistic personality structure. The narcissist is fundamentally insecure and needs the validation of others in order to feel any sense of self-esteem. This fragile sense of self-identity among individuals has led, among other things, to a fear of commitment and of lasting relationships, a dread of ageing and a boundless admiration for fame and celebrity. People's relationships have become determined by the competition for obtaining the symbols of wealth and the 'right' lifestyle, and they relate to one another through intense forms of social competition. Every human activity is aimed at achieving the symbols of material wealth, which appear to provide protection against dropping down the hierarchical pecking order. The result of this is that any form of community (and by this Lasch means any form of collective grouping, including the family, professions, a team, and friendships) is undermined or destroyed by competition, and the individual becomes completely atomized and alone.

In answer to the question posited by Wernick, Lasch would probably answer: behind the mask is a narcissistic self. People have become primarily focused on themselves, and the communities that once surrounded us and provided a sense of identity, belonging and security are systematically destroyed by this self-obsession. As communities are undermined, interpersonal relationships are rendered shallow and superficial.

Lifestyles: consumer freedom and new forms of association

The same processes identified above as eroding authentic personal relationships can, however, also be interpreted in a more positive light. Theorists who suggest a shift towards **late-modern** (as opposed to **post-modern**) social arrangements and individualization draw on the concept of lifestyle to emphasize how consumer culture offers people 'new freedoms' in defining who they are and with whom they associate (refer to Chapter 1 for a discussion of the **individualization thesis**). For these theorists, consumption permits new opportunities to buy into and display a particular lifestyle; rather than a harmful process this is presented as an issue of 'choice' and 'self-expression' (Bauman, 1988; Featherstone, 1991; Giddens, 1991).

Central in these accounts is the claim that social class no longer provides the basis for sense of self-identity and attachment to social groups. Industrialization had produced societies where occupation, wealth and collective interests were linked to social class. Social class thus became a fundamental basis of identity and association. Profound social changes during the latter third of the twentieth century are held to have weakened this alignment such that class has lost its relevance in terms of helping to define who a person is (identity) and who they identify (associate) with (Southerton, 'Boundaries of "Us" and "Them"', 2002).

Lash and Urry (1987) identify three key processes that have contributed to the diminished significance of social class in determining who a person can be or how they can live. First, mass production and consumption have resulted in the availability of a growing quantity and wider range of consumer goods at relatively affordable prices. Not only have high levels of consumption become available to the vast majority of people in Western societies, but the range of goods available offers many opportunities for consumers to express their personal tastes (as discussed above). Second, the emergence of subcultural lifestyles, particularly formed around young people – such as 'Mod' and 'Hippie' subcultures in the 1960s – transformed consumption into a means of expressing a collective identity, or group membership, irrespective of social class. The third key process is the decline of manufacturing and the rise of service- and information-related occupations in advanced capitalist societies. These three processes have worked to blur the boundaries between traditional class cleavages, between blue collar (manual) and white collar (office-based) occupations. At the same time, traditional class-based political alignments have become weaker, and have been replaced by the politics of new social movements concerned with global crises and specific issues, such as the environment and animal welfare (for an in-depth discussion of new social movements, please refer to Gemma Edwards's chapter in the present volume).

For Zygmunt Bauman (1988), once the shackles of class-based identities have been loosened and the range of consumer goods and services have expanded and diversified, a 'consumer attitude' begins to form. The consumer attitude has, according to Bauman, come to represent a fundamental orientation towards the consumption of things. It is an attitude in which the market, by which he means the places where people buy goods and services, provides solutions to all of life's problems (and sometimes even produces in people the sense that there *is* a problem that requires solution), and as such it becomes the consumers' duty to avail themselves of those solutions: 'Bit by bit, problem by problem, the consumer attitude renders the whole of life to the market, it orients every desire and each effort in the search for a tool or an expertise one can buy' (Bauman, 1990, p. 204). The consumer attitude creates a way of being that presents all of life as a set of problems to be solved by purchasing the right product or products from the shops. This attitude also comes to reflect self-identity, so that consumption choices come to represent, both to the self and to others, who a person is. We do not make these choices on our own, however, because consumption choices have been formed into lifestyles (styles of consumption), from which consumers make the choice that they feel best reflects who they are (Giddens, 1991). The various experts of the market – advertisers, celebrities, fashion forecasters, retailers, journalists and the media – all offer advice, guidance and persuasion to help with these consumer choices, to coordinate those choices into a coherent lifestyle, and provide solutions and reassurance should the consumer make the wrong choices. Or, as Bauman puts it, these 'market experts' provide ready-assembled lifestyle 'models' to help guide consumer choices: what he calls 'DIY identitykits'.

The consumer attitude thus represents new freedoms in the process of identity formation. As people are released from traditional forms of identity (such as class), anyone – providing they have the economic means – can mould their lifestyle according to their personal preference and in accordance with their desired identity. However, this freedom is double-edged because consumers find themselves in a situation where they have no choice but to choose, and even opting out of a style of consumption becomes a lifestyle in itself. The new freedoms found in consumer culture thus become a duty to select the right goods in order to assemble a style of life reflective of one's self-identity. For Bauman (1990, p. 205), the consumer attitude reduces identity to a matter of consumption: 'It seems in the end as if I were made up of the many things I buy and own: tell me what you buy, in what shops you buy it, and I'll tell you who you are' (Bauman, 1990, p. 205).

These new freedoms of consumer culture have contributed to the collapse of traditional sources of identity and association. Mike Featherstone (1991) describes the new middle classes (generally young urban professionals) fully embracing the concept of lifestyle as 'heroic consumers' who adopt a form of calculated hedonism to embark upon a conscious project of lifestyle creation. This involves taking the consumer attitude and applying it to all aspects of style through the 'assemblage of goods, clothes, practices, experiences, appearance and bodily dispositions' (Featherstone, 1991, p. 59), which allows for the narration of unified consumption styles. This, according to Featherstone, generates a process that he calls the 'aestheticization of everyday life', which describes the principle that even the most mundane goods and practices can be stylized and hold symbolically meaningful qualities. In this view, consumer cultures do not undermine authentic values (as suggested by both Baudrillard and Wernick), but produce lifestyles that are an expressive, playful and unrestricted exercise in individual consumption. It is a process which breaks down old hierarchical distinctions such that the social world becomes flattened: anything goes and old class-based distinctions are rendered obsolete. And it is not only class divisions that matter – even the elderly and the retired (as opposed to only the young urban professional) can enjoy expressive and playful lifestyles (see Box 12.1).

Box 12.1   Ageing, retirement and lifestyles

The process of ageing has often been met with dread and fear, presented as a negative process as one's body (and mind) prevents active engagement in social life. Since the 1970s, this assumption has come under increasing scrutiny, not least because of the emergence of consumer lifestyles for the elderly. Health clubs, diets, exercise machines and sunbeds, together with a range of other goods and services that promise an 'active lifestyle', have all been harnessed for the promotion of positive images of ageing. Today, retirement is presented as a period of leisure and consumption.

Featherstone and Hepworth's (1995) analysis of ageing builds on Featherstone's (1991) earlier accounts of the 'aestheticization of everyday life', whereby all aspects of lifestyle, even the most mundane of activities, can be turned into a symbolic, meaningful and expressive lifestyle. They analysed a magazine, called *Retirement Choice*, initially produced to provide information on planning for retirement. It emerged at a time when society was perceived to be 'ageist'. This ageism contained two key elements: old people were viewed with a mixture of negative emotions of pity, fear, disgust, condescension and neglect; and, age discrimination in areas like job markets and access to leisure services was widespread.

Originally aiming to overturn negative images of old age, by 1974, the magazine shifted in emphasis. It was re-titled *Pre-retirement Choice*, with the stated aim of promoting 'youthful old age', with features on 'older' celebrities, and an emphasis on making new leisure and lifestyle choices with retirement approaching. By the 1980s, the magazine had firmly established itself as a lifestyle magazine that informed about consumer lifestyles – filled with images of youthful retirement, hobbies, leisure and consumption. Old age had become something to be embraced and viewed as 'an extended plateau of active middle age typified in the imagery of positive aging as a period of usefulness and active consumer lifestyles' (Featherstone and Hepworth, 1995, p. 46).

While Featherstone and Hepworth can be criticized for focusing on media images and representations (as opposed to actual experiences of old age) and therefore overlooking the reality that ageing bodies can and do restrict 'youthful' lifestyles, they do illustrate how consumer culture penetrates all ages and stages of life. Ageing and retirement have become a matter of lifestyle choice where consumer goods and leisure practices are moulded into expressive styles of consumption that are unified by the aesthetic of 'youthful retirement'.

Under such conditions, people no longer associate with or build a sense of belonging towards others based on social class, but rather come to build 'neo-tribal' affiliations based around styles of consumption. Neo-tribes can be defined as specialized small groups that form around particular styles of consumption. They are elective (you choose to join or leave), affectual (create a strong sense of association and familiarity) and transitory (because anyone can join or leave at any moment). Examples include New Age travellers (Hetherington, 1992), youth 'subcultures' such as 'ravers', new social movements such as environmental groups, fans of sports clubs or music groups, enthusiasts of food, gardening, classic cars and so on. Belonging to a neo-tribe requires little more than the adoption of a specific lifestyle by choosing from the range of different styles and images available. Given the sheer variety of styles available in the marketplace and the lack of restrictions to joining, individuals can also be affiliated to a number of neo-tribes at any one moment. Being a member of a neo-tribe is a matter of choosing and appropriating the 'identity symbols' of that group or buying the right DIY identikit.

Theories of late-modern consumer culture present identity as a personal duty that involves choosing goods from the marketplace and assembling them into a lifestyle. People are free to choose who they are and who they want to be seen as, and are no longer constrained by traditional social structures such as social class. People are also free to associate with whichever lifestyle group they like, can choose more than one, and change which 'neo-tribal' group they wish to belong to on the basis of their selection of consumer lifestyles from the marketplace.

Consumer culture and social distinction

Whether the new freedoms of identity and lifestyle formation afforded by consumer culture can actually provide for satisfactory senses of belonging is debatable. Theories of late-modern consumer culture only talk about a sense of belonging to a social group in terms of buying into a lifestyle. As Alan Warde (1994) argues, it remains doubtful whether 'buying' into a particular consumption style is enough to provide for group acceptance or the competence to 'carry off' an affiliation. Others must notice, read and understand the significance and meanings of the lifestyle that is being projected if a satisfactory sense of belonging is to be achieved. Warde is also critical of the idea that people are free to choose which lifestyle groups they want to belong to. It is not just that others may not recognize the lifestyle being displayed but that friends, family and associates may socially sanction those who adopt a lifestyle incorrectly or in an inauthentic way. Imagine if you suddenly decided to buy into a lifestyle or identity that markedly differed from your current one. How do you think your friends and family would react to this new identity you were trying to express? And what impact would this have in terms of your sense that you were 'really' the person you were hoping to be? From this perspective, identities, styles of life and senses of belonging are shared and negotiated within interpersonal relationships, and the acceptance of others plays a crucial role in which identities a person *can* choose.

Drawing on Pierre Bourdieu's (1984) account of taste and social distinction, Warde argues that social class continues to play an important part in identity, even within consumer culture. This is because consumption and lifestyle are an expression of class-based identities, forms of association and social differentiation. For Bourdieu, social class can be understood in terms of the volumes of economic (money), cultural (knowledge of cultural activities) and social (networks) resources (what he calls 'capital') possessed by individuals. How much of each resource a person has depends largely on their occupation, level of education and social status.

Following extensive survey analysis of French society in the 1960s (see Bennett *et al.*, 2009, for a more recent analysis of British cultural tastes), Bourdieu shows that consumer tastes map on to volumes of economic, cultural and social capital. In other words, people with similar amounts of these forms of capital tend to express similar tastes for food, music and clothing, for example. Not only are patterns of consumption in this way stratified by class, but class groupings develop tastes which help distinguish them from other class groups. For example, Bourdieu describes the working class as having a 'taste for necessity', while they reject the tastes of those with high economic and cultural capital as wasteful and extravagant. He demonstrates this through food consumption. The working classes in his study favoured foods like pie and chips over more 'fancy' foods, such as nouvelle cuisine. The middle classes, however, with more economic resources (who can, therefore, afford more expensive foods) and cultural resources (a knowledge of fine cuisines) rejected pie and chips as poor-quality, stodgy and tasteless food.

Such processes of distinction help reproduce social inequalities. Tastes provide for a sense of belonging to a group or a social class which shares the same orientations towards consumption, and they also differentiate those who do not. A person's tastes are therefore constrained by the volumes of economic, cultural and social capital he or she has access to. Tastes also act to mark out the boundaries of class groups. And this extends beyond class: tastes in consumption reveal the distinctions between other social groupings, such as those based around ethnicity. The way we come to 'learn' how to be good consumers, particularly during childhood, plays an important role in reproducing such social divisions (see Box 12.2). In other words, consumer choices do not represent freedom from social class, as the theorists of late-modern consumer culture propose, but rather help to reproduce class-based social distinctions.

Box 12.2   Learning to consume: consumer culture and children

In his study of the market of ready-made child clothing in the USA, Daniel Cook (2004) provides a detailed history of how consumer markets construct the boundaries between 'adulthood' and 'childhood'. He reveals how the child clothing market utilized 'medical-psychological' theories of child development – particularly the importance of correctly sized and appropriately styled clothing for children to 'fit in' with their peers – through which new childhood categories, such as 'the toddler', were produced. By the 1930s the category of toddler emerged within marketing parlance, which was accompanied by a general shift towards seeing consumption from the 'child's point of view'. Ideals of consumer taste and individual choice were extended to the youngest members of society, and it was increasingly through their consumption that children developed their sense of who they were and how they might relate to others.

The shift towards seeing consumption from the 'child's point of view' indicates another important aspect of consumer culture in the lives of children and their parents: the parental role in teaching their children to become competent consumers. For very young children, parents take the role of selecting styles of consumption on their children's behalf, but as those children grow older they come to expect, if not demand, greater autonomy (Zelizer, 2002). As children grow older parents adopt many strategies to enable their children to learn and thus develop competent consumer skills. From selecting, within a given monetary budget, Christmas and birthday presents from catalogues through to offering pocket money that children can spend at their own discretion, parents guide children into developing their own tastes and styles of consumption (Schor, 2004). In doing so, parents impart their own judgements of 'good taste', thus, arguably, reproducing the social group distinctions (Martens et al., 2004), that Bourdieu (1984) and others identify when analysing consumption patterns.

It is also interesting to observe how children relate to consumer culture and what their use of consumer goods reveals about the social group distinctions that are salient in their lives. Chin's (2001) study is an example of the ways in which Afro-American girls personalize white Barbie dolls by working on their hair to make it look like their own and, in the process, reveal social group distinctions related both to gender and ethnicity.

Concluding remarks

This chapter began with a relatively simple observation that contemporary society is characterized by consumer culture, a condition in which consumption becomes increasingly central to our sense of identity, associations and personal relationships. Processes such as urbanization and a shift towards the valuing of the symbolic properties of consumption were identified as critical to the emergence of consumer culture.

Most accounts of the significance of consumer culture for personal life focus on the implications of this for people's sense of identity and association.

Post-modern accounts argue that the meanings of commodities have become so detached from reality that reality disappears to become little more than simulations, leading to a promotional culture, which in turn breeds an incessant scepticism about everything and everybody. In addition, consumer culture is thought to produce a narcissistic personality structure that results in feelings of personal isolation.

Accounts that characterize consumer culture as a feature of late-modern societies present it as a form of freedom, albeit a freedom with certain conditions attached. The consumer attitude means that people have a duty to constantly seek out (with the help of market experts) the right consumer goods (or ready-to-assemble identitykits) that capture who they are as individuals. Any sense of group belonging and personal attachment is formed through neo-tribal lifestyles, which amount to little more than groups who share a playful affinity through the lifestyle goods that they acquire and display.

Finally, accounts influenced by the theories of Bourdieu provide a different interpretation of consumption. They agree that consumer lifestyles have become the principal way through which people form their identities and identify with others. However, this does not amount to freedom or consumer choice, because a person's choices are constrained by their social class. This means that people identify with those who share the same consumer tastes and distinguish themselves from those who do not. Consumption therefore reproduces social divisions and inequalities.

The different prognoses of personal life under conditions of consumer culture tend to focus on rather negative outcomes, whether they be narcissism, the obligation to choose or the reproduction of social inequalities. Yet, consumer culture does have more positive sides, as captured by Daniel Miller's discussion of the importance of consumption for expressing love and care:

> When a mother shops for her child she may feel that there are a hundred garments in that shop that would be fine for all her friends' children but she loves her own child enough that the exact balance between what his or her school friends will consider 'cool' and what her family will consider respectable matters hugely to her, enough for her to reject the lot and keep on searching until she finds the one article that satisfies this subtle and exacting need. A woman who feels her boyfriend has paid sufficient attention that he can successfully buy her a pair of suitable shoes while unaccompanied feels she has a boyfriend to treasure. (Miller, 2001, p. 231)

Consumer culture is, thus, more than simply individualized materialism, the pursuit of lifestyles and social distinction. It also permits, particularly through exchanges of gifts, expressions of intimacy and opportunities for personalizing mass consumer goods in ways that forge and maintain interpersonal relationships.

Questions for discussion

- What is consumer culture? What is meant by the term 'symbolic consumption'?
- In what ways might consumer culture lead to a promotional culture and a culture of narcissism?
- What are some of the arguments for and against the view that lifestyles and styles of consumption are increasingly a matter of free personal choice?
- In what ways might consumption be an expression of love and intimacy?

Personal Life and Politics

Gemma Edwards

13

Introduction

Personal life and politics are often studied as two distinct areas in sociology. In fact, on examining their subject matter you could be forgiven for thinking that they are opposites. Studying 'the personal' leads us to look at the **'private sphere'** of particular, emotional relationships between family and friends. Studying 'the political', on the other hand, leads us to look at the **'public sphere'** of general, rational relationships between states and citizens.

In reality, however, the boundaries of our social lives are not so exact, and, as we have already seen in Vanessa May's Chapter 10, personal life transgresses both private and public spheres. Contemporary examples of this are not hard to come by. We can point, for example, to a number of political struggles across the globe which are deeply rooted in personal existence: pro-life and pro-choice groups debating abortion, gay rights groups challenging discrimination, fathers' rights groups bringing to the public eye the issue of access to children after divorce, campaigns against domestic and sexual abuse, and movements mobilizing around health and ageing. These examples, and you are likely to be able to think of several more, illustrate the way in which people's personal lives cross the boundaries into public, political debate and action.

It is the intersection between personal life and politics that is the subject of this chapter. The cases that could be used to examine it are many and varied. This chapter argues that there is good reason to start with the case of 'social movements' (groups or networks that act collectively around issues of public contention). First, it examines how an iconic social movement of the 1970s in the USA and the UK – the second-wave feminist movement – transformed personal life into a 'stake' and a 'site' of political struggle. It looks at their struggle as a 'new' form of politics concerned with personal identity and lifestyle that became characteristic of 'new social movements' more generally. The second part of the chapter turns 'the personal is political' idea on its head to suggest that the political is also very much personal. Not only are friends and family crucial in people's decisions about whether to participate in social movements, but our political values and behaviour are shaped by our personal relationships. In the case of personal life and politics, opposites attract.

The opposition between the personal and the political

To understand personal life, do we need to explicitly talk about politics? After all, in political philosophy personal life and politics were traditionally placed in 'separate spheres'. Personal life was associated with the 'private sphere' and politics with the 'public sphere'. This goes as far back as Aristotle, who put politics in the public world of men and the family household in the private world of women (Mansbridge and Okin, 1995, p. 272). Public and private spheres are divided up, therefore, on the basis of the *different types of relationships and interactions* that they involve. The private sphere is constituted by particularized, emotional relationships, such as those between family and friends that have traditionally been studied under the rubric of 'personal life' – and the public sphere by generalized, rational relationships, such as those between states and citizens that have traditionally been studied under the rubric of 'politics' (see Vanessa May's Chapter 10 for a discussion of how this 'separate spheres' thinking has influenced the distinction that is made between public and private spaces).

It is also important to note that, in much social theory, politics – which is fundamentally about relationships structured by power – has been placed in 'public spheres' of the state and the economy rather than private spheres of everyday interpersonal relations (Fraser, 1989). As we will see below, however, it is necessary to critically engage with the way in which the boundaries between private and public have been drawn.

Feminist theorists have shown, for example, that these boundaries are highly contentious and are largely the product of the gender bias of 'malestream' social theory, that is, theories about the world which have been produced by men and from a male perspective (see Elshtain, 1981; Pateman, 1988). They argue that the notion of 'separate spheres' does not point to any natural distinction between public and private, but reflects gendered assumptions about men and women and their place in the world. The public sphere of men is defined as distinct from the family home, operating on the basis of rational rather than emotional action. The separate spheres argument was used in political philosophy to justify why women could not be given public office or the vote and become 'citizens' on the same basis as men (for example, because they think irrationally, belong at home and so forth).

What does such a recognition of the gendered assumptions of separate spheres mean? Well, we could argue that, rather than the personal and political being 'opposites', the whole theoretical notion of separate spheres is itself a product of politics – it is a product of the unequal power relationships between men and women.

It is also necessary for us to challenge the picture that the separate spheres

argument draws of personal life as entirely 'private' and, thus, without relationships structured by power (see Fraser, 1989). Most contemporary sociologists
would concede that our personal lives are inherently 'political' in the sense that
they – more often than not – involve inequalities of power. Families are not
always 'sanctuaries' that offer protection from the outside world, but can
involve domination, exploitation, violence and the reproduction of inequalities
(Greer, 1970). And friendships too – as Katherine Davies's chapter in the present volume shows – can have a 'dark side' to them, where people can exploit
and be exploited rather than adhere to expectations of reciprocity.

'Private' life is also influenced in a variety of ways by the public sphere –
for example, by government policies and public debates about how people
should live. Think of the important changes in personal lives that have been
enabled by changes in the law – the right of women to file for divorce, the
introduction of same-sex marriage and policies on adoption, to name but a
few. In fact, many of the changes in personal life that are examined in this
book cannot be comprehended without an awareness of the ways in which
personal lives are politically constituted and politically constrained.

In reality therefore, the boundaries of our social lives are not as easy to
draw as the theory of public/private spheres would suggest. Most contemporary sociologists accept this, but how has this change come about? How have
theorists moved from placing the personal and the political in opposite categories, to acknowledging their deep intersection? It is this chapter's contention
that to tackle this question we should start by looking at social movements –
that is, collective actions around issues of public contention. In particular, it
suggests that we need to look at the Women's Liberation movement of the
1970s. After all, it was this movement that announced to the world that 'the
personal is political' and inspired the kind of feminist theorising that critiqued
the idea of separate spheres.

The personal is political

The Women's Liberation movement – established in 1969 in the USA and 1970
in the UK – is a very good place to start when considering the ways in which the
personal and political are interrelated. More than any other social movement of
its time (with the exception of the Gay Liberation Front, perhaps), feminists
explicitly centred their struggle on the notion that 'the personal is political'.

This 'second wave' of **feminism** (which came after the 'first-wave' suffrage
campaigns for women's right to vote) challenged the idea of separate spheres
in a fundamental way. The argument was not only about admitting women to
public life on an equal footing with men – for instance, Equal Pay for Equal
Work – but for a redefinition of 'politics' itself. Feminists did this by arguing
that relationships of power are not limited to the institutions of the public
sphere, but are present in all aspects of life. This included the personal, and
even sexual, relationships between men and women.

In fact, feminists argued that the private sphere and the public sphere were interconnected because the male domination of women within the family and heterosexual relationships helped to ensure the subordination of women within public spheres of work and politics as well (Walby, 1990). Kate Millett's *Sexual Politics* (1970) posed the question, 'Is it possible to regard the relation of the sexes in a political light at all?' Her answer was that it depended upon 'how one defines politics'. If we define politics as 'power-structured relationships' (Millett, 1970) that allow some groups to dominate over others, then the systematic domination of men over women in all areas of life – referred to as **'patriarchy'** – could be seen as a 'political' issue. The private as well as the public can be thought of, then, as inherently political.

This realization had important implications. The first was that aspects of private life that caused women grief (like norms and expectations around sex, marriage and domestic roles) did not have to be seen as natural and unchangeable, but could be opened up to public debate. Women's 'private' problems could be redefined not as personal failings, but as symptoms of a male-dominated society. In the 'consciousness raising' groups of the Women's Liberation movement, small groups of women would meet to discuss their so-called 'private troubles' – with sex and contraception, with marriage and child care, with work and housework, and with the pressures around femininity. In relating their private troubles to wider public issues, feminists were doing what C. Wright Mills in *The Sociological Imagination* (1959) had urged sociologists to do: to situate the personal narratives and problems of the individuals they researched within wider public concerns, and to focus on the ways in which individual woes are structured by the society and times in which people live. It was C. Wright Mills, therefore, who inspired the feminist slogan 'the personal is political'.

In the wake of the separation between private life and politics, this statement was, however, controversial. Carol Hanisch commented that while it was sometimes accepted that women needed further rights relating to work and pay, 'they [men] belittled us no end for trying to bring our so-called "personal problems" into the public arena – especially "all those body issues" like sex, appearance and abortion' (Hanisch, 2006, p. 1). Consciousness-raising also made another important link between the personal and political. Through these groups, political knowledge and action was to arise from, and be grounded within, women's personal experience. Women were encouraged to understand their problems in the context of unequal power relationships with men. And they did not need to understand complex political philosophy to grasp this; all they needed was to reflect upon their own lives.

If the personal is not private and individual, but influenced by society and politics, then solutions to women's personal troubles required a *collective* movement to change things (Hanisch, 1970). Personal life therefore became the site as well as the stake in a wider political struggle. Feminists, for example, troubled aspects of personal identity, rejecting the dominant meanings attached to being a 'woman', or being 'feminine', or being a 'wife' and a 'mother', and constructed alternative images of themselves. This produced a 'collective culture' among feminists, which gave women an alternative way of knowing, representing and relating to themselves and to men (Rowbotham, 1997).

In the USA and Britain, feminist magazines like *Ms* and *Spare Rib* acted as outlets for this alternative culture, challenging conventional gender norms and sex roles. Feminists produced alternative music, art and poetry. They dressed differently, and argued that the way in which everyday language was used mattered (Spender, 1980). They challenged, for example, the use of words like 'mankind' to refer to both men and women, and suggested that historians should retrace the hidden voices of '*his*tory' to produce '*her*story'. Feminist politics also inspired radically different lifestyles, like lesbianism and communal living.

The feminist struggle therefore instigated new ways of living, being and thinking that represented a new form of political struggle which was much more deeply rooted in personal existence. It was also a politics which played itself out in people's everyday lives and sought to reshape the norms and expectations that governed them. For those involved 'it seemed as if politics and culture had melted into one' (Rowbotham, 1997, p. 398). This 'new' form of politics was characteristic, however, of a much broader range of social movements that emerged around the same time as feminism in the 1970s and have been referred to as 'new social movements'.

New social movements

Social movements like Women's Liberation pointed to the fact that political struggle is not *just* about organized groups demanding rights and concessions from the government through protests and campaigns. Political struggle can also be present within people's personal lives and the wider culture of society. This kind of political struggle involves a challenge to the dominant definitions of who we are and how we should live. It can be much less visible than those organized groups who take to the streets with placards, as much of the resistance that takes place does so through personal attempts to do things differently. Where there are more collective efforts, these too tend to happen by way of informal networks of people striving to construct a new collective identity (like, for example, the feminist consciousness-raising groups where women got together to create new ideas about who they were and how they might conduct their lives). These kinds of networks – in which new personal and collective identities form – are very much 'submerged' in everyday life and are not as obvious as the big bureaucratic organizations involved in political confrontations with the state (Melucci, 1989).

The Women's Liberation movement of the 1970s, then, signalled a novel form of politics and a very different kind of social movement compared with the political movements of the past, like those concerned with labour and civil rights. These 'old' groups centred much more on conflict with the state and tended to operate through large organizations and political parties. Women's Liberation was not the only social movement in the 1970s to take a 'new' form, however. The Gay Liberation movement, Student movement, Environmental and Peace movements, and self-help groups (like Anti-Psychiatry) also emerged at this time with an emphasis upon personal identity and lifestyle, and engaged in political struggle through 'counter-cultural' activities. These movements have been referred to as 'new social movements'. Unlike other social movements, new social movements argue that to change the world you have to change *yourself* first.

Several theories were put forward to explain why new social movements emerged. Alain Touraine (1974), for example, argued that they arose as a reaction to a new set of social conflicts that appeared in Western capitalist societies in the late 1960s and 1970s. Touraine wrote about a fundamental shift in societies at this time which came about because of a change in how they produced goods and generated wealth. From the 1970s onwards, capitalist societies moved from an industrial economy based upon manufacturing (for example, producing goods in factories) to a 'post-industrial' economy based much less on producing goods and much more on producing services (for example, financial services and welfare services). In industrial society, political conflict had centred on the working class, who were exploited in factories, and involved their clashes with the capitalist class who owned the factories and pocketed the profit. Touraine's argument was that the shift to post-industrial society had lessened the conflict between capitalists and workers and replaced it with a 'new' conflict. The new conflict was 'post-material' in nature (so not about material issues of work and pay) and led to new kinds of social movements. But what exactly was this new conflict? And how did it create a fusion between politics and personal life?

Alberto Melucci (1980) suggested that conflicts in post-industrial society spread well beyond the sphere of work and are experienced by people in every aspect of their life. This spread has come about because of changes in capitalism. Capitalist societies now face several challenges if they are to survive: they must continually generate profit and wealth and they must keep their citizens in order. By the 1970s, however, capitalism badly needed to find new ways of doing these things. It needed to convince people to keep buying goods and services (when often their initial needs had been met), and it needed citizens to keep behaving in line with the norms and expectations that supported capitalist society (like the desire to conform, the work ethic, the consumer attitude and so forth). In order to do these things, economic and state institutions started to take control of far more than the process of production: they began to extend their reach into the culture of society and into people's personal existence.

Culture consists of all sorts of symbols (words, images, and so on) and to control it would to be to control the meaning that things have for people, including the meaning they give to their life, relationships and self. In post-industrial societies, then, it becomes harder and harder to retain an autonomous sense of self – a sense of who you are as an individual – that is not defined for you 'from above' (that is, in accordance with dominant definitions and norms) (Melucci, 1989). It thus becomes difficult to hold an identity that lies outside of imposed social categories (like, for example, a woman who does not see herself as feminine or motherly). The result, Melucci argues, is that, in post-industrial society:

> Personal identity – that is to say, the possibility on the biological, psychological, and interpersonal levels, of being recognized as an individual – is the property which is now being claimed and defended; this is the ground in which individual and collective resistance is taking root. (Melucci, 1980, p. 218)

Melucci's analysis of post-industrial society therefore points to a new type of social conflict that deeply implicates personal identity. In fact, Jürgen Habermas (1981) has argued that new social movements largely arise when people's identities and lifestyles come under attack. In post-industrial societies, for example, the state and the capitalist market interfere more and more in everyday life (a process he calls 'colonization'). The welfare state takes over a host of family functions, like child care, healthcare and education. The capitalist marketplace also grows, spreading consumption into more areas of life. There are many reasons, therefore, why people might feel that their ways of living and their personal identities are under threat of being redefined, and they participate in new social movements primarily as a way of defending them.

Explanations of new social movements suggest, therefore, that the personal and political have become intertwined due to wider social and economic changes in capitalist societies that started to take place in the late 1960s and 1970s. The emergence of new social movements reflects this growing intersection and marks the 'end of the separation between public and private spheres' (Melucci, 1980, p. 219). Personal life is no longer a private matter but a stake in political struggle. And politics, too, is transformed by an agenda that arises from personal life – from issues of sex and bodies to ageing and consumption.

Although these explanations of new social movements offer interesting reasons for why personal life becomes the focus of political struggle in post-industrial society, it is important to note that they have also been criticized for overstating their case. Personal identity and lifestyle are not necessarily separate from material issues that people face at work (Edwards, 2004). And it would not be accurate to describe the Women's Liberation movement as 'post-material' (that is, no longer concerned with material issues but rather more abstract issues of identity) because it campaigned very strongly around issues of work and pay.

Nevertheless, the idea of 'new social movements' has been influential in contemporary research. Touraine, Melucci and Habermas perhaps spotted a trend (if not a break) in the nature of social conflicts that continues to generate contemporary social movements whose concerns lie at the intersection between personal life and politics. For example, the idea of new social movements has been recently applied to health, where the bodily experience of illness radically shapes personal identity and can lead to political struggles on the part of sufferers for recognition and dignity (Kelleher, 2001). Health-related new social movements also contest dominant ideas about how particular illnesses should be defined, treated and prevented. This is the case in recent movements around breast cancer and mental health, for instance (Brown *et al.*, 2004).

The political is also personal

So far we have looked at social movements – and the new social movements in particular – to highlight the ways in which 'the personal is political'. Feminism has shown that in order to properly understand personal life we need to locate it within public issues. This section argues that the same is also true the other way round – in order to properly understand politics we need to locate political attitudes and behaviour within personal life. This is because people's personal social networks – that is, the web of kinship and friendship relations in which their lives are embedded – have a crucial role to play in forming their political attitudes and behaviour.

Let us take, for example, the question of political participation. How do people become politically active? Today, many people say that they care about the environment, but only a minority are members of groups like Greenpeace, and even fewer will actually turn up to a demonstration against tree felling, or road building. One way to address the question of why some people become involved and not others is to concentrate upon individual political attitudes. We could ask, for example, how people come to hold the kind of beliefs and values that lead to political activism. What starts as a question about the individual, however, quickly turns into a question about people's interconnections. This is because personal relationships have a great deal of influence over the development of political attitudes and behaviour. People do not become politically active (or apathetic) in isolation, but in the context of their everyday interactions with significant others.

The first example of this involves the way in which emotional ties to others can supply people with the motivation to take part in social movements in the first place. Interpersonal relationships involve strong feelings for significant others (like parents, children, partners and friends). People are often compelled to participate in political action when they think it will help to ease the suffering of their significant others, or bring the perpetrators of their suffering to justice. For example, Deborah Gould's (2009) study of ACT UP ('Aids Coalition to Unleash Power', formed in 1987 in the USA) showed that personal experience of a partner suffering from Aids supplied the emotional motivation for participation in public action. At certain times in the campaign, grief born out of witnessing loved ones suffer and die from Aids led to anger at the public handling of the crisis. It not only motivated activism, but also influenced the way in which people campaigned. ACT UP, for example, conducted 'political funerals' where the ashes of loved ones who had died from Aids were scattered in front of government buildings as a way of making the politicians aware of their great personal losses.

The second example comes from a much older study of voting behaviour conducted at Columbia University in the USA in the 1940s called *The People's Choice* (Lazarsfeld *et al.*, 1948), which has remained highly influential because it challenged the individual approach to explaining political action. Against the image of voters as individual actors who calculate the pros and cons of various political parties when making a decision about which to support, the Columbia study showed that people actually make up their minds about politics within the context of their close personal relationships. Paul Lazarsfeld, Bernard Berelson and Hazel Gaudet (1948) found that people's political values and choices were influenced by the others with whom they interacted on a daily basis, especially those they were intimate with.

Lazarsfeld and colleagues' findings are supported by a wealth of literature from the 1950s onwards on the nature of political **socialization** (see Niemi and Sobieszek, 1977, for a review). Although a question of some debate, the family continues to be seen as an important factor in political socialization. As discussed in more detail in Box 13.1, by influencing their children, parents transmit political dispositions down the generations.

While the emphasis has traditionally been upon how parents influence their children's politics (as in the study described in Box 13.1), there is also a growing awareness of the fact that adolescent children sometimes influence their parents' politics (McDevitt and Chaffee, 2002). Friends, too, can be just as important as family for political socialization (Kotler-Berkowitz, 2005). One of the reasons why family and friends are important in shaping political views is because the family household and friendship group tend to be the key spaces in which people talk about politics. Everyday conversations, like those between husband and wife or cohabiting partners, provide the primary context in which people make up their minds about issues ranging from which party to vote for to whether abortion is right or wrong (Zuckerman *et al.*, 2005). Married couples therefore tend to hold similar political views (Stoker and Jennings, 1995).

Interestingly, Nina Eliasoph (1998) has argued that apathy – a form of political disengagement – is also reproduced in everyday personal interactions. She found that when people fail to talk about politics with their family and friends, they find politics less and less relevant to their lives.

Finally, research on social movements has also found that personal networks of kinship and friendship are very important when it comes to recruiting people to political activism (Passy, 2003). In fact, whether there is a prior personal connection to somebody already in the movement turns out to be one of the best predictors of participation. This observation was first made in a

---

Box 13.1   Political socialization in the family

M. Kent Jennings, Laura Stoker and Jake Bowers (2009) investigate the nature of political socialization in American families using a statistical analysis of longitudinal data.
They draw upon data from the parent–child political socialization project conducted
at the University of Michigan's Survey Research Center and Center for Political
Studies. The data were collected in four waves in 1965, 1973, 1982 and 1997, using a
mixture of interviews and survey questionnaires. In 1997, they reinterviewed children
of the original cohort, and collected data about their children. Their sample, therefore,
included three generations of Americans, and 636 parent–child pairs.

Jennings and colleagues used the interview and survey data to measure the similarity between parent and child pairs with respect to variables such as which political
party they supported, who they voted for and levels of political interest. They found
high levels of transmission between parent and child pairs in the sample when it came
to issues like which political party they supported and who they voted for. For example, the estimated effect of the parent upon the child's party identification was 0.55
(on a scale between 0 and 1). This result was the same for vote choice. For political
knowledge it was also strong at 0.42, but was less so for political trust (0.14) and political interest (0.10).

They also analysed whether these parental transmission effects would still be significant when they accounted for other important factors like family income, the education of parents, the sex and ethnicity of the child and local contextual factors such
as the type of school the child went to. They found that on issues of party identification and vote choice, the strong influence from parents remained, despite these other
factors being added. Interestingly, they found that neither parental attributes nor the
local context correlated strongly with a child's *level* of political interest. They argue that
levels of political interest are best explained instead by the children's levels of participation in clubs and organizations inside and outside of school.

---

survey of university students in the USA conducted by David Snow, Louis
Zurcher and Sheldon Ekland-Olson (1980), which found that 63 per cent of
students had been recruited to political movements on campus through their
personal social networks, compared with 30 per cent through the mass media,
7 per cent in public places and 0 per cent by mail/telephone (Snow *et al.*, 1980,
p. 125).

Why is it, then, that personal social networks are so influential when it
comes to participation in politics? Doug McAdam and Ronnelle Paulsen
(1993) address this question in their research on the participation of white college students in the 1964 Freedom Summer Project. This project was part of
the Civil Rights movement in the USA, and involved college students travel-
ling to Mississippi to help register black voters and run Freedom Schools.
Students had to apply in advance to participate in the project and by the time
it started some had dropped out.

McAdam and Paulsen's research followed up on the differences between the
students who went on Freedom Summer and those who were 'no shows'. They

Box 13.2   The social network of Emmeline Pankhurst

What role do family and friends play in political activism? Is it accurate to say that family and friends 'pull you in' to activism? Or that some families are 'political' families? These questions have been the focus of a historical research project that I have been involved in with other sociologists at the University of Manchester.[1] In this project, we examined the role of social networks in the political activism of British Suffragettes (1903–14). In particular we looked at the Women's Social and Political Union (WSPU), which was founded by Emmeline Pankhurst in Manchester in 1903 to campaign for votes for women. The project mapped and analyzed Emmeline Pankhurst's 'personal network' of family and friends before she founded the WSPU. We also traced the key leading members of the WSPU between 1903 and 1914 when it ceased.

Figure 13.1 – which looks rather like a thick spider's web because it depicts a very dense network – shows Emmeline Pankhurst's personal social network before she founded the WSPU in October 1903. The diagram has also added in the people who became key leading members of the WSPU at some time between 1903 and 1914. We can see by the circles that several of Emmeline Pankhurst's existing family and friends became leading activists (note in particular her three daughters, Christabel, Sylvia, and Adela, who each had an important role to play in the campaign for women's suffrage). We can also see by the triangles that most of the other leading members of the WSPU at one time or another in the campaign were friends of existing friends. Indeed, only four leading members – shown by the diamonds – had no prior personal connection to Emmeline Pankhurst. The results of this exercise suggest that the core of this political group (the rank-and-file being a different matter of course) largely grew out of an existing personal network of family and friends.

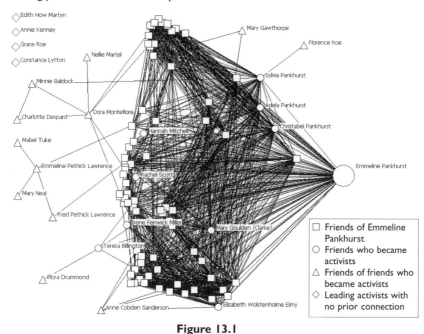

Figure 13.1

argued that the key factor was the extent to which the student had close personal relationships that were supportive of their involvement. The 'no shows' reported much less support from their family, friends and peers. This made participation difficult for them, according to McAdam and Paulsen, because we depend upon close personal relationships to sustain the predominant image we hold of ourselves. If family and friends do not support the 'new' identity that a person takes on through political involvement, then it can unsettle a person's sense of self and make it more likely that they will drop out. In Box 13.2, we explore in more detail the role that family and friends can play in a person becoming politically active.

This section has suggested that relationships with family and friends can help to explain people's political values and participation – for example, who they vote for and whether they become involved in social movements. Friends and family may directly influence your political values, and they may also 'pull you in' to political activities that they are already involved with. Furthermore, social movements often recruit not individuals but 'blocs', like a circle of friends or a family unit (Obershall, 1973). It is also important to remember, however, that while people may come to political activity via friends and family, they also make friends and family out of political activity. Intense interactions with political comrades can forge bonds that are similar to those of kinship and friendship. In her study of the Italian Red Brigades, a left-wing terrorist movement in the 1970s and 1980s, Donatella della Porta (1992), for example, found that underground political groups became like surrogate families for those involved.

Concluding remarks

This chapter has examined the ways in which personal life intersects with politics. We have seen that the opposition in political philosophy between 'the personal' and 'the political' is a false one. Instead, we need to look beyond 'separate spheres' to the ways in which personal life and politics intersect. In order to do this, the chapter has concentrated upon the case of social movements. It has argued that social movements are a good place to start when considering the intersection between personal life and politics, not least because it was the Women's Liberation movement that first suggested that 'the personal is political'. Women's Liberation was part of a wider set of movements, however, which emerged in Western capitalist countries in the 1970s and converted personal identity and everyday life into 'stakes' in political struggle. We considered these movements as 'new social movements' which responded to the social conflicts of post-industrial society.

Finally, we turned the 'personal is political' on its head to look at some of the ways in which the 'political is also personal'. We found evidence to suggest that political attitudes and behaviour are embedded in personal social networks. Friends and family have a crucial role to play in political activism, and friends and family are also forged in the course of political activism. This chapter has put forward a number of arguments, therefore, to suggest that in order to understand personal life we must look at politics – and in order to understand politics, we must look at personal life.

Questions for discussion

■ What did the Women's Liberation movement mean in 1970 when it declared that 'the personal is political'? Is this slogan still relevant today?
■ Does politics influence who you are and how you live? If so, in what ways?
■ How is the idea of 'new social movements' useful for understanding the nature of contemporary political struggles?
■ In what ways, and to what extent, do family and friends shape a person's political values and behaviour?

Researching Personal Life

Vanessa May

14

Introduction

You have, in the previous chapters, been introduced to a whole range of sociological writings on different aspects of personal life. Many of these are based on empirical research, that is, they derive from empirical data that a researcher has collected and analysed. There are numerous different kinds of data that sociologists can use in their research, ranging from in-depth qualitative interviews and observations to survey methods and statistical modeling. This chapter offers some tips to students on how to go about researching personal life. Its focus is on the collection, rather the analysis, of data.

We begin with a few suggestions on where to start when planning a research project, followed by a short discussion of the difference between quantitative and qualitative methods of data collection and analysis, before moving on to discuss examples from research that has been conducted by members of the Morgan Centre for the Study of Relationships and Personal Life (henceforth the Morgan Centre) at the University of Manchester. The chapter does not aim, however, to provide a full step-by-step 'how to' guide to sociological research. For further advice on how to design and conduct a research project, and for examples of sociological empirical research see Mason (*Qualitative Researching*, 2002), Silverman (2005), Treiman (2009), Neuman (2005) and Devine and Heath (2009).

It is important to keep in mind that doing research is not merely a question of learning appropriate techniques, but also of applying 'a playfulness of mind' and 'a truly fierce drive to make sense of the world' (Mills, 1959, p. 211). Thus, becoming a good researcher is not simply a matter of training or of pure technical skill, but involves also the development of what C. Wright Mills calls a sociological imagination (see Mills, 1959, pp. 212–17, for tips on how one can exercise and develop this imagination).

Finding and honing a topic

The first thing you need to do when embarking upon a research project is to choose a topic. It is always better to pick a topic that interests and intrigues you in 'real life'. Is there something you go around thinking about and speculating 'Why is that so?' or 'I wonder what that is like?' The reason why it is better to start from a question that interests you personally is because any research project requires a significant investment of time and effort, and you are more likely to remain motivated if the topic genuinely fascinates you.

The next step is to formulate your initial interest into a focused research question to which you want to find the answer (Jennifer Mason, *Qualitative Researching*, 2002, calls this an intellectual puzzle). It is important that such a research question is practical to implement – in other words, avoid questions that aim to explore a broad social phenomenon in its totality. Instead, try to find a specific aspect of your topic that you want to study, and try to find a clearly defined place, situation or setting where whatever it is you are interested in studying is going on. So, for example, if you were interested in researching interactions in public space, you would need to decide who, what, when and where is to be the focus of your study – whose interactions, which type of interaction, taking place in which public spaces and when. You will only have limited time and financial resources to carry out the study, which should also be reflected in the scope of your research question – student projects are generally much more specific and narrow in scope than research projects that are funded over several years and involve a research team. You will at this point want to also think about which sociological theories you will use to explore your topic. The chapters in this book will have given you some ideas of theories that can be used to shed light on personal life.

Quantitative or qualitative?

Already, when constructing your research question, you will have to think about whether you wish to use quantitative or qualitative methods. A somewhat simplified definition of quantitative research is that it is concerned with quantifying the extent and location of phenomena, and the inter-relationships between phenomena. If you are wanting to find the answer to questions such as 'How many people get married, and at what age?' or 'On average, how many hours do people spend at work?', and in both cases 'How does this vary across different groups in the population?', you will have to use quantitative methods. In an equally simplified manner, qualitative research can be characterized as focusing on the micro level, with the aim of understanding, for example, the meanings that people attach to their experiences or the interactions between people. Questions that you could answer with the help of qualitative methods are 'How do people reason over their decision to divorce?' or

'What meanings do people attach to their work?' Furthermore, qualitative research aims to understand thought and action in their context – for example, why in certain societies divorce might be frowned upon, whereas in others it is seen as generally acceptable.

Much of quantitative research aims to be statistically representative. This means that the sample of research respondents is chosen in such a way that it represents a larger population (for example, the population of a country or a region), which in turn means that the findings of the study can be said to reflect the whole population, not merely the sample itself. To ensure that a sample is representative, the population being studied must be sampled in such a way that each individual has a known likelihood of being included (a so-called known probability sample), and to get accurate estimates for the population the sample needs to be large in size. For example, many nationally representative surveys collect responses from thousands and sometimes tens of thousands of individuals. Qualitative research does not aim to be statistically representative, and can therefore use smaller samples. This is perhaps why qualitative methods are relatively popular among undergraduate students who have limited resources to use on their research (though see below about the possibility of using existing datasets).

The above brief description of quantitative and qualitative methods is an oversimplification, and the difference between quantitative and qualitative is not necessarily this stark. It is, however, important to keep in mind that these methods tend to answer different types of question. This allows for a different focus in research: in quantitative research the focus is on aggregate patterns (that is, what people in a particular group or country tend to do or the differences between different groups), in qualitative research the focus is more on understanding individual thought and action within its social context.

Collecting data

The next step, once you have decided on your topic, research question and overall methodological approach, is to decide what type of data you will use, where and how you can access the data and how you will analyse them. If you have opted for a quantitative approach, you can choose between using available datasets or collecting your own data. For example, you can consider using census data that are collected in many countries, such as the UK and the USA, usually every ten years. Data are collected about every person living in that country at the time of the census, and information such as their age, gender, ethnicity, religion, nationality, marital status, number of children, occupation, housing status and so on are recorded. Such data can be a good way of exploring, for example, whether there are differences between ethnic groups in marriage rates or the type of housing they live in.

You can also consider whether you could use data collected by large-scale surveys such as the National Survey of America's Families or the National

Survey of Families and Households in the USA. In the UK, key surveys include the National Child Development Study, the British Household Panel Survey and the Millenium Cohort Study. All of the above are large-scale longitudinal surveys or panel studies – that is, they collect data from the same people over a number of years at certain intervals (sometimes adding new respondents as time goes on). These surveys are designed to provide answers to particular sets of questions (for example, about family formation or life transitions), and therefore they can provide more detailed information – for example, of people's experiences of family life or work – than census surveys. These large datasets are usually available to researchers upon application. In the UK, for example, the major national surveys are archived at the Economic and Social Data Service (which also houses a number of qualitative datasets). The ease of using such surveys lies in the fact that the data are already collected, though it can be difficult to find a survey that can provide answers to your research questions.

One such survey is the English Longitudinal Study of Ageing (ELSA) that is based on a nationally representative sample of respondents over 50 years of age. ELSA data collection was begun in 2002 with a sample of 12,100 respondents. It is a longitudinal survey that returns to the same people every two years (and keeps adding a new representative sample of people who have turned 50 since the previous wave of data collection). The survey is designed to investigate various aspects of the ageing process, including physical and mental health, social networks and economic impact. We will return to this survey in the section below.

Quantitative research can also be conducted using smaller surveys with, say, only a hundred or a few hundred respondents. These surveys are usually very specific and focused on a particular topic, such as how families adjust to life after divorce. Students can devise their own questionnaire and collect data themselves, and this has become increasingly more realistic with the help of the internet that enables the use of web-based surveys (Nesbary, 2000). You might, for example, want to find out what fellow students at your university think about their friends and whether their friendship networks have significantly changed since coming to university. Or you might want to find out how people in your home town think about racial segregation. It is worth noting that constructing a good questionnaire is an art-form in itself and requires much thought (Fink, 2008). The benefit of using your own survey is that you can design a questionnaire that enables you to collect data that answer your specific research questions.

Perhaps the most popular qualitative method used by sociologists is the face-to-face in-depth interview that is aimed at exploring an individual's experiences of the topic at hand (Kvale, 2007). Interviews can focus on, for example, how children have experienced their parents' divorce (Smart and Neale, 1999), how people think about and structure their time (Southerton, 'Temporal Rhythms', 2009b), or the meaning that pets have in their life (Tipper, '"A Dog Who I Know Quite Well"', 2011). The analysis of such data can focus on *how* a research participant has expressed themselves over a particular topic, what things they talk about and which things they leave outside their account, what matters to this person and why, and so on. You might also want to study practices; that is, what people do in their personal life – for example, how things are passed on from generation to generation (Finch and Mason, 2000) – and what these practices mean to people. Examples of further qualitative research methods are provided in the following section.

Examples from our research

The studies discussed in this section are mentioned in the previous chapters, but here we will examine *how* the research involved was conducted rather than on the findings that emerged from these. Some of these studies are still ongoing at the time of writing. What follows is by no means an exhaustive list of qualitative methods, or indeed of the present-day landscape of sociology of personal life research, but a selection of examples showing the application of 'sociological imagination' to the study of personal life, namely finding imaginative ways of conducting qualitative interviews; alternative sources of data; and the use of several sources of data in one study.

As mentioned above, the in-depth interview is perhaps the most popular method of qualitative data collection within sociology. There are, however, many imaginative ways in which interviews can be conducted in order to collect better-quality data – for example, via the use of vignettes, visual elicitation techniques and group interviews.

Using vignettes within interviews means providing research participants with possible scenarios that they are then asked to comment on. For example, in a study of how family members negotiate their obligations to one another, Janet Finch and Jennifer Mason (1993) employed vignettes as a way of accessing people's thoughts about how family members 'should' take responsibility over one another (irrespective of how family obligations had been dealt with in their own lives). Vignettes can also offer research participants a safe place where they can talk about an issue that has affected their lives without requiring them to disclose their own experiences. Carol Smart, Bren Neale and Amanda Wade (2001) used this technique when interviewing children about their experiences of life after their parents' divorce. The children were provided, for example, with a vignette of a child whose parents cannot amicably agree over how much time she should spend with each, and were asked to talk about what they thought of this situation. This allowed the children to explore such potentially painful topics without necessarily having to talk about their own experiences.

There are also a range of visual elicitation techniques that can be used within qualitative interviewing. In a study of how children reason about who counts as 'kin', Jennifer Mason and Becky Tipper ('Being Related', 2008) used a photo elicitation method where they provided children with disposable cameras and asked them to take photographs that somehow represented the people that mattered to them and whom they counted as kin. In subsequent interviews, the children were asked to talk about these photographs and about the relationships that they represented. The children were also given the opportunity to draw maps of people close to them on concentric circles, with the most important people on the inner circles, or to draw pictures of their family. In a study about family resemblance, Jennifer Mason and Katherine Davies ('Coming to Our Senses?', 2009) conducted interviews that involved looking through research participants' family photograph albums, and in a study of family traditions, Jennifer Mason and Stewart Muir provided their research participants with video cameras so that they could film, for example, how they spend Christmas.

Interviews need not always be conducted with individuals, but can be conducted in pairs or in groups. Brian Heaphy, Carol Smart and Anna Einarsdottir are currently conducting a study of same-sex marriage entitled 'Just like Marriage? Young Couples' Civil Partnerships'. Couples are interviewed both together and separately to explore everyday relational practices. This approach, which is rarely taken up in couple studies, allows a new and dynamic way of exploring what kind of stories couples tell about their relationships and married life, and how these are negotiated between the spouses.

Group interviews have been used in a project called 'Critical Associations' which focuses on different aspects of personal relationships (please see Katherine Davies's chapter in this volume for more information on this study). This study, which was carried out by Davies, Heaphy, Mason and Smart, included so-called 'memory workshops'. Each workshop consisted of a group of participants with a shared experience; of being a member of a British academic feminist network in the 1970s or 'coming out' as non-heterosexual. Such group interviews can be a useful way of tapping into how people talk about an issue in interaction, and the shared narratives or memories that are told, and how these are negotiated in the group, as well as the group dynamics that emerge. Or, you may wish to adopt a 'participant observation' approach, which means observing the interactions between individuals in a particular setting.

A researcher of personal life need, of course, not limit themselves to talking to (or observing) people, but can use any number of other sources of data, including official records, data collected on how people spend their time and money, or letters and diaries and other forms of biographical writings. In a study about parents who had taken their dispute over their children to the courts, Smart, May, Furniss and Wade (2003) analysed court records[1] to find out the stated reasons for why parents take their disputes to court and what happens to these cases once they enter the legal system. In a cross-national comparative study over how practices of consumption (for example, eating family meals together) have changed since the 1970s in five different countries, Dale Southerton used time-diary data that involved respondents recording their activities in a specifically designed diary over a particular period of time (Cheng et al., 2007). In his current work, Southerton is exploring the impact that personal relationships and social networks have on taste and consumer behaviour. One of his sources of data is the transactional data that many shops now collect through loyalty card schemes.

Gemma Edwards has been exploring how personal social networks affect participation in social movements such as, for example, the suffragette movement in the UK (Edwards and Crossley, 2009). To do so, she has used a methodological technique known as social network analysis (SNA) to explore these questions using historical sources (auto/biographies, letters and diaries). By analysing the content of diaries of suffragettes she has explored the significance of the family home for interpersonal relationships and the suffrage campaign. Using the quantitative techniques of SNA – that is, mapping and measuring the network of suffragettes – she has been able to create a diagram (called a sociogram) of the network and how it changed over time.

The 'Critical Associations' research team mentioned above also commissioned a Mass Observation Project directive on friendship (for a closer look at this aspect of the study, see Katherine Davies's Chapter 7). The Mass Observation Project, which began in 1981, is an example of a qualitative longitudinal study and houses a collection of responses from a panel of respondents on a variety of topics ranging from pocket money, food and clothing, to relationships, sex and belonging. The Mass Observation Project is housed at the University of Sussex and is open to researchers by special appointment.

A researcher is never limited to using just one method of data collection (or analysis). One aim of such use of 'mixed methods' is to explore a social phenomenon from a variety of angles in order to get a fuller picture of not only what goes on, but also what this means to the people involved. Most of the studies mentioned so far have, in fact, used a variety of data sources. For example, in their study of family obligations, Finch and Mason (1993) collected data through both quantitative survey interviews and in-depth qualitative interviews. In their study of court disputes between parents, Smart and colleagues (2005) also interviewed parents who had been involved in these cases in order to get an understanding of how they had experienced the court case, and whether going to court had helped resolve the dispute. The findings from the first stage of the study focusing on the court process were used to identify key issues to explore in the interviews with the parents.

Mason, Smart, Heaphy and Davies (the 'Critical Associations' team mentioned above) have conducted a sub-project of relationships in, and to, a particular place. This sub-project used qualitative interviews, ethnography and secondary analysis of archived written and photographic memories to explore personal associations with friends, neighbours, family members, acquaintances and others among people who were moved out of inner-city housing to a more rural 'overspill' estate during a major slum clearance programme in an English city in the 1960s and 1970s.

A further example of the use of mixed methods is the study 'Inter/ Generational Dynamics', conducted by Mason, Nazroo, May and Muir.[2] This study is interested in older people's perceptions of their ageing and in intergenerational relationships, and uses data from the ELSA survey mentioned above. The focus is on a very particular part of the ELSA survey, namely the information it provides on the quality and quantity of respondents' relationships with spouses, children, other family and friends, as well as their relationship to their local area. In addition to this, the research team conducted a linked qualitative study with a small sub-sample of ELSA respondents, focusing on issues such as how people experience their ageing bodies, and how ageing impacts on their relationship to family and friends, as well as to place. To this end, research participants were interviewed twice. The first interview focused on the participants' experiences of ageing, their hobbies and their relationship to technology. The participants were then asked to fill in an interaction diary over a period of seven days, noting every interaction they had (or as many as possible) whether face-to-face or over phone, text, email, Skype or letter. In a subsequent interview, we asked the participants to talk us through their diary in order to get an idea of the types of interaction their everyday lives are made up of, and where these interactions take place and what they mean to them. We also conducted focus groups (that is, group interviews) with older people in the Greater Manchester area, focusing on their relationship to technology. Together with the survey data from ELSA, these data allow us to better understand how ageing impacts on people's relationships with the surrounding world.

Concluding remarks

A sociology of personal life is interested in how personal life and social structures interlink. Any student will need to be mindful of these in their own project, and be able to discuss how personal life is embedded in a particular historical and social context. This means that both quantitative and qualitative approaches are invaluable in the study of personal life. This chapter has aimed to give the reader an insight into the immense variety of data collection methods that can be utilized in the study of personal life, plus some practical tips on how to go about conducting such research.

Conclusion: Why a Sociology of Personal Life?

Vanessa May

15

The personal and the social

In this chapter, we return to some of the key ideas introduced by David Morgan in Chapter 2, and bring together and further develop some of the theoretical concepts that have constituted the backbone of this book. Our aim has been to introduce the reader to a *sociology* of personal life – that is, to what is sociological about personal life. As the study of people *in* society, sociology tries to understand not only the individual experience but also how this experience is shaped by the social context in which it takes place. For example, in most Western societies, a young working-class man in the 1950s would have faced very different opportunities compared to today – in terms of the jobs available to him or the chances of gaining a university education. Throughout this book the reader will have gained an understanding of how Western societies have changed in the last 100 years or more, as well as what impact these **social changes** have had on personal life.

These broad social patterns may seem like something completely separate from the individual experience, but the argument we have been putting forward in this book is that the two are, in fact, intertwined. To use Georg Simmel's (1950, pp. 7–9) analogy, if we think of society as a painting, the closer we get to it, the more clearly we can distinguish the individual people in the picture. But as we move further away, we can no longer see the details so clearly, and can instead appreciate the overall structure of the painting. We may interpret this as observing two separate entities (individual people and society), but both are, in fact, views of the same thing seen differently, depending on our distance from it. If we view people and society in this manner, it becomes clear that the two cannot be understood independently of each other.

Concerning personal life, which to each of us tends to feel private and unique, a sociological approach is thus interested in exploring the ways in which even the most 'private' of experiences are shaped by the socio-cultural context in which they occur. For example, how a person views her or his marriage is not only the consequence of how well they get on with their spouse, but is also coloured by social expectations around marriage. In contemporary Western societies, where marriage is meant to be based on romantic love and mutual emotional disclosure, a person not experiencing these things in their own marital relationship may feel that their marriage is not as it should be. As pointed out in the Introduction, this is true also for the term 'personal' itself – what we mean by it, and how we experience it, is not a universal given, but culturally and socially shaped.

If we look at personal life in the aggregate, we can see patterns and structures emerging: people in a particular society or section of society tend to do things similarly and at similar times in their lives. For example, there are trends regarding when people in a given society marry and how many children they have, and the age at which they do so – and these trends shift over time. It is this shifting patterning that sociologists are interested in describing and explaining.

But, in addition, a sociologist studying personal life is also interested in understanding how this aggregate picture affects how individuals live their lives and the meanings they attach to their experiences. For example, how do people view their 'work' time and 'leisure' time, and what activities do they feel are appropriate under these different times? Do women and men feel differently about 'work' and 'leisure' time, and, if so, why? Why do some people place such high value on 'quality' time with family, while for other groups such notions seem foreign?

Treading a fine line

As pointed out in the Introduction, sociologists are always treading a fine line between saying that individuals are socially shaped and that their lives are predetermined. In other words, while exploring how the ways in which people understand fundamental aspects of their self (such as their gender, sexuality, social class or ethnicity) are socially constructed (that is, had they been born into another culture or in another historical period, they would understand themselves differently), it is also important to remain mindful of the fact that people's lives are not fully determined in advance. If they were, there would be little to distinguish between people from the same background and children would become carbon copies of their parents. This way, people's lives would be highly predictable and there would be no social change.

How can we then claim that people's lives are, to an extent, socially shaped if Mary, a daughter of working-class parents, goes to university and becomes a lawyer, while her sister Ann leaves school at 18 and works in a shop? Elias (1991) argues that this is because the instincts of every child are unique, and consequently each child responds differently to the **socialization** processes that they are subject to. For example, two children will each respond differently to being scolded or to receiving affection. According to Elias, it is this individual dialogue between a person and his or her environment that helps shape the person they are. In other words, when explaining what becomes of a person, we cannot explain this as the result of social shaping or individual choice alone. Instead, we must appreciate that a person's life is the result of a complex interaction between individual personality and social context, as well as pure luck and circumstance. Hence, the different paths that Mary's and Ann's lives follow.

People are, thus, not mere automatons or puppets to be shaped by social forces, but have a degree of volitional control over their lives. In other words, they have agency. It is partly thanks to this individual agency that people react to their surroundings in not only varied but also unpredictable ways, which in turn helps explain why society is constantly changing. It is this interplay between individual agency and being shaped by social forces beyond our control that is of key interest within sociology, and is also the focus of much sociological debate (sometimes called the 'structure–agency' debate). You will, in this book, have read about this issue in relation to, for example, the debate surrounding the **individualization** (or **de-traditionalization**) **thesis**, which claims that old structures have given way to increased individual choice in almost all aspects of life. You will also have gathered that a sociology of personal life is always mindful of the mixture of individual choice and social shaping that is involved in making personal life what it is.

A relational view of society

One key concept that has run through this book is that of relationality. In previous chapters we have discussed how people are relational, gaining their sense of self in relationships with and in relation to other people. Let's now extend this relational view to encompass also how we understand society.

While reading sociological texts, one would be forgiven for thinking that society is a 'thing', an entity that 'really' exists out there, independent of the human interactions that constitute it. It is such a reading that leads some students to depict society as an entity that can act – as exemplified by statements such as 'society makes us do X'. However, according to Simmel (1950, pp. 9–10), this is a misunderstanding of the nature of society; it is something that individuals *do* rather than a thing or a concrete substance. Simmel proposed that society is the result of interactions between individuals, and the elements of society we have come to see as 'permanent' (such as the state, family or social class – also called **social structures**) are nothing but actions that have become to some extent fixed (Burkitt, 2004, p. 220).

Society can therefore be understood not as something that *is*, but as something that we *do* in our personal lives. Society is also relational because it is something that we do in interaction *with other people*. To take the example of family, 'family' does not exist out there as a thing independent of the family practices that constitute it. In other words, if people did not *do* family – by, for example, getting married, having children and calling this 'family' – there would be no family. These social structures also often become institutional-ized. That is, they become regular practices of established social institutions – for example, in the form of family policy or legislation on marriage.

Elias (1991) made a similar point by proposing that society should not be viewed as something separate from the relationships that constitute it. In other words, society is not a force that exists outside of people, but is rather made up of the relationships between people. Consequently, neither individuals nor society can be understood independently of each other, which is why Elias urged sociologists to focus on the relationship between them. He used an anal-ogy comparing society to a house and individuals to the bricks that constitute it (Elias, 1991, p. 19). Elias argued that we cannot understand the shape of the house by examining individual bricks independently of their relations to each other, and, conversely, we must understand the structure of the whole if we are to understand the relationship between the individual parts. Furthermore, he warned against thinking of either society or the individual as more important than the other, because society could not exist without individuals, while indi-viduals do not exist separate from society.

The interconnectedness of spheres

As noted by David Morgan in Chapter 2, the word 'personal' carries with it several meanings, many of them in contrast with the meanings attached to the word 'public'. Questioning and critically exploring this distinction that is gen-erally drawn between 'private/personal' and 'public/official' is also a key theme running through the present volume. As we have seen, this distinction has led to a particular view of the world which is divided into 'personal' home and 'public' work and politics. These in turn tend to be gendered so that the home has traditionally been seen as women's sphere, while the **public sphere** remains masculine. This has had a significant impact on personal life, restrict-ing women's access to paid employment or political life for centuries, as well as leaving women with the main responsibility for unpaid work such as child care and household work. The effects of these gendered divisions can still be felt today. What the chapters in this book have also demonstrated are the many ways in which this often taken-for-granted distinction between public and private, and all of its consequences, are socially constructed and therefore liable to change.

In addition, the authors have discussed many examples of how the bound-ary between public and private is porous. This means not only that the public and **private spheres** are interconnected, in that 'public' actions such as politics affect personal life (and vice versa), but also that personal activities take place in public settings and vice versa. Capitalism is a prime example of a shift that has occurred in the 'public' sphere that has had a significant impact on per-sonal life. Capitalism evolved hand-in-hand with **industrialization**, and partic-ular modes of producing goods, mainly in factories. This had a significant impact on the lives of countless people who moved from the countryside into towns and cities in order to work in factories for a wage. Industrialization also came with the production of increasing volumes of goods. We now live in societies dominated by consumption to the extent that even our identities or lifestyles can, according to some theorists, be bought. Think of the ways in which you signal who you are – for example, through the clothes you wear, the music you listen to, or the food you eat. Thus, it can be argued that even our identity, which probably, to many of us, feels purely 'personal', is in fact to some extent the product of capitalist market forces.

Concluding remarks

To sum up, our argument in this book has been that it is important to understand both the personal and the social in order to examine not only personal life but also society. Although 'the personal' is seemingly private and therefore not 'social', and consequently perhaps not something that sociology could or should study, in fact the most private moments of our lives are, to an extent, shaped by social forces. In other words, personal life says something about both us as individual people, and the social context in which we live. Conversely, what we do in our personal lives has an impact on the social: social structures or broader patterns in society are nothing more than the aggregate of numerous individual acts. Personal life is therefore an important field of study for sociology.

Glossary of Terms

Commodification: A term denoting the process whereby something becomes a commodity. In this process, something that was previously not given a monetary value now becomes measured in terms of economic value. As a result, this thing can now be bought and sold at a certain price. Not only concrete products but also abstract ideas (such as time) can become commodified.

Conspicuous consumption: A form of consumption the aim of which is to convey wealth and social status visibly. As such, it must be conspicuous, i.e.clearly noticeable by others who are then meant to draw the right conclusion as to the person's social status. In addition, what is consumed must be expensive, luxurious or otherwise unattainable to the large majority of people. Expensive sports cars are an example of conspicuous consumption.

Consumer culture: Contemporary Western societies are said to be consumer cultures, i.e. they are characterized by high volumes of goods produced and consumed. In consumer culture, more and more things are available for consumption, and consumption has become increasingly important in people's lives. Even lifestyles and identities can be said to be bought in the form of, for example, clothing and music.

Demography: A discipline that studies statistics, i.e. aggregate patterns of birth, death, marriage, income, and so on.

De-traditionalization thesis. See *individualization thesis*.

Empirical research: Research that is based on data that have been collected through **qualitative** or **quantitative** methods.

Ethnomethodology: A school of thought within sociology that is interested in studying the common-sense knowledge within a society. For example, the focus can be on how people use language to make sense of their everyday experiences. Or, an ethnomethodologist can be interested in how people create social order, for example social order on the streets, where most people can be seen to behave as if according to some unwritten and taken-for-granted rules.

Families of choice: A term that is used by sociologists to highlight the fact that families are not necessarily defined by blood and marital ties, but rather who counts as kin can also be a question of choice. A person's family of choice is made up of people who matter most to them, irrespective of whether they are related by blood or marriage.

Feminism: Both a social movement and a theoretical tradition. Second-wave feminism began in 1960s in the US and the UK, and has had a significant impact on women's lives by campaigning for equal rights in working life and in families. The theoretical strand of feminism has been closely linked to the social movement side, and many feminist theorists have also been political activists. There are many different schools of thought within feminism, but one of the key foci has been to analyse critically the nature and workings of inequalities between men and women, and the impact these have had on women's lives.

Functionalism: A school of thought within sociology that dominated the discipline in the 1950s and 1960s. Depicts society as an organization (much like an organism)

173

where every constituent part (or social institution) has its own function to perform that helps ensure the proper functioning of the whole. So, for example, the family is seen to have a key function in ensuring the stability and social cohesion of society.

Globalization: A term used to denote the increasing international influence that certain organizations and businesses have gained over the last decades. Whereas beforehand economic, social and political systems were thought of as national, many now have a global reach. There is even talk of the emergence of a single global market, as exemplified by the increasing power of multinational conglomerates.

Homophily: A term that is used to describe the fact that people tend to associate with – i.e. be friends and enter into intimate relationships with – people who are similar to them. So, for example, people's networks of friends tend to consist of people from a similar social class background, or a similar ethnic background.

Individualization thesis (also called *detraditionalization* thesis): A thesis that has become a central focus of debate within the social sciences. The main thrust of the argument is that, as a result of the weakening of traditions in contemporary societies, individuals are freer to make their own life choices.

Industrialization: A process that began in the eighteenth century in Britain that transformed pre-industrial societies into industrialized ones. Central to this process was the development of machine-based forms of production, which meant that production was increasingly centralized in large factories that produced hitherto unseen volumes of goods. In addition, developments in transportation meant that these goods could be transported across vast distances by train or boat. Industrialization also led to significant social change, as increasing numbers of people moved to towns and cities and incomes rose.

Kin: A term widely used within anthropology to denote a person's 'extended family' as it were, i.e. relatives beyond the nuclear family group (for example, grandparents, aunts and cousins).

Late modernity: A term that is used to describe contemporary Western societies, which are said to have moved to a new stage of modernity that can be characterized as late modern, i.e. a continuation of some of the aspects of modernity. For example, some institutions such as capitalism continue to be in a key position within late modern societies. (Compare with '*Postmodernity*'.)

Modernity: Through industrialization, Western societies are said to have entered a stage of modernity characterized by an increasing emphasis on rationality, reason and science; the rise of capitalism and nation-states; and the increased social mobility of people.

Moral panic: One of the mechanisms through which a social phenomenon gets labelled as a 'social problem' is through the construction of a moral panic. In other words, a social phenomenon is labelled (for example, by the mass media or politicians) as something that gives rise to concern, and a cause behind this 'problem' is identified. These are termed 'moral' panics because they often focus on issues of morality (the 'right' and 'wrong' way to do things).

Patriarchy: The systematic domination of women by men that extends to all areas of life, including family, work and politics. This is a structure, i.e it is not necessary for every man to dominate every woman, but rather this is viewed on a broader scale of men as a group in society dominating over women as a group. This is still clearly visible in statistics that show that women earn on average less than men (for the same work even), women rarely reach top positions in business or politics, and women take care of most of the housework or domestic labour such as child care and cleaning.

Post-industrialization: A term used to describe contemporary Western societies that are no longer dominated by the manufacturing industries (as they were when they were industrialized nations). Instead, the service sector has increased in significance and the countries are now more reliant on the financial sector.

Postmodernity: A term that is used to describe contemporary Western societies, which are said to have emerged from a period of modernity into a new period of postmodernity. In contrast with theories of late modernity, the concept of postmodernity is used to indicate that there has been distinct break away from modernity to a period characterized by fragmentation, insecurity and superficiality. (Compare with '*Late modernity*'.)

Private sphere: The private sphere is usually depicted in contrast to the public sphere (see below). The private sphere is most commonly associated with the home. This distinction between the private sphere and public sphere is the result of industrialization which separated production from homes into factories, thus creating a distinction between home and employment.

Public sphere: The public sphere is usually depicted in contrast to the private sphere (see above). The public sphere is most commonly thought to exist outside the home, for example employment and politics are public sphere activities. This distinction between the private sphere and public sphere is the result of industrialization, which separated production from homes into factories, thus creating a distinction between home and employment.

Pure relationship: A term coined by Anthony Giddens to describe what he saw as a key characteristic of contemporary intimate relationships, namely that they are no longer bound by tradition such as marriage but last only for as long as the two parties are satisfied with the relationship.

Qualitative: Refers to research that is conducted with the help of qualitative methods of data collection and analysis. The label 'qualitative research' covers a range of approaches and methods. Broadly speaking, qualitative research aims to understand the meanings that people attach to their experiences, and to understand thought and action in their social context.

Quantitative: Refers to research that is conducted with the help of quantitative methods of data collection and analysis. Quantitative research aims to quantify the extent to which a social phenomenon occurs within a society, and to locate where in society it is taking place, as well as how it relates to other social phenomena.

Queer: The term was originally a derogatory term used to describe non-heterosexuals and has since become a term adopted by non-heterosexuals as a sign of defiance against such stigma. Social scientists began also to use this term to denote a particular approach to the study of human life: called 'queer theory'. The focus of queer theory is mainly forms of sexuality that fall outside 'the norm' of heterosexuality.

Rationalization: A process that underpinned the development of modern capitalism and industrialization. It is characterized by an increasing reliance on knowledge in order to make different forms of human activity more efficient. For example, in factories the production of goods was made more efficient through the adoption of the conveyor belt. Efficiency is now a key aim throughout society, as exemplified by how large bureaucracies are run (for example, university teaching regularly undergoes 'rationalization' exercises). In other words, we can say that many aspects of our lives have become rationalized.

Relational self: A term that denotes the self not as separate or autonomous from others but as inherently connected to other people. The relational self gains a sense of self in relationships with and in relation to other people.

Social capital: There are various definitions of social capital, but the one used in this book derives from the work of Pierre Bourdieu, who defined social capital as the benefits a person can gain through the people he or she knows. A person's social network can, for example, afford them access to various resources such as information.

Social change: This is a broad term that in sociology is used to denote not only significant shifts in how people think and act (i.e. in social norms and practices) but also in social institutions (such as religion or industry) and systems of governance (for example, the shift from feudal states to democratic republics).

Social constructionism: An approach within the social sciences that takes a particular view of the nature of reality. Rather than accepting social reality at face value, social constructionists would argue that much of the social reality we come to know and take for granted is in fact socially constructed, i.e. the product of human thought and activity. For example, 'adolescence' is a stage in the lifecourse that many would take to 'just exist' – but in fact the concept of adolescence emerged at a particular time and in a particular place and is therefore not a universal concept. Instead, it is socially constructed.

Social norm: A term used to describe how there exist in any society certain socially shared expectations as to how people should behave. For example, the expectation that people not laugh at a funeral reflects a social norm of appropriate behaviour.

Social order: This is a key interest of many sociologists, namely how society and social life are ordered along particular patterns. This happens both on the macro level (as seen if we look at statistics of, for example, men and women's employment patterns) and on the micro level (exemplified by, for example, studies of how people tend to interact with one another according to certain unwritten rules while out in public).

Social structure: A concept used within sociology to describe (semi-) permanent patterns of social life. An example of a social structure is gender: our societies are to an extent organized around gender. Men and women are seen to have different roles, for example within families and at work. These social structures are perhaps most clearly visible if we use statistics to examine the patterning of social life. It is, for example, clear that women look after children more than men do, while a higher proportion of men work outside the home, and command bigger salaries at work than women do.

Socialization: A process that children go through as they learn the 'correct' manner of behaviour for their particular society. In other words, children become socialized (in the first instance by their parents) to become acceptable members of their social group who can act 'appropriately' in social situations. (See *Social norm*.)

Symbolic interactionism: A sociological tradition that investigates how meaning is created in interaction. Symbolic interactionists tend to be interested in studying face-to-face interactions between individuals, focusing, for example, on how those individuals come to define the situation.

Symbolic value: If a good such as a table has symbolic value, its value is in other words determined by the symbolic meanings attached to it, such as whether or not the table is an antique or a fashion item. (Compare with '*Use value*'.)

Use value: The use value of a good such as a table is determined by the quality of craftsmanship and raw materials that went into producing it, as well as by its usefulness to the person buying it. (Compare with '*Symbolic value*' above.)

Notes

4 'Marriage' and the Personal Life of Same-sex Couples

1. The Office for National Statistics' *Social Trends 38* (2008) revealed that, in 2007, the proportion of people living alone in Britain (12 per cent) was double that found in 1971 and the Census of 2001 showed that the majority of single-person households were made up by pensioners, typically women.

5 What It Means to be Related

1. While at the time of writing, same-sex couples can legally marry in ten countries (Argentina, Belgium, Canada, Iceland, Netherlands, Norway, Portugal, South Africa, Spain and Sweden) and in a few jurisdictions of two countries (United States and Mexico), most countries only recognize marriage between a husband and a wife. Instead, many countries have introduced special legislation which formally recognizes same-sex relationships as civil partnerships, civil unions or registered partnerships. This is why this chapter places the term 'marriage' in quotation marks, but later dispenses with these for the ease of reading. Yet, readers should be mindful of this fact when the chapter discusses 'same-sex marriage' because this is, in many ways, what it amounts to in practice and in common parlance.
2. See note, Table 5.1.
3. Queer is a form of resistance, a refusal of labels and pathologies. Queer challenges all socially constructed categories such as 'gender' and 'sexuality'.
4. The author's doctoral study was based on the following: (a) a survey which was sent to everyone who had entered into a Civil Partnership in Iceland between 27 June 1996 and 18 November 2004; (b) interviews with professionals who were involved in the legislative process; (c) interviews with women who had entered into a Civil Partnership; and (d) analysis of official documents and newspaper coverage.

8 Pets and Personal Life

1. Sources: US figures are for 2009 and from the American Pet Products Association (http://americanpetproducts.org); UK figures are for 2009 and come from the Pet Food Manufacturers' Association (http://www.pfma.org.uk); Canadian figures are from T. Perrin (2009), 'The Business of Urban Animals Survey: The Facts and Statistics on Companion Animals in Canada', *The Canadian Veterinary Journal*, 50(1), 48–52; Australian figures refer to 2005 and are from the Australian Veterinary Association (http://www.ava.com.au).

2. UK figure is from http://news.bbc.co.uk/1/hi/business/5040140.stm; US source as above.
3. Source: http://news.bbc.co.uk/1/hi/8021027.stm.

13 Personal Life and Politics

1. The Covert Social Movement Networks study was conducted by Nick Crossley, Gemma Edwards, Rachel Stevenson and Ellen Harries in 2009–10 at the University of Manchester.

14 Researching Personal Life

1. Official records such as court records are not automatically accessible to researchers; access must be negotiated with the relevant authority, in this case the Ministry of Justice and the individual courts involved.
2. This study was called Inter/Generational Dynamics (http://www.socialsciences.manchester.ac.uk/realities/research/generations) and it was conducted under the larger project of Realities (RES-576-25-0022), which was part of the ESRC National Centre for Research Methods. The study was conducted between October 2008 and September 2011. The project team comprised Jennifer Mason, James Nazroo, Vanessa May and Stewart Muir.

Bibliography

Ackroyd, J. and Pilkington, A. (1999) 'Childhood and the Construction of Ethnic Identities in a Global Age: A Dramatic Encounter', *Childhood*, 6(4), 443–54.

Adam, B. (1995) *Timewatch: The Social Analysis of Time* (London: Polity).

Alanen, L. (1992) *Modern Childhood? Exploring the 'Child Question' in Sociology*, Research Report No. 50 (Jyväskylä: University of Jyväskylä).

Alger, J. and Alger, S. (1997) 'Beyond Mead: Symbolic Interaction between Humans and Felines', *Society and Animals*, 5(1), 65–81.

Allan, G. (1996) *Kinship and Friendship in Modern Britain* (Oxford: Oxford University Press).

Allan, G. and Crow, G. (eds) (1989) *Home and Family: Creating the Domestic Sphere* (Basingstoke: Macmillan).

Anderson, E. (1990) *Streetwise: Race, Class and Change in an Urban Community* (Chicago, IL: University of Chicago Press).

Anderson, M. (1980) *Approaches to the History of the Western Family: 1500–1914* (Cambridge: Cambridge University Press).

Anderson, P. (2003) 'A Bird in the House: An Anthropological Perspective on Companion Parrots', *Society and Animals*, 11(4), 393–418.

Arluke, A. and Sanders, S. (1996) *Regarding Animals* (Philadelphia, PA: Temple University Press).

Australian Institute of Family Studies (2007) *A Snapshot of How Australian Families Spend Their Time*, http://www.aifs.gov.au/institute/pubs/snapshots/familytime.html

Baldwin, P. C. (2002) '"Nocturnal Habits and Dark Wisdom": The American Response to Children in the Streets at Night, 1880–1930', *Journal of Social History*, 35(3), 593–611.

Banks, J. (1954) *Prosperity and Parenthood: A Study of Family Planning Amongst the Victorian Middle Classes* (London: Routledge & Kegan Paul).

Bartlett, B. (2005) *The Hanged Man: A Story of Miracle, Memory and Colonialism in the Middle Ages* (Princeton, NJ: Princeton University Press).

Baudrillard, J. (1988) *Selected Writings* (Cambridge: Polity Press).

Bauman, Z. (1988) *Freedom* (Milton Keynes: Open University Press).

Bauman, Z. (1990) *Thinking Sociologically* (Oxford: Blackwell).

Beattie, I., Christopher, K., Okamoto, D. and Way, S. (2005) 'Momentary Pleasure: Social Encounters and Fleeting Relationships at a Singles Dance', in C. Morrill, D. A. Snow and C. H. White (eds), *Together Alone: Personal Relationships in Public Spaces* (Berkeley, CA: University of California Press).

Beck, U. (1992) *Risk Society: Towards a New Modernity* (London: Sage).

Beck, U. and Beck-Gernsheim, E. (1995) *The Normal Chaos of Love* (Cambridge: Polity).

Beck, U. and Beck-Gernsheim, E. (2002) *Individualization* (London: Sage).

Bengtson, V. L., Biblarz, T. J. and Roberts, R. E. L. (2002) *How Families Still Matter: A Longitudinal Study of Youth in Two Generations* (Cambridge: Cambridge University Press).

Ben-Moshe, L. and Powell, J. J. W. (2007) 'Sign of Our Times? Revis(it)ing the International Symbol of Access', *Disability & Society*, 22(5), 489–505.

Bennett, T., Savage, M., Silva, E., Warde, A., Gayo-Cal, M. and Wright, D. (2009) *Culture, Class, Distinction* (London: Routledge).

Bittman, M. and Wajcman, J. (2000) 'The Rush Hour: The Character of Leisure Time and Gender Equity', *Social Forces*, 79(1), 165–89.

Booth, A., and Crouter, A. C. (eds) (2002) *Just Living Together* (Hillside, NJ: Erlbaum Associates).

Bottero, W. (2005) *Stratification: Social Division and Inequality* (London: Routledge).

Bourdieu, P. (1984) *Distinction: A Social Critique of the Judgment of Taste* (London: Routledge).

Brandzel, A. L. (2005) 'Queering Citizenship? Same-Sex Marriage and the State', *GLQ: A Journal of Lesbian and Gay Studies*, 11(2), 171–204.

Brannen, J. and O'Brien, M. (eds) (1996) *Children in Families: Research and Policy* (London: Falmer).

Brannen, J., Moss, P. and Mooney, A. (2004) *Working and Caring Over the Twentieth Century: Change and Continuity in Four-Generation Families* (Basingstoke: Palgrave Macmillan).

Breedveld, K. (1998) 'The Double Myth of Flexibilization: Trends in Scattered Work Hours, and Differences in Time Sovereignty', *Time & Society*, 7(1), 129–43.

Brickell, C. (2001) 'Whose "Special Treatment"? Heterosexism and the Problems with Liberalism', *Sexualities*, 4(2), 211–35.

Brooks, R. (2005) *Friendship and Educational Choice: Peer Influence and Planning for the Future* (Basingstoke: Palgrave Macmillan).

Brown, P., Zavestoski, S., McCormick, S., Mayer, B., Morello-Frosch, R. and Gasior Altman, R. (2004) 'Embodied Health Movements: New Approaches to Social Movements in Health', *Sociology of Health and Illness*, 26(1), 50–80.

Brownlow, A. (2006) 'An Archaeology of Fear and Environmental Change in Philadelphia', *Geoforum*, 37, 227–45.

Bryceson, D. and Vuorela, U. (2002) *The Transnational Family: New European Frontiers and Global Networks* (Oxford: Berg).

Burkitt, I. (2004) 'The Time and Space of Everyday Life', *Cultural Studies*, 18(2), 211–27.

Burkitt, I. (2008) *Social Selves: Theories of Self and Society* (London: Sage).

Carmichael, K. (1991) *Ceremony of Innocence: Tears, Power and Protest* (London: Macmillan).

Carro, D., Valera, S. and Vidal, T. (2010) 'Perceived Insecurity in the Public Space: Personal, Social and Environmental Variables', *Quality and Quantity*, 44(2), 303–14.

Carsten, J. (2004) *After Kinship* (Cambridge: Cambridge University Press).

Cassanello, R. (2008) 'Avoiding "Jim Crow": Negotiating Separate and Equal on Florida's Railroads and Streetcars and the Progressive Era Origins of the Modern Civil Rights Movement', *Journal of Urban History*, 34(3), 435–57.

Chamberlain, M. (ed.) (1998) *Caribbean Migration: Globalised Identities* (London: Routledge).

Charles, N. and Davies, C. A. (2008) 'My Family and Other Animals: Pets as Kin', *Sociological Research Online*, 13(5), http://www.socresonline.org.uk/13/5/4.html.

Charles, N., Davies, C. A. and Harris, C. (2008) *Families in Transition: Social Change, Family Formation and Kin Relationships* (Bristol: Policy Press).

Cheal, D. J. (1991) *Family and the State of Theory* (New York, NY: Harvester Wheatsheaf).

Cheng, S. L., Olsen, W., Southerton, D and Warde, A. (2007) 'The Changing Practice of Eating: Evidence from UK Time Diaries, 1975 and 2000', *British Journal of Sociology*, 58(1), 39–61.

Chin, E. (2001) *Purchasing Power: Black Kids and American Consumer Culture* (Minneapolis, MN: University of Minnesota Press).

Clarke, L. and Roberts, C. (2004) 'The Meaning of Grandparenthood and its Contribution to the Quality of Life of Older People', in A. Walker and C. Hagan Hennessy (eds), *Growing Older: Quality of Life in Old Age* (Milton Keynes: Open University Press).

Cohen, A. P. (1994) *Self Consciousness: An Alternative Anthropology of Identity* (London: Routledge).

Collins, D. C. A. and Kearns, R. A. (2000) 'Under Curfew and Under Siege? Legal Geographies of Young People', *Geoforum*, 32, 389–403.

Cook, D. (2004) *The Commodification of Childhood: The Children's Clothing Industry and the Rise of the Child Consumer* (Durham, NC: Duke University Press).

Cook, H. (2004) *The Long Sexual Revolution, English Women, Sex and Contraception 1800–1975* (Oxford: Oxford University Press).

Daly, K. (1996) *Families and Time: Keeping Pace in a Hurried Culture* (London: Sage).

Daly, M. and Rake, K. (2003) *Gender and the Welfare State: Care, Work and Welfare in Europe and the USA* (Cambridge: Polity).

Darier, E. (1998) 'Time to be Lazy: Work, the Environment and Subjectivities', *Time & Society*, 7(2), 193–208.

Dawkins, C. J. (2005) 'Evidence on the Intergenerational Persistence of Residential Segregation by Race', *Urban Studies*, 42(3), 545–55

Day, K. (2001) 'Constructing Masculinity and Women's Fear in Public Space in Irvine, California', *Gender, Place & Culture*, 8(2), 109–27.

della Porta, D. (1992) 'Political Socialization in Left-wing Underground Organizations. Biographies of Italian and German Militants', in D. della Porta (ed.), *International Social Movements Research: Social Movements and Violence – Participation in Underground Organizations, Volume 4* (Greenwich, CO: JAI Press).

Delphy, C. and Leonard, D. (1992) *Familiar Exploitation: A New Analysis of Marriage in Contemporary Western Societies* (Cambridge: Polity).

Denzin, N. (1977) *Childhood Socialisation* (San Francisco, CA: Jossey-Bass).

Dermott, E. (2008) *Intimate Fatherhood: A Sociological Analysis* (London: Routledge).

DeVault, M. L. (2000) 'Producing Family Time: Practices of Leisure Activity Beyond the Home', *Qualitative Sociology*, 23(4), 485–503.

Devine, F. and Heath, S. (eds) (2009) *Doing Social Science: Evidence and Methods in Empirical Research* (Basingstoke: Palgrave Macmillan).

Douglas, G. and Murch, M. (2000) *How Parents Cope Financially on Marriage Breakdown*, Report No. 480 (York: Joseph Rowntree Foundation).

Duncan, S. and Phillips, M. (2009) 'People Who Live Apart: How Different are They?', *Sociological Review*, 58(1), 112–34.

Durkheim, E. (1970[1897]) *Suicide: A Study in Sociology* (London: Routledge).

Durkheim, E. (1979[1911]) 'Childhood', in W. F. Pickering (ed.) *Durkheim: Essays on Morals and Education* (London: Routledge).

Dye, J. L. (2008) *Fertility of American Women: June 2008*, Current Population Reports, P20-563 (Washington, DC: US Census Bureau).

Edwards, G. (2004) 'Habermas and Social Movements: What's "New"?', in N. Crossley and J. M. Roberts (eds), *After Habermas: New Perspectives on the Public Sphere* (Oxford: Blackwell/Sociological Review).

Edwards, G. and Crossley, N. (2009) 'Measures and Meanings: Exploring the Ego-net of Helen Kirkpatrick Watts, Militant Suffragette', *Methodological Innovations Online*, 4, 37–61.

Edwards, J. (2000) *Born and Bred: Idioms of Kinship and New Reproductive Technologies in England* (Oxford: Oxford University Press).

Edwards, R., Hadfield, L. and Mauthner, M (2006) *Sibling Identity and Relationships: Brothers and Sisters* (London: Routledge).

Elder, G., Wolch, J. and Emel, J. (1998) '*Le pratique sauvage*: Race, Place and the Human–Animal Divide', in J. Wolch and J. Emel (eds), *Animal Geographies: Place, Politics and Identity in the Nature-Culture Borderlands* (London: Verso).

Elias, N. (1991) *The Society of Individuals* (New York, NY: Continuum).

Eliasoph, N. S. (1998) *Avoiding Politics: How Americans Produce Apathy in Everyday Life* (Cambridge: Cambridge University Press).

Elshtain, J. B. (1981) *Public Man, Private Woman: Women in Social and Political Thought* (Princeton, NJ: Princeton University Press).

Engels, F. (1986[1884]) *The Origin of the Family, Private Property and the State* (Harmondsworth: Penguin).

Ettelbrick, P. L. (1997) 'Since When is Marriage a Path to Liberation?', in M. Blasius and S. Phelan (eds), *We Are Everywhere: A Historical Sourcebook of Gay and Lesbian Politics* (London: Routledge).

Etzioni, A. and Bloom, J. (eds) (2004) *We Are What We Celebrate: Understanding Holidays and Rituals* (New York, NY: New York University Press).

Fairchild, K. and Rudman, L. A. (2008) 'Everyday Stranger Harassment and Women's Objectification', *Social Justice Research*, 21(3), 338–57.

Featherstone, M. (1991) *Consumer Culture and Postmodernism* (London: Sage).

Featherstone, M. and Hepworth, M. (1995) 'Images of Positive Aging: A Case Study of Retirement Choice Magazine', in M. Featherstone and A. Wernick (eds), *Images of Aging: Representations of Later Life* (London: Routledge).

Finch, J. (1989) *Family Obligations and Social Change* (Cambridge: Polity).

Finch, J. (2006) 'Kinship as 'Family' in Contemporary Britain', in F. Ebtehaj, B. Lindley and M. Richards (eds), *Kinship Matters* (Oxford: Hart).

Finch, J. (2007) 'Displaying Families', *Sociology*, 41(1), 65–81.

Finch, J. (2008) 'Naming Names: Kinship, Individuality and Personal Names', *Sociology*, 42(4), 709–25.

Finch, J. and Mason, J. (1993) *Negotiating Family Responsibilities* (London: Routledge).

Finch, J. and Mason, J. (2000) *Passing On: Kinship and Inheritance in England* (London: Routledge).

Finch, J. and Summerfield, P. (1991) 'Social Reconstruction and the Emergence of Companionate Marriage, 1945–59' in D. Clark (ed.), *Marriage, Domestic Life & Social Change* (London: Routledge).

Fink, A. (2008) *How to Conduct Surveys: A Step-By-Step Guide* (London: Sage).

Finnie, R. (1993) 'Women, Men, and the Economic Consequences of Divorce: Evidence from Canadian Longitudinal Data', *Canadian Review of Sociology and Anthropology*, 30, 205–41

Fisher, K. (2006) *Birth Control, Sex and Marriage in Britain, 1918–1960* (Oxford: Oxford University Press).

Fox, R. (2006) 'Animal Behaviours, Post-human Lives: Everyday Negotiations of the Animal–Human Divide in Pet-keeping', *Social and Cultural Geography*, 7(4), 525–37.

Francis, D. (2000) 'The Significance of Work Friends in Late Life', in J. F. Gubrium and J. A. Holstein (eds), *Aging and Everyday Life* (Malden, MA: Blackwell).

Franklin, A. (1999) *Animals and Modern Cultures: A Sociology of Human–Animal Relations in Modernity* (London: Sage).

Franklin, S. and McKinnon, S. (eds) (2001) *Relative Values: Reconfiguring Kinship Studies* (Durham and London: Duke University Press).

Fraser, N. (1989) *Unruly Practices: Power, Discourse and Gender in Contemporary Social Theory* (Cambridge: Polity Press).

Freund, P. (2001) 'Bodies, Disability and Spaces: The Social Model and Disabling Spatial Organisations', *Disability & Society*, 16(5), 689–706.

Frosh, S., Phoeniz, A. and Pattman, R. (2002) *Young Masculinities: Understanding Boys in Contemporary Society* (Basingstoke: Palgrave Macmillan).

Gadsden, B. (2010) ' "The Other Side of the *Milliken* Coin": The Promise and Pitfalls of Metropolitan School Desegregation', *Journal of Urban History*, 36(2), 173–96.

Garfinkel, H. (1967) *Studies in Ethnomethodology* (Englewood Cliffs, NJ: Prentice-Hall).

Gaule, S. (2005) 'Alternating Currents of Power: From Colonial to Post-apartheid Spatial Patterns in Newtown, Johannesburg', *Urban Studies*, 42(13), 2335–61.

Gershuny, Jonathan (2005) 'Busyness as the Badge of Honour for the New Superordinate Working Class', *Working Papers of the Institute for Social and Economic Research*, Paper 2005–9 (Colchester: Institute for Social and Economic Research).

Gershuny, J., Godwin, M. and Jones, S. (1994) 'The Domestic Labour Revolution: A Process of Lagged Adaptation', in M. Anderson, F. Bechhofer and J. Gershuny (eds), *The Social and Political Economy of the Household* (Oxford: Oxford University Press).

Giddens, A. (1984) *The Constitution of Society: Outline of the Theory of Structuration* (Cambridge: Polity).

Giddens, A. (1991) *Modernity and Self-Identity. Self and Society in the Late Modern Age* (Cambridge: Polity).

Giddens, A. (1992) *The Transformation of Intimacy: Sexuality, Love and Eroticism in Modern Societies* (Cambridge: Polity).

Gillis, J. R. (1992) 'Gender and Fertility Decline Among the British Middle Classes', in J. R. Gillis, L. Tilly and D. Levine (eds), *The European Experience of Declining Fertility, 1850–1970* (Cambridge, MA: Blackwell).

Gillis, J. (1997) *A World of the Their Own Making: Myth, Ritual, and the Quest for Family Values* (Oxford: Oxford University Press).

Gittins, D. (1982) *Fair Sex: Family Size and Structure, 1930–39* (London: Hutchison).

Glennie, P., and Thrift, N. (1996) 'Reworking E. P. Thompson's "Time, Work-Discipline and Industrial Capitalism" ', *Time & Society*, 5(3), 275–99.

Goffman, E. (1963) *Behavior in Public Places: Notes on the Social Organization of Gatherings* (New York, NY: Free Press).

Gotham, K. F. (2000) 'Urban Space, Restrictive Covenants and the Origins of Racial Residential Segregation in a US City, 1900–50', *International Journal of Urban and Regional Research*, 24(3), 616–33.

Goulbourne, H. (1999) 'The Transnational Character of Caribbean Kinship in Britain', in S. McRae (ed.), *Changing Britain: Families and Households in the 1990s* (Oxford: Oxford University Press).

Gould, D. (2009) *Moving Politics: Emotion and ACT UP's Fight Against Aids* (Chicago: University of Chicago Press).

Green, E., and Singleton, C. (2006) 'Risky Bodies at Leisure: Young Women Negotiating Space and Place', *Sociology*, 40(5), 853–71.

Greenebaum, J. (2004) 'It's a Dog's Life: Elevating Status from Pet to Fur Baby at Yappy Hour', *Society and Animals*, 12(2), 117–35.

Greer, G. (1970) *The Female Eunuch* (London: Paladin Grafton).

Grier, K. C. (2002) ' "The Eden of Home": Changing Understandings of Cruelty and Kindness to Animals in Middle-class American Households 1820–1900', in M. J. Henninger-Voss (ed.), *Animals in Human Histories: The Mirror of Nature and Culture* (Rochester, NY: University of Rochester Press).

Griffiths, M. (1995) *Feminisms and the Self: The Web of Identity* (London: Routledge).

Gronow, J. (1997) *The Sociology of Taste* (London: Routledge).

Habermas, J. (1981) 'New Social Movements', *Telos*, 49, 33–7.

Hajnal, J. (1965) 'European Marriage Patterns in Perspective', in D. V. Glass and D. E. C. Eversley (eds), *Population in History: Essays in Historical Demography* (London: Edward Arnold).

Hanisch, C. (1970) 'The Personal is Political', in S. Firestone and A. Koedt (eds), *Notes from the Second Year – Women's Liberation: Major Writings of the Radical Feminists* (New York, NY: pamphlet published by S. Firestone and A. Koedt).

Hanisch, C. (2006) 'The Personal is Political: Introduction', http://www.carolhanisch.org/CHwritings/PersonalisPol.pdf

Haraway, D. (2003) *The Companion Species Manifesto: Dogs, People and Significant Otherness* (Chicago, IL: Prickly Paradigm Press).

Hardey, M. (2007) 'Poking Intimacies', *Practicing a Proper Social Demeanour: A Guide to Facebook Etiquette*, http://www.properfacebooketiquette.blogspot.com/2007/10/poking-intimacies.html

Hawkes, G. (1996) *A Sociology of Sex and Sexuality* (Oxford: Oxford University Press).

Hebdige, D. (1979) *Subcultures: The Meaning of Style* (London: Routledge).

Hendrick, H. (1997) *Children, Childhood and English Society 1880–1990* (Cambridge: Cambridge University Press).

Hetherington, E. M. (2003) 'Social Support and the Adjustment of Children in Divorced and Remarried Families, *Childhood*, 10(2), 217–36.

Hetherington, E. M. and Kelly, J. (2002) *For Better or for Worse: Divorce Reconsidered* (New York, NY: W. W. Norton).

K. Hetherington, K. (1992) 'Stonehenge and its Festivals: Spaces of Consumption', in R. Shields (ed.), *Lifestyle Shopping: The Subject of Consumption* (London: Routledge).

Hochschild, A. R. (1983) *The Managed Heart: Commercialization of Human Feeling* (Berkeley, CA: University of California Press).

Hochschild, A. R. (1997) *The Time Bind: When Work becomes Home and Home Becomes Work* (New York, NY: Metropolitan).

Holden, K. C. and Smock, P. J. (1991) 'The Economic Costs of Marital Dissolution: Why Do Women Bear a Disproportionate Cost?' *Annual Review of Sociology*, 17, 51–78.

Holdsworth, C. and Morgan, D. (2005) *Transitions in Context: Leaving Home, Independence and Adulthood* (Maidenhead: Open University Press).

Howell, S. and Marre, D. (2006) 'To Kin a Transnationally Adopted Child in Norway and Spain: The Achievement of Resemblances and Belonging', *Ethnos*, 71(3), 293–316.

ILGA (2010) 'Marriage or Substitutes to Marriage', http://www.ilga.org/

Irvine, L. (2004) *If You Tame Me: Understanding Our Connection with Animals* (Philadelphia, PA: Temple University Press).

Irvine, L. (2007) 'The Question of Animal Selves: Implications for Sociological Knowledge and Practice', *Qualitative Sociology Review*, 3(1), 5–22.

Irwin, S. (2005) *Reshaping Social Life* (Abingdon: Routledge).

James, A. and Prout, A. (eds) (1990) *Constructing and Reconstructing Childhood*, 2nd edn (London: Falmer Press).

Jamieson, L. (1998) *Intimacy: Personal Relationships in Modern Societies* (Cambridge: Polity Press).

Jamieson, L. (1999) 'Intimacy Transformed: A Critical Look at the Pure Relationship', *Sociology*, 27, 201–20.

Jamieson, L. (2003) 'The Couple: Intimate and Equal?', in J. Weeks, J. Holland and M. Waites (eds), *Sexualities and Society: A Reader* (Cambridge: Polity Press).

Jamieson, L., Wasoff, F. and Simpson, R. (2009) 'Solo-living, Demographic and Family Change: The Need to Know More About Men', *Sociological Research Online*, 14(2), http://www.socresonline.org.uk/14/2/5.html.

Javors, I. and Reimann, R (2001) 'Building Common Ground: Strategies for Grassroots Organizing on Same-sex Marriage', in M. Bernstein and R. Reimann (eds), *Queer Families Queer Politics: Challenging Culture and the State* (New York: Columbia University Press).

Jennings, M. K., Stoker, L. and Bowers, J. (2009) 'Politics Across Generations: Family Transmission Reexamined', *Journal of Politics*, 71(3), 782–99.

Johnston, L. (1997) 'Queen(s') Street or Ponsonby Poofters? Embodied HERO Parade Sites', *New Zealand Geographer*, 53(2), 29–32.

Johnston, L. and Valentine, G. (1995) 'Wherever I Lay My Girlfriend, That's My Home: The Performance and Surveillance of Lesbian Identities in Domestic Environments', in D. Bell and G. Valentine (eds), *Mapping Desire: Geographies of Sexualities* (London: Routledge).

Kanter, R. M. (1977) *Men and Women of the Corporation* (New York, NY: Basic Books).

Karsten, L. (2002) 'Mapping Childhood in Amsterdam: The Spatial and Social Construction of Children's Domains in the City', *Tijdschrift voor Economische en Sociale Geografie*, 93(3), 231–41.

Katz, S., Eekelaar, J. and Maclean, M. (2000) *Cross Currents: Family Law and Policy in the US and England* (Oxford: Oxford University Press).

Kelleher, D. (2001) 'New Social Movements in the Health Domain', in G. Scambler (ed.), *Habermas, Critical Theory and Health* (London: Routledge).

Kelly, J. B. (2003) 'Changing Perspectives on Children's Adjustment Following Divorce: A View from the United States', *Childhood*, 10(2), 237–54.

Ketokivi, K. (2008) 'Biographical Disruption, the Wounded Self, and the Reconfiguration of Significant Others', in E. D. Widmer and R. Jallinoja (eds), *Beyond the Nuclear Family: Families in a Configurational Perspective* (Bern: Peter Lang).

Kiernan, K. (2002) 'Cohabitation in Western Europe: Trends, Issues and Implications', in A. Booth and A. Crouter (eds), *Just Living Together: Implications of Cohabitation on Families, Children and Social Policy* (Hillside, NJ: Lawrence Erlbaum Associates).

Kiernan, K., Land, H. and Lewis, J. (1998) *Lone Motherhood in Twentieth Century Britain: From Footnote to Front Page* (Oxford: Clarendon Press).

Kitchin, R. (1998) ' "Out of Place", "Knowing One's Place": Space, Power and the Exclusion of Disabled People', *Disability & Society*, 13(3), 343–56.

Klein, H. (2004) *A Population History of the United States* (Cambridge: Cambridge University Press).

Kotler-Berkowitz, L. (2005) 'Friends and Politics: Linking Diverse Friendship Networks to Political Participation', in A. Zuckerman (ed.), *The Social Logic of Politics: Personal Networks as Contexts for Political Behavior* (Philadelphia, PA: Temple University Press).

Kvale, S. (2007) *Doing Interviews* (London: Sage).

La Fontaine, J. S. (1985) 'Persons And Individuals: Some Anthropological Reflections', in M. Carrithers, S. Collins and S. Lukes (eds), *The Category of the Person: Anthropology, Philosophy, History* (Cambridge: Cambridge University Press).

Lamb, M. E. (2010) *The Role of the Father in Child Development* (Hoboken, NJ: Wiley & Sons).

Landes, D. (1983) *Revolution in Time: Clocks and the Making of the Modern World* (Cambridge, MA: Harvard University Press).

Lasch, C. (1979) *The Culture of Narcissism: American Life in an Age of Diminishing Expectations* (New York, NY: Norton).

Lash, S. and Urry, J. (1987) *The End of Organized Capitalism* (Cambridge: Polity Press).

Lawler, S. (2008) *Identity: Sociological Perspectives* (Cambridge: Polity Press).

Lazarsfeld, P. F., Berelson, B. and Gaudet, H. (1948) *The People's Choice: How the Voter Makes Up His Mind in a Presidential Campaign* (New York, NY: Columbia University Press).

Lesthaeghe, R. (1994) 'The Second Demographic Transition in Western Countries: An Interpretation', in K. Oppenheim Mason and A.-M. Jensen (eds), *Gender and Family Change in Industrialized Countries* (Oxford: Clarendon Press).

Levin, I. (2004) 'Living Apart Together: A New Family Form', *Current Sociology*, 52(2), 223–40.

Lewis, J. (2001) *The End of Marriage? Individualism and Intimate Relations* (Cheltenham: Edward Elgar).

Lienhardt, G. (1985) 'Self, Public, Private: Some African Representations', in M. Carrithers, S. Collins and S. Lukes (eds), *The Category of the Person: Anthropology, Philosophy, History* (Cambridge: Cambridge University Press).

Linder, S. B. (1970) *The Harried Leisure Class* (New York, NY: Columbia University Press).

Lofland, L. H. (1973) *A World of Strangers: Order and Action in Urban Public Space* (New York, NY: Basic).

Lofland, L. H. (1998) *The Public Realm: Exploring the City's Quintessential Social Territory* (New Brunswick, NJ: Aldine Transactions).

Lupton, D. (1998) *The Emotional Self: A Sociocultural Exploration* (London: Sage).

Maclean, M. and Eekelaar, J. (1997) *The Parental Obligation: A Study of Parenthood Across Households* (Oxford: Hart).

Mansbridge, J. and Okin, S. M. (1995) 'Feminism', in R. Goodin and P. Pettit (eds), *A Companion to Contemporary Political Philosophy* (Oxford: Blackwell).

Mansfield, P. and Collard, J. (1988) *The Beginning of the Rest of Your Life? A Portrait of Newly-Wed Marriage* (London: Macmillan).

Manzo, J. (2005) 'Social Control and the Management of "Private" Space in Shopping Malls', *Space & Culture*, 8(1), 83–97.

Marsiglio, W. (ed.) (1995) *Fatherhood: Contemporary Theory, Research and Social Policy* (London: Sage).

Martens, L., Southerton, D. and Scott, S. (2004) 'Bringing Children (and Parents) into the Sociology of Consumption: Towards a Theoretical and Empirical Agenda', *Journal of Consumer Culture*, 4 (2), 155–82.

Marx, K. (1976[1867]) *Capital, Vol. I.* (London: Penguin).

Mason, J. (1999) 'Living Away from Relatives: Kinship and Geographical Reasoning', in S. McRae (ed.), *Changing Britain: Families and Households in the 1990s* (Oxford: Oxford University Press).

Mason, J. (2002) *Qualitative Researching*, 2nd edn (London: Sage)

Mason, J. (2004) 'Managing Kinship Over Long Distances: The Significance of "the Visit"', *Social Policy and Society*, 3(4), 421–9.

Mason, J. (2008) 'Tangible Affinities and the Real Life Fascination of Kinship', *Sociology*, 42(1), 29–45.

Mason, J. and Davies, K. (2009) 'Coming to Our Senses? A Critical Approach to Sensory Methodology', *Qualitative Research*, 9(5), 587–603.

Mason, J. and Tipper, B. (2008) 'Being Related: How Children Define and Create Kinship', *Childhood*, 15(4), 441–60.

Mathews, T. J. and Hamilton, B. E. (2009) *Delayed Childbearing: More Women Are Having Their First Child Later in Life*, NCHS data brief, no. 21 (Hyattsville, MD: National Center for Health Statistics).

Matthews, S. H. (1986) *Friendships Through the Lifecourse: Oral Biographies in Old Age* (Beverly Hills, CA: Sage).

Mayall, B. (ed.) (1994) *Children's Childhoods Observed and Experienced* (London: Falmer Press).

McAdam, D. and Paulsen, R. (1993) 'Specifying the Relationship Between Social Ties and Activism', *American Journal of Sociology*, 99(3), 640–67.

McDevitt, M. and Chaffee, S. (2002) 'From Top-down to Trickle-up Influence: Revisiting Assumptions about the Family in Political Socialization', *Political Communication*, 19(3), 281–301.

McPherson, M., Smith-Lovin, L. and Cook, J. M. (2001) 'Birds of a Feather: Homophily in Social Networks', *Annual Review of Sociology*, 27, 415–44.

Mead, G. H. (1934) *Mind, Self and Society* (Chicago, IL: University of Chicago Press).

Melucci, A. (1980) 'The New Social Movements: A Theoretical Approach', *Social Science Information*, 19(2), 199–226.

Melucci, A. (1989) *Nomads of the Present: Social Movements and Individual Needs in Contemporary Society* (London: Hutchinson).

Milardo, R. M. (2010) *The Forgotten Kin: Aunts and Uncles* (Cambridge: Cambridge University Press).

Miller, D. (2001) 'The Poverty of Morality', *Journal of Consumer Culture*, 1(2), 225–44.

Miller, T. (2010) *Making Sense of Fatherhood* (Cambridge: Cambridge University Press).

Millett, K. (1970) *Sexual Politics* (New York, NY: Doubleday).

C. W. Mills (1959) *The Sociological Imagination* (Oxford: Oxford University Press).

Moinian, F. (2009) '"I'm Just Me!" Children Talking Beyond Ethnic and Religious Identities', *Childhood*, 16(1), 31–48.

Morgan, D. H. J. (1996) *Family Connections: An Introduction to Family Studies* (Cambridge: Polity).

Morgan, D. H. J. (2008) 'The Gentle Art of Name-dropping: Acquaintanceship and the Auto/biographical Self', in A. C. Sparkes (ed.), *Auto/Biographical Yearbook, 2008* (Durham: British Sociological Association).

Morgan, D. H. J. (2009) *Acquaintances: The Space Between Intimates and Strangers* (Maidenhead: Open University Press).

Morgan, D. H. J. (2011) *Family Practices Revisited* (Basingstoke: Palgrave Macmillan).

Moxnes, K. (2003) 'Risk Factors in Divorce: Perceptions by the Children Involved', *Childhood*, 10(2), 131–46.

Nagle, J. (2003) *Race, Ethnicity, and Sexuality: Intimate Intersections, Forbidden Frontiers* (Oxford: Oxford University Press).

Nast, H. (2006) 'Loving … Whatever: Alienation, Neoliberalism and Pet-love in the Twenty-first Century', *ACME: An International E-Journal for Critical Geographies*, 5(2), 300–27.

National Statistics (2004) *Social Trends No. 34*, http://www.statistics.gov.uk/downloads/theme_social/Social_Trends34/Social_Trends34.pdf.

Nesbary, G. (2000) *Survey Research and the World Wide Web* (Boston, MA: Allyn & Bacon).

Neuman, W. L. (2005) *Social Research Methods: Quantitative and Qualitative Approaches*, 6th edn (Boston, MA: Allyn & Bacon).

Niemi, R. G. and Sobieszek, B. I. (1977) 'Political Socialization', *Annual Review of Sociology*, 3, 209–33.

Noack, T., Seierstad, A. and Weedon-Fekjær, H. (2005) 'A Demopraphic Analysis of Registered Partnerships (Legal Same-sex Unions): The Case of Norway', *European Journal of Population*, 21, 89–109.

Oberschall, A. (1973) *Social Conflict and Social Movements* (Englewood Cliffs, NJ: Prentice-Hall).

O'Brien, M., Jones, D., Sloan, D., and Rustin, M. (2000) 'Children's Independent Spatial Mobility in the Urban Public Realm', *Childhood*, 7(3), 257–77.

Office for National Statistics (2006) 'Report: Divorces in England and Wales during 2005', *Population Trends 125*, http://www.statistics.gov.uk/downloads/theme_population/PT125_main_part3.pdf.

Office for National Statistics (2008) *Social Trends 38*, http://www.statistics.gov.uk/downloads/theme_social/Social_Trends38/Social_Trends_38.pdf.

Office for National Statistics (2010a) *Average Age of Mother at Childbirth: Social Trends 33*, http://www.statistics.gov.uk/StatBase/ssdataset.asp?vlnk=6372&Pos=1&ColRank=2&Rank=272.

Office for National Statistics (2010b) '*Births & Deaths: Later Start and Fewer Children for Families*', http://www.statistics.gov.uk/CCI/nugget.asp?ID=1309&Pos=6&ColRank=2&Rank=352.

Office for National Statistics (2010c) *Statistical Bulletin: Civil Partnerships in the UK 2009*, http://www.statistics.gov.uk/pdfdir/cpuk0810.pdf.

Office for National Statistics (2010d) *Statistical Bulletin: Marriages in England and Wales 2008*, http://www.statistics.gov.uk/pdfdir/marr0210.pdf.

O'Malley, M. (1992) 'Time, Work and Task Orientation: A Critique of American Historiography', *Time and Society*, 1(3), 341–58.

Pahl, R. (2000) *On Friendship* (Cambridge: Polity).

Parsons, T. (1955) 'The American Family: Its Relations to Personality and the Social Structure', in T. Parsons and R. F. Bales, *Family, Socialization and Interaction Process* (Glencoe, IL: Free Press).

Passy, F. (2003) 'Social Networks Matter. But How?', in M. Diani and D. McAdam (eds), *Social Movements and Social Networks* (Oxford: Oxford University Press).

Pateman, C. (1988) *The Sexual Contract* (Stanford, CA: Stanford University Press).

Pinchbeck, I. and Hewitt, M. (1973) *Children in English Society, Vol II* (London: Routledge & Kegan Paul).

Plummer, K. (2003) *Intimate Citizenship: Private Decisions and Public Dialogues* (London: University of Washington Press).

Putnam, R. (2000) *Bowling Alone: The Collapse and Revival of American Community* (New York, NY: Simon & Schuster).

Quillian, L. and Campbell, M. E. (2003) 'Beyond Black and White: The Present and Future of Multiracial Friendship Segregation' *American Sociological Review*, 68(4), 540–66.

Qvortrup, J. (ed.) (1993) *Childhood Matters* (Aldershot: Avebury).

Reisch, L. (2001) 'Time and Wealth: The Role of Time and Temporalities For Sustainable Patterns of Consumption', *Time and Society*, 10 (2/3), 387–405.

Reynolds, T. (2010) 'Transnational Family Relationships, Social Networks and Return Migration Among British-Caribbean Young People', *Ethnic and Racial Studies*, 33(5), 797–815.

Richards, L. (1990) *Nobody's Home: Dreams and Realities in a New Suburb* (Melbourne: Oxford University Press).

Ritvo, H. (1987) *The Animal Estate: English and Other Creatures in the Victorian Age* (Cambridge, MA: Harvard University Press).

Robinson, J. and Godbey, G. (1997) *Time for Life: The Surprising Ways that Americans Use Their Time* (University Park, PA: Pennsylvania State Press).

Rollin, B. and Rollin, M. (2003) 'Dogmatisms and Catechisms: Ethics and Companion Animals', in S. Armstrong and R. Botzler (eds), *The Animal Ethics Reader* (London: Routledge).

Rose, A. M. (1962) 'A Systematic Summary of Symbolic Interaction Theory', in A. M. Rose (ed.), *Human Behaviour and Social Processes: An Interactionist Approach* (London: Routledge & Kegan Paul).

Roseneil, S. and Budgeon, S. (2004) 'Beyond the Conventional Family: Intimacy, Care and Community in the 21st Century', *Current Sociology*, 52(2), 135–59.

Rosser, C. and Harris, C. C. (1965) *The Family and Social Change* (London: Routledge & Kegan Paul).

Rothblum, E. D. (2005) 'Same-sex Marriage and Legalized Relationships: I Do, or Do I?', *Journal of GLBT Family Studies*, 1(1), 21–31.

Rowbotham, S. (1997) *A Century of Women: The History of Women in Britain and the US* (London: Viking Penguin).

Samara, T. R. (2010) 'Order and Security in the City: Producing Race and Policing Neoliberal Spaces in South Africa', *Ethnic and Racial Studies*, 33(4), 637–55.

Saunders, P. (1989) 'The Meaning of "Home" in Contemporary English Culture', *Housing Studies*, 4, 177–92.

Savage, M., Barlow, J., Dickens, P. and Fielding, T. (1992) *Property, Bureaucracy and Culture: Middle-Class Formation in Contemporary Britain* (London: Routledge).

Savage, M., Bagnall, G. and Longhurst, B. (2005) *Globalization and Belonging: The Suburbanization of Identity* (London: Sage).

Schor, J. (1992) *The Overworked American: The Unexpected Decline of Leisure* (New York, NY: Basic Books).

Schor, J. (1998) 'Work, Free Time and Consumption. Time, Labour and Consumption: Guest Editor's Introduction', *Time & Society*, 7(1), 119–27.

Schor, J. (2004) *Born To Buy: The Commercialized Child and the New Consumer Culture* (New York, NY: Scribner).

Scott, S., Jackson, S. and Backett-Milburn, K. (1998) 'Swings and Roundabouts: Risk Anxiety and the Everyday Worlds of Children', *Sociology*, 32(4), 689–705.

Seccombe, W. (1993) *Weathering the Storm: Working-Class Families from the Industrial Revolution to the Fertility Decline* (London: Verso).

Sedgwick, E. K. (1991) *Epistemology of the Closet* (London: Harvester Wheatsheaf).

Seidman, S. (1997) 'Introduction', in S. Seidman (ed.), *Queer Theory/Sociology* (Oxford: Blackwell).

Shaw, A. (2000) *Kinship and Continuity: Pakistani Families in Britain* (Amsterdam: Harwood Academic).

Shaw, C. R. (1966[1930]) *The Jack-Roller* (Chicago: University of Chicago Press).

Silverman, D. (2005) *Doing Qualitative Research: A Practical Handbook*, 2nd edn (London: Sage).

Simmel, G. (1950) 'The Field of Sociology', in G. Wolff (ed. and trans.), *The Sociology of Georg Simmel* (New York, NY: Free Press).

Simmel, G. (1970[1903]) 'The Metropolis and Mental Life', in D. Levine (ed.), *On Individuality and Social Form* (Chicago, IL: Chicago University Press).

Slater, D. (1997) *Consumer Culture and Modernity* (Cambridge: Polity Press).

Smart, C. (1984) *The Ties That Bind: Law, Marriage and the Reproduction of Patriarchal Relations* (London: Routledge & Kegan Paul).

Smart, C. (2007) *Personal Life: New Directions in Sociological Thinking* (Cambridge: Polity).

Smart, C. and Neale, B. (1999) *Family Fragments?* (Cambridge: Polity).

Smart, C. and Shipman, B. (2004) 'Visions in Monochrome: Families, Marriage and the Individualization Thesis', *British Journal of Sociology*, 55(4), 491–509.

Smart, C., Neale, B. and Wade, A. (2001) *The Changing Experience of Childhood: Families and Divorce* (Cambridge: Polity).

Smart, C., May, V., Furniss, C. and Wade, A. (2003) *Residence and Contact Disputes in Court, Volume 1*, Research Series No. 6/03 (London: Department for Constitutional Affairs).

Smart, C., May, V., Furniss, C. and Wade, A. (2005) *Residence and Contact Disputes in Court, Volume 2*, Research Series 4/5) (London: Department for Constitutional Affairs).

Smart, C., Davies, K., Heaphy, B. and Mason, J. (2010) ' "I Have Found it Hard to Make Real Friends Since This Time": Difficult Friendships, Guilt and Ontological Insecurity', unpublished paper presented at the British Sociological Association Annual Conference, Glasgow Caledonian University, 7–9 April.

Smets, P. (2005) 'Living Apart or Together? Multiculturalism at a Neighbourhood Level', *Community Development Journal*, 41(3), 293–306.

Smith, A., Taylor, N. and Tapp, P. (2003) 'Rethinking Children's Involvement in Decision-making after Parental Separation', *Childhood*, 10(2), 201–16.

Smith, J. (2003) 'Beyond Dominance and Affection: Living with Rabbits in Post-humanist Households', *Society and Animals*, 13(8), 181–97.

Smock, P. J. and Gupta, S. (2002) 'Cohabitation in Contemporary North America' in A. Booth and A. Crouter (eds), *Just Living Together: Implications of Cohabitation on Families, Children and Social Policy* (Hillside, NJ: Lawrence Erlbaum Associates).

Smock, P. J., Manning, W. D. and Gupta, S. (1999) 'The Effects of Marriage and Divorce on Women's Economic Wellbeing', *American Sociological Review*, 64(6), 794–812.

Smyth, B. and Weston, R. (2000) *Financial Living Standards After Divorce*, Research Paper No. 23 (Melbourne: Australian Institute of Family Studies).

Snow, D., Zurcher, L. and Ekland-Olson, S. (1980) 'Social Networks and Social Movements', *American Sociological Review*, 45(5), 787–801.

Solomon, S. E., Rothblum, E. D. and Balsam, K. F. (2004) 'Pioneers in Partnership: Lesbian and Gay Male Couples in Civil Unions Compared with Those Not in Civil Unions and Married Heterosexual Siblings', *Journal of Family Psychology*, 18(2), 275–86.

Southerton, D. (2002) 'Boundaries of "Us" and "Them": Class, Mobility and Identification in a New Town', *Sociology*, 36(1), 171–93.

Southerton, D. (2003) ' "Squeezing Time": Allocating Practices, Co-ordinating Networks and Scheduling Society', *Time & Society*, 12(1), 5–25.

Southerton, D. (2007) 'Time Pressure, Technology and Gender: The Conditioning of Temporal Experiences in the UK', *Equal Opportunities International*, 26(2), 113–28.

Southerton, D. (2009a) 'Changing Times: Quantitative Analyses of Time Use', in F. Devine and S. Heath (eds), *Doing Social Science: Evidence and Methods in Empirical Research*, 2nd edn (Basingstoke: Palgrave Macmillan).

Southerton, D. (2009b) 'Temporal Rhythms: Comparing Daily Lives of 1937 with Those of 2000 in the UK', in E. Shove, F. Trentmann and R. Wilk (eds), *Time, Consumption and Everyday Life: Practice, Materiality and Culture* (Oxford: Berg).

Southerton, D. and Tomlinson, M. (2005) ' "Pressed for Time" – The Differential Impacts of a "Time Squeeze" ', *Sociological Review*, 53(2), 215–39.

Spencer, L. and Pahl, R. (2006) *Rethinking Friendship: Hidden Solidarities Today* (Princeton, NJ and Oxford: Princeton University Press).

Spender, D. (1980) *Man Made Language* (London: Routledge & Kegan Paul).

Spilsbury, J. C. (2002) ' "If I Don't Know Them I'll Get Killed Probably": How Children's Concerns About Safety Shape Help-seeking Behaviour', *Childhood*, 9(1), 101–17.

Stack, C. (1974) *All Our Kin: Strategies for Survival in a Black Community* (New York, NY: Basic Books).

Stalp, M. C., Williams, R., Lynch, A. and Radina, M. E. (2009) 'Conspicuously Consuming: The Red Hat Society and Midlife Women's Identity', *Journal of Contemporary Ethnography*, 38(2), 225–53.

Steinbugler, A. C. (2005) 'Visibility as Privilege and Danger: Heterosexual and Same-sex Interracial Intimacy in the 21st Century', *Sexualities*, 8(4), 425–43.

Stoddard, T. B. (1997) 'Why Gay People Should Seek the Right to Marry', in M. Blasius and S. Phelan (eds), *We Are Everywhere: A Historical Sourcebook of Gay and Lesbian Politics* (London: Routledge).

Stoker, L. and Jennings, M. K. (1995) 'Life-cycle Transitions and Political Participation: The Case of Marriage', *American Political Science Review*, 89(2), 421–33.

Sullivan, A. (ed.) (2004) *Same-Sex Marriage. Pro and Con: A Reader*, rev. edn (New York, NY: Vintage).

Sullivan, O. (1997) 'Time Waits for No (Wo)men: An Investigation of the Gendered Experience of Domestic Time', *Sociology*, 31(2), 221–40.

Swabe, J. (2005) 'Loved to Death? Veterinary Visions of Pet-keeping in Modern Dutch Society', in J. Knight (ed.), *Animals in Person: Cultural Perspectives on Human–Animal Intimacies* (Oxford: Berg).

Sycamore, M. B. (ed.) (2004) *That's Revolting! Queer Strategies for Resisting Assimilation* (Brooklyn, NY: Soft Skull Press).

Taylor, F. (1911) *The Principles of Scientific Management* (New York, NY: Harper & Brothers).

Thomas, W. I. and Znaniecki, F. (1958) *The Polish Peasant in Europe and America, Volumes 1 & 2*, 2nd edn (New York, NY: Dover).

Thompson, C. (1996) 'Caring Consumers: Gendered Consumption Meanings and the Juggling Lifestyle', *Journal of Consumer Research*, 22, 388–407.

Thompson, E. P. (1967) 'Time, Work-Discipline and Industrial Capitalism: Past and Present', reproduced in M. Flinn and T. Smout (eds) (1974), *Essays in Social History* (Oxford: Clarendon Press).

Tilley, C. (1994) *A Phenomenology of Landscape: Places, Paths and Monuments* (Oxford: Berg).

Tillyard, S. (1995) *Aristocrats: Caroline, Emily, Louisa and Sarah Lennox, 1750–1832* (London: Vintage).

Tipper, B. (2011) ' "A Dog Who I Know Quite Well": Everyday Relationships Between Children and Animals', *Children's Geographies*, 9(2), 145–165.

Touraine, A. (1974) *The Postindustrial Society* (London: Wildwood House).

Treiman, D. J. (2009) *Quantitative Data Analysis: Doing Social Research to Test Ideas* (San Francisco, CA: Jossey-Bass).

Trinder, L., Feast, J. and Howe, D. (2005) *The Adoption Reunion Handbook* (Chichester: Wiley & Sons).

Urry, J. (2007) *Mobilities* (Cambridge: Polity).

Valentine, G. (1993) '(Hetero)sexing Space: Lesbian Perceptions and Experiences of Everyday Spaces', *Environment and Planning D: Society and Space*, 11, 395–413.

Valentine, G. (2002) 'Queer Bodies and the Production of Space', in D. Richardson and S. Seidman (eds), *Handbook of Lesbian and Gay Studies* (London: Sage).

Veblen, T. (1925[1899]) *The Theory of the Leisure Class: An Economic Study of Institutions* (London: Allen & Unwin).

Vogler, C., Brockmann, M. and Wiggins, R. (2006) 'Intimate Relationships and Changing Patterns of Money Management at the Beginning of the Twenty First Century', *British Journal of Sociology*, 57(3), 455–82.

Waaldijk, K. (2001) 'Small Change: How the Road to Same-sex Marriage Got Paved in the Netherlands', in R. Wintemute and M. Andenaes (eds), *Legal Recognition of Same-Sex Relationships: A Study of National, European and International Law* (Oxford: Hart).

Wacquant, L. (2008) *Urban Outcasts: A Comparative Sociology of Advanced Marginality* (Cambridge: Polity).

Walby, S. (1990) *Theorising Patriarchy* (Oxford: Blackwell).

Warde, A. (1994) 'Consumption, Identity-formation and Uncertainty', *Sociology*, 28(4), 877–98.

Warde, A., Cheng, S.-L., Olsen, W. and Southerton, D. (2007) 'Changes in the Practice of Eating: A Comparative Analysis of Time-use', *Acta Sociologica*, 50(4), 365–87.

Warner, M. (2000) *The Trouble with Normal: Sex, Politics, and the Ethics of Queer Life* (Cambridge, MA: Harvard University Press).

Warr, M. (1984) 'Fear of Victimization: Why are Women and The Elderly More Afraid?', *Social Science Quarterly*, 65(3), 681–702.

Warren, T. (2003) 'Class- and Gender-based Working Time? Time Poverty and the Division of Domestic Labour', *Sociology*, 37(4), 733–52.

Wasoff, F., Jamieson, L. with Smith, A. (2005) 'Solo Living, Individual and Family Boundaries: Findings from Secondary Analysis', in L. McKie, S. Cunningham-Burley and J. Campling (eds), *Families in Society: Boundaries and Relationships* (Bristol: Policy Press).

Weeks, J. (1991) *Against Nature: Essays on History, Sexuality and Identity* (London: Rivers Oram Press).

Weeks, J. (2003) *Sexuality*, 2nd edn (London: Routledge).

Weeks, J. (2007) *The World We Have Won* (Abingdon: Routledge).

Weeks, J., Heaphy, B. and Donovan, C. (2001) *Same Sex Intimacies: Families of Choice and other Life Experiments* (London: Routledge).

Wellman, B. and Hogan, B. (2004) 'The Internet in Everyday Life', in W. S. Bainbridge (ed.), *The Berkshire Encyclopedia of Human Computer Interaction* (Great Barrington, MA: Berkshire).

Wernick, A. (1991) *Promotional Culture: Advertising, Ideology And Symbolic Expression* (London, Sage).

Weston, K. (1991) *Families We Choose: Lesbians, Gays, Kinship* (New York, NY: Columbia University Press).

Widmer, E. D. and Jallinoja, R. (eds) (2008) *Beyond the Nuclear Family: Families in a Configurational Perspective* (Bern: Peter Lang).

Wilkinson, S. and Kitzinger, C. (2006) 'In Support of Equal Marriage: Why Civil Partnership is Not Enough', *The Psychology of Women Section Review*, 8(1), 54–7.

Willis, P. (1978) *Learning to Labour* (Aldershot: Ashgate).

Woods, R. (1992) *The Population of Britain in the Nineteenth Century* (Cambridge: Cambridge University Press).

Wrigley, E. and Schofield, R. (1989) *The Population History of England 1541–1871* (Cambridge: Cambridge University Press).

Wrigley, E., Davies, R., Oeppen, J. and Schofield, R. (1997) *English Population History from Family Reconstitution: 1580–1837* (Cambridge: Cambridge University Press).

Young, M. and Schuller, T. (eds) (1988) *The Rhythms of Society* (London: Routledge).

Zelizer, V. (2002) 'Kids and Commerce', *Childhood*, 9(4), 275–96.

Zuckerman, A., Fitzgerald, J. and Dasovic, J. (2005) 'Do Couples Support the Same Political Parties?', in A. Zuckerman (ed.), *The Social Logic of Politics: Personal Networks as Contexts for Political Behavior* (Philadelphia, PA: Temple University Press).

Index

Note: page numbers in **bold** indicate a table or figure in the text.

Veblen, Thorstein, 135

Wade, Amanda, 102, 164, 165
Wajcman, Judy, 127
Warde, Alan, 142, 143
Warr, Mark, 111
Weeks, Jeffrey, 4, 53, 68, 76, 81, 83
Wernick, Andrew, 137–8
Weston, Kath, 4, 53, 68

Women's Liberation movement, 149,
 150, 151–2, 153, 159
work
 and gender, 126–8
 flexible working, 129–30
 time spent at, 124–8
 work–life balance, 128–9, 130

Znaniecki, Florian, 2–3